FASHION DOLL
Fantasy™

PUBLISHER / Donna Robertson
EDITORIAL DIRECTOR / Carolyn Brooks Christmas
DESIGN DIRECTOR / Fran Rohus
PRODUCTION DIRECTOR / Ange Workman

EDITORIAL

EDITORS / Jennifer A. Simcik, Janet Tipton
COORDINATING EDITOR / Joni Sheedy
ASSOCIATE EDITORS / Nancy Clevenger, Nancy Harris,
   Kristine Hart-Kirst, Susan Koellner, Sharon Lothrop,
   Pauline Rosenberger, Marianne Telesca
EDITORIAL ASSISTANT / Janice Kellenberger

PHOTOGRAPHY

ART DIRECTORS / Glenda Chamberlain, Minette Collins Smith,
   Greg Smith
PHOTOGRAPHERS / Renée Agee, Tammy Cromer-Campbell,
   Mary Craft
PHOTO STYLIST / Ruth Whitaker
COVER PHOTO / Tammy Cromer-Campbell

PRODUCTION

PRODUCTION MANAGER / Glenda Chamberlain
PRODUCTION TEAM / Jamie Hendry, Diane Simpson,
   Jean Schrecengost

PRODUCT DESIGN

DESIGN COORDINATOR / Brenda Wendling

BUSINESS

CHIEF EXECUTIVE OFFICER / John Robinson
VICE PRESIDENT / CUSTOMER SERVICE / Karen Pierce
VICE PRESIDENT / MARKETING / Greg Deily
VICE PRESIDENT / M.I.S. / John Trotter

CREDITS

Sincerest thanks to all the designers, manufacturers and other
professionals whose dedication has made this book possible. Special
thanks to Klaus Rothe of Sullivan Rothe Design, Berne, IN, and Mark
Levasseur of Quebecor USA, Leominster, MA.

Library of Congress Cataloging-in-Publication Data
ISBN: 0-9638031-4-X
First Printing: 1994
Library of Congress Catalog Card Number: 94-66884
Published and Distributed by *The Needlecraft Shop, LLC*
Printed in the United States of America.

For more than 30 years, fashion dolls have been the imaginative play things of the young and the young at heart around the world. Dolls bring out the kid in all of us, and needlework and crafts are expressions of our individual style and creativity.

Even famous fashion designers love creating doll clothes. Paris designer Yves Saint Laurent has said that he did not realize when he made clothing for his sister's dolls as a child that something so fun and carefree would lead to his vocation.

Somehow, doll play stirs our imaginations in visionary worlds where dreams always come true.

So, if you love crafts and stitchery and fashion dolls, you are going to love this book! It is chock full of patterns with clear, step-by-step instructions, helpful diagrams and full color charts to help you make fashion doll fantasies into realities.

Our designers have created projects featuring needlework and novelty craft techniques that are sure to dazzle and delight doll lovers everywhere. So, if you've been wanting to learn something new, like crochet or plastic canvas needlepoint, now is the time to get started. We have lots of small projects that can be completed quickly and six pages of detailed, basic instructions on pages 120-126 that will be helpful to beginners and experienced stitchers alike.

Our team of art directors here at The Needlecraft Shop included an avid fashion doll collector. Minette Smith (she and her husband, Greg, also designed some of the patterns) combined her talents with her enjoyment of dolls to show off our collection of projects in photo scenes of fantasies we've all dreamed about.

And who doesn't daydream about an outing at the beach, a relaxing afternoon sipping tea beside a cozy fire, or the medieval world of fair maidens, winged horses and unicorns?

Janet

Contents

Fancy Boudoir

NIGHTGOWN & ROBE

Designed by Sue Childress

TECHNIQUE: Crochet
SIZE: Fits 11"-11½" fashion doll.
MATERIALS FOR BOTH: Size 5 crochet cotton — 100 yds. white; Eyelash novelty yarn — 100 yds. white; ⅔ yd. white ⅛" satin ribbon; Size 4/0 snap; White sewing thread; Sewing needle; No. 1 steel, F and K crochet hooks or sizes needed to obtain gauges.
GAUGES: No. 1 hook, 7 hdc sts = 1"; 4 hdc rows = 1". F hook, 4 shells = 3"; 7 shell rows = 3". K hook, 5 dc sts = 2"; 4 dc rows = 3½".

NIGHTGOWN

Row 1: With No. 1 hook and crochet cotton, ch 26, sc in 2nd ch from hook, sc in each ch across, turn (25 sc).

Row 2: Ch 1, sc in first st, (sc in next st, 2 sc in next st) 6 times, (2 sc in next st, sc in next st) 6 times, turn (37).

Row 3: Ch 2, (hdc in next st, 2 hdc in next st) across, turn (55).

Row 4: Ch 2, hdc in each st across, turn.

Row 5: Ch 2, hdc in next 8 sts; for **first armhole,** ch 1, skip next 8 sts; hdc in next 21 sts; for **second armhole,** ch 1, skip next 8 sts; hdc in last 9 sts, turn (39 hdc, 2 ch sps).

Row 6: Ch 2, hdc in each st and in each ch across, turn (41).

Rows 7-8: Ch 2, hdc in each st across, turn.

Rnd 9: Working in rnds, ch 3, dc in each st around, join with sl st in top of ch-3, **turn.**

NOTES: For **beginning shell (beg shell),** ch 3, (dc, ch 1, 2 dc) in same st or ch sp.

For **shell,** (2 dc, ch 1, 2 dc) in next st or ch sp.

Rnd 10: With F hook, beg shell in first st, (skip next st, shell in next st) around, join (21 shells).

Rnds 11-23: Sl st in next st, sl st in next ch sp, beg shell in same sp, shell in ch sp of each shell around, join.

Row 24: Sl st in next st, sl st in next ch sp, ch 3, 4 dc in same sp, sc in sp between last worked shell and next shell, (5 dc in next shell, sc in sp between last worked shell and next shell) around, join, fasten off.

Starting at center front, weave ribbon through every other st on rnd 9.

Sew snap to top of back opening.

ROBE

Row 1: With K hook and eyelash yarn, ch 15, dc in 4th ch from hook,

Continued on page 10

BEADED ACCESSORIES

Designed by Carol Krob

TECHNIQUE: Plastic Canvas
SIZE: Tote is ⅜" x 1¼" x 1½" tall, not including handles; Evening Bag is ⅝" x 1", not including handle; Jewelry Box is ¾" x 1¼" x ⅜" tall; Hand Mirror is ⅝" x 1½"; Vanity Tray is ¾" x 1¼" x ¼" tall.
MATERIALS: ½ sheet of 14-count plastic canvas; 174 white, 86 blue, 83 pink and 46 yellow pearl seed beads; One gold rocaille bead; Three pink and three blue 6-mm. flower-shaped beads; One pink, one blue and two gold pony beads for jars; One pink, one blue and two gold 5-mm. beads for lids; 13 x 18-mm. oval acrylic mirror; Small snap; Scrap of pink felt; #10 crewel needle; #24 tapestry needle; White quilting thread; Craft glue or glue gun; 1/16" ribbon thread or six-strand embroidery floss (for amounts see Color Key on page 8).

CUTTING INSTRUCTIONS:

NOTE: Graphs and diagrams on page 8.

A: For Tote front and back, cut one each 16 x 20 holes.

B: For Tote sides and bottom, cut two 4 x 20 holes and one 4 x 16 holes (no graphs).

C: For Evening Bag, cut one according to graph.

D: For Jewelry Box lid and bottom, cut one each 12 x 16 holes (no bottom graph).

E: For Jewelry Box sides, cut two 4 x 16 holes and two 4 x 12 holes (no graphs).

F: For Hand Mirror, cut one according to graph.

G: For Vanity Tray sides, cut two 4 x 16 holes and two 4 x 12 holes (no graphs).

H: For Vanity Tray bottom, cut one 12 x 16 holes (no graph).

I: For Jewelry Box and Vanity Tray linings, using H as a pattern, cut two from felt ⅛" smaller at all edges.

STITCHING INSTRUCTIONS:

NOTES: Bottom D and H pieces are unworked.

Continued on page 8

Lacy, Feminine Accents & Accessories Make Sweet Dreams Come True

Nightgown & Robe (page 6); Beaded Accessories (page 6); Puppy
(page 9); Lace Pillows (page 9); Vanity & Stool (page10)

Beaded Accessories

Continued from page 6

For best results, use 18" or shorter lengths of ribbon; keep ribbon smooth and flat by guiding it between the thumb and forefinger of your free hand while completing each stitch. Drop needle occasionally to let ribbon unwind, and check your work on the wrong side. Use a shallow, rimmed dish to hold beads.

1: With crewel needle and quilting thread, using Beaded Half Cross Stitch (see Stitch Illustration) and seed bead colors indicated, work A, C, lid D and F pieces according to graphs. Using ribbon colors and stitches indicated, work A, C, lid D and F pieces according to graphs. Using white and Slanted Gobelin Stitch over narrow width, work B, E and G pieces.

2: Using green and Straight Stitch, embroider leaves on front A and lid D as indicated on graphs. With quilting thread and yellow seed beads, sew flower beads to front A and lid D as indicated.

3: For Tote, with white ribbon, Whipstitch A and B pieces together according to Tote Assembly Diagram; Overcast unfinished edges. For handles, attach ribbon to top edges of front and back according to diagram.

4: For Evening Bag, with quilting thread, sew half of snap to C as indicated. Folding C wrong sides together to join front and back (see Evening Bag Folding Diagram), easing to fit, with white ribbon, Whipstitch together; Overcast unfinished edges. Sew remaining half of snap to corresponding area on wrong side of flap.

5: For handle, secure quilting thread at top edge on one side of Evening Bag; thread ten white, two blue, three pink, two blue and ten white beads onto strand; secure thread on opposite side.

6: For Jewelry Box, with white ribbon, Whipstitch D and E pieces together according to Jewelry Box Assembly Diagram. Sew gold rocaille bead to center top on front side (see diagram). Glue one I inside bottom of box.

7: For Hand Mirror, with white ribbon, Overcast unfinished edges of F. Glue mirror behind beaded area.

8: For Vanity Tray, with white ribbon, Whipstitch G and H pieces together according to Vanity Tray Assembly Diagram. Glue remaining I inside Tray. For jars, glue one 5-mm. bead to top of each pony bead as shown in photo, and glue beads in Tray.

BEADED ACCESSORIES COLOR KEY:

$^1/_{16}$" ribbon thread	Amount
White/Pastel Variegated	15 yds.
Green Metallic	1 yd.

STITCH KEY:
- — Backstitch/Straight Stitch
- ◆ White Bead
- ◆ Yellow Bead
- ◆ Pink Bead
- ◆ Blue Bead
- ○ Pink Flower Bead
- ○ Blue Flower Bead
- ○ Snap Attachment

F – Hand Mirror
(cut 1) 8 x 20 holes

C – Evening Bag
(cut 1) 28 x 29 holes

Beaded Half Cross Stitch Illustration

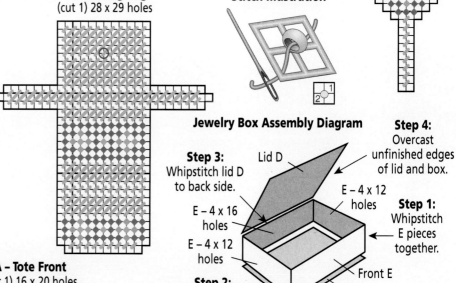

Jewelry Box Assembly Diagram

Step 3: Whipstitch lid D to back side.

Lid D

E – 4 x 16 holes

E – 4 x 12 holes

E – 4 x 12 holes

Step 4: Overcast unfinished edges of lid and box.

E – 4 x 12 holes

Step 1: Whipstitch E pieces together.

Front E

Bottom D

Step 2: Whipstitch sides and bottom D together.

Evening Bag Folding Diagram

A – Tote Front
(cut 1) 16 x 20 holes

D – Jewelry Box Lid
(cut 1) 12 x 16 holes

A – Tote Back
(cut 1) 16 x 20 holes

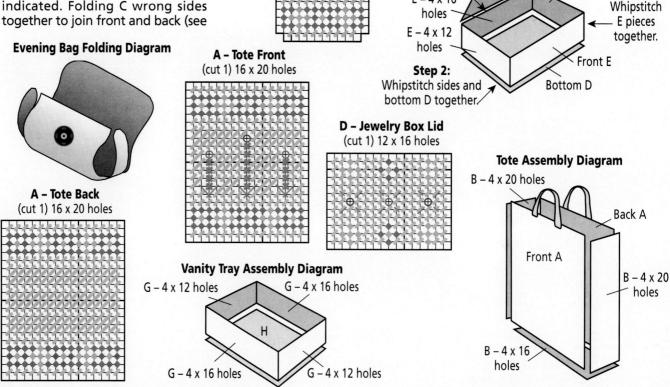

Vanity Tray Assembly Diagram

G – 4 x 12 holes

G – 4 x 16 holes

H

G – 4 x 16 holes

G – 4 x 12 holes

Tote Assembly Diagram

B – 4 x 20 holes

Back A

Front A

B – 4 x 20 holes

B – 4 x 16 holes

PUPPY

Designed by Fran Rohus

TECHNIQUE: Novelty Craft
SIZE: 3½" x 3½".
MATERIALS: One 18" white 38-mm. curly loop chenille stem; Two white 15-mm. bump chenille stems; One black 3-mm. pom-pom.

CUTTING INSTRUCTIONS:
1: From curly chenille, cut one 5" piece and one 6½" piece for body and one 3" piece for head.
2: From bump chenille, cut one 2½" piece (be sure to include one thin part and one thick part of chenille stem) for tail.
NOTE: Remaining piece of bump chenille will be used for ears.

ASSEMBLY INSTRUCTIONS:
1: Assemble Puppy according to Puppy Assembly Diagram.
2: For nose, glue pom-pom to head as shown in photo.

LACE PILLOWS

Designed by Rosemarie Walter

PHOTO on page 7
TECHNIQUE: Sewing
SIZE: Square Pillow is 3½" x 3½"; Round Pillow is 3½" across; Bolster Pillow is 4½" long.
MATERIALS: ⅛ yd. lavender fabric; ⅛ yd. white lace fabric; 1½ yds. white ¼" flat double-edged lace; 1½ yds. each of white and lavender ⅛" satin ribbon; Sewing needle; Purple and white sewing thread.

CUTTING INSTRUCTIONS:
1: From lavender fabric, cut one 2" x 30" piece for square pillow, two 4¼" circles for round pillow and one 2" x 25" piece for bolster pillow.
2: From lace fabric, cut two 3" squares for square pillow covering, two 3½" circles for round pillow covering, two 1¾" x 18" pieces for square and round pillow ruffles and one 4" x 7" piece for bolster pillow covering.

STITCHING INSTRUCTIONS:
1: For square pillow, fold 2" x 30" piece of fabric into 2" x 2" square. Position fabric square between wrong sides of lace covering; baste lace together. Trim seams to ¼".
2: For ruffle, fold one 1¾" x 18" piece of lace fabric in half lengthwise with wrong sides together.

Gather unfinished edges to fit around outside edge of pillow; stitch in place on top of ¼" seam allowance of pillow covering.
3: For trim, cut one 9" length of double-edged lace. Position on top of ruffle; stitch in place.
4: For bows, cut four 4" lengths of each color of ribbon. Tie each into small bows and tack one of each color to corners of pillow as shown in photo.
5: For round pillow, run a row of gathering stitches ¼" from outside edges of circles. Pull up gathers and position in center. Position circles wrong sides together with gathers in center; slip stitch together.
6: Finish lace covering and ruffle same as square pillow. For bows, cut one 16" length of each color of ribbon; fold ribbons in half at center top of pillow; tack in place. Make several loops of each color and tack in place as shown in photo. Tack streamers to bottom edge of pillow.
7: For bolster pillow, roll 2" x 25" piece of fabric, slip stitch together. Fold under 1¼" on each 7" edge of lace covering; slip stitch making a 4" x 4½" piece. Cover fabric roll with lace covering, extending hemmed edge of lace for ruffles. Fold under unfinished edge of lace; slip stitch together.
8: For trim, cut two 7" lengths of double-edged lace; tie around each end of bolster pillow.
9: For bows, cut two 16" lengths of each color of ribbon; tie over trim with four loops on each ribbon; tack in place.

Puppy Assembly Diagram

Step 1: For first section of body, bend 5" curly chenille to form oval; twist ends together.

Step 2: For second section of body, bend 6½" curly chenille to form oval; twist ends together.

Step 3: For tail, twist thin part of 2½" bump chenille around end of both ovals.

Step 5: For ears, bend remaining piece of bump chenille to shape ears; twist ends together.

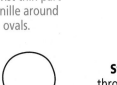

Step 4: For head, bend 3" curly chenille to form circle; twist ends together.

Step 6: Slip one ear through assembled head; twist long ends of head and ears around body to secure.

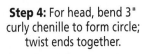

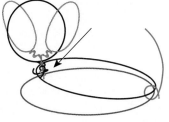

VANITY & STOOL

Designed by Rosemarie Walter

PHOTO on page 7
TECHNIQUE: Plastic Canvas & Sewing
SIZE: Vanity is 4" x 6¼" x 3⅝" tall; Stool is 2⅜" x 2⅜" x 2¾" tall.
MATERIALS: One sheet of lavender 7-count plastic canvas; ½ yd. lavender fabric; ½ yd. white lace fabric; 2½ yds. white ¼" flat double-edged lace; 1½ yds. each of white and lavender ⅛" satin ribbon; Craft batting; Tapestry needle; Sewing needle; Lavender and white sewing thread; Worsted-weight or plastic canvas yarn (for amount see Color Key).

VANITY & STOOL
CUTTING INSTRUCTIONS:

A: For Vanity top, cut one according to graph.

B: For Vanity base side, cut two 22 x 26 holes (no graph).

C: For Vanity base end, cut two 13 x 22 holes (no graph).

D: For Stool top, cut one according to graph.

E: For Stool base, cut one 16 x 48 holes.

STITCHING INSTRUCTIONS:
NOTE: Pieces are unworked.

1: For Vanity base, with rose, Whipstitch B and C pieces together and to A as indicated on graph and according to Vanity Assembly Diagram.

2: For Stool base, overlapping four holes, Whipstitch ends of E together; Whipstitch D and E pieces together.

VANITY & STOOL COVERS
CUTTING INSTRUCTIONS:

1: From lavender fabric, cut one 7½" x 37" piece for Vanity skirt and one 5½" x 15" piece for Stool skirt; using plastic canvas Vanity and Stool top pieces as patterns, cut one Vanity cover and one Stool cover ½" larger around all edges.

2: From lace fabric, cut one Vanity top cover and one Stool top cover same as fabric pieces. Cut one 3¾" x 40" piece for Vanity skirt and one 2¾" x 16" for Stool skirt.

3: From craft batting, using plastic canvas Vanity and Stool top pieces as patterns, cut one Vanity pad and one Stool pad.

STITCHING INSTRUCTIONS:

1: For Vanity cover, with right sides together and with ½" seam, stitch short edges of 7½" x 36" piece together, forming ring. Fold in half lengthwise with wrong sides together; press. With right sides together and with ½" seams, stitch short edges of 3¾" x 40" piece together, forming ring. Place lace skirt over fabric skirt and stitch together along unfinished edges, gathering to fit around outer edge of plastic canvas Vanity top; sew to outer edge of Vanity top. Tack Vanity pad to top of Vanity. Place lace top over fabric top and stitch together along unfinished edges, gathering to fit over unfinished edges of skirt; place over Vanity pad and sew to skirt.

2: For trim, from double-edged lace, cut one 18" length and one 40" length; sew 18" length around top seam and 40" length around bottom edge of lace skirt.

3: For bows, cut two 12" lengths of each color of ribbon; tie into bows and tack to each side of Vanity as shown.

4: For Stool cover, using 5½" x 15" piece and 2¾" x 16" piece, plastic canvas Stool top and Stool pad, follow Step #1.

5: For trim, from double-edged lace, cut one 8½" length and one 16" length; sew 8½" length around top seam and 16" length around bottom edge of lace skirt.

6: For bows, cut one 9" length of each color of ribbon; tie into bows and tack to one side of Stool as shown.❧

VANITY & STOOL COLOR KEY:

	Worsted-weight	Nylon Plus™	Need-loft™	Yarn Amount
☐	Rose	#12	#05	3 yds.

STITCH KEY:
☐ Vanity Base Attachment

Vanity Assembly Diagram

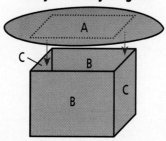

Nightgown & Robe
Continued from page 6

2 dc in each ch across, turn (24 dc).

Row 2: Ch 3, dc in next st, 2 dc in next st, (dc in each of next 2 sts, 2 dc in next st) across, turn (32).

Row 3: Ch 3, dc in next 4 sts; for **first armhole,** ch 4, skip next 5 sts; dc in next 12 sts; for **second armhole,** ch 4, skip next 5 sts; dc in last 5 sts, turn (22 dc, 2 ch sps).

Row 4: Ch 3, dc in each st and in each ch across, turn (30).

Row 5: Ch 3, dc in each st across, turn.

Row 6: Ch 3, dc next 2 sts tog, dc in each st across to last 3 sts, dc next 2 sts tog, dc in last st, turn (28).

Rows 7-11: Ch 3, dc next 2 sts tog, dc in each st across to last 4 sts, dc next 2 sts tog, dc in next st leaving last st unworked, turn (25, 22, 19, 16, 13). Fasten off at end of last row.❧

A – Vanity Top
(cut 1) 26 x 41 holes

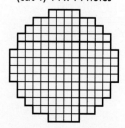

D – Stool Top
(cut 1) 14 x 14 holes

Enjoy a Lazy Afternoon in a Room Tastefully Appointed with a Sofa Bed and Homey Accents

VAZARA
Hill vo Roses
Dinh Welah
Olhyschu

Lounging Around

SOFA BED

Designed by Joyce Bishop

TECHNIQUE: Crochet
SIZE: 5½" x 6½" x 8½".
MATERIALS: Worsted-weight yarn — 10 oz. rust; One sheet of 7-count plastic canvas; Styrofoam® — three 1" x 3½" x 8" pieces and one 1" x 2" x 8" piece; Craft glue; Tapestry needle; G crochet hook or size needed to obtain gauge.
GAUGE: 4 sc sts = 1"; 4 sc rows = 1".

CUTTING INSTRUCTIONS:

A: For back, from plastic canvas, cut one 34 x 54 holes.
B: For arms, from plastic canvas, cut two 23 x 30 holes.

BACK CUSHION & SEAT CUSHION (make 1 each)

Row 1: Ch 33; working in **one lp** only, sc in 2nd ch from hook, sc in each ch across, turn (32 sc).
Rows 2-14: Ch 1, sc in each st across, turn. **Do not** turn at end of last row.
Rnd 15: Working around outer edge, in ends of rows and in sts, ch 1, sc in each row across to row 1; working in **one lp** only, sc in each ch across, sc in each row across to row 14; working in **back lps** only, sc in each st across, join with sl st in first sc (92).
Rnds 16-18: Ch 1, sc in each st around, join. **Turn** at end of last rnd.
Row 19: Working in **front lps** this row only, ch 1, sc in first 32 sts leaving remaining sts unworked, turn (32).
Rows 20-32: Ch 1, sc in each st across, turn. Fasten off at end of last row.

BOTTOM & BACK COVER

NOTE: Label pieces as you are working on them to help with assembly.

Rows 1-14: Starting at **inside bottom**, repeat same rows of Back Cushion & Seat Cushion.
Row 15: Ch 1, sc in end of each row across to row 1; working in **one lp** only, sc in each ch across, sc in end of each row across leaving sts of row 14 unworked, turn (60).
Rows 16-18: Ch 1, sc in each st across, turn. Fasten off at end of last row.
Row 19: For **outer bottom,** with wrong side of row 18 facing you, skip first 14 sts; working in **front lps** this row only, join with sc in next st, sc in next 31 sts leaving last 14 sts unworked, turn (32).
Rows 20-36: Repeat row 16.
Row 37: For **back cushion rest,** with wrong side of row 14 facing you, working in **front lps** only, join with sc in first st, sc in each st across, turn (32).
Rows 38-40: Ch 1, sc in each st across, turn.
Row 41: Working in **back lps** this row only, ch 1, sc in each st across, turn.
Rows 42-44: Repeat row 38.
Row 45: For **front of back cover,** working in **front lps** this row only, repeat row 38.
Rows 46-57: Repeat row 38.
Row 58: For **back of back cover,** working in **front lps** this row only, repeat row 38.
Rows 59-78: Repeat row 16.

ARM COVERS (make 2)

Row 1: Ch 19, sc in 2nd ch from hook, sc in each ch across, turn (18).

SOFA BED ASSEMBLY DIAGRAM #1

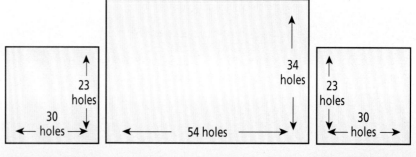

Rows 2-14: Ch 1, sc in each st across, turn.

Row 15: Working in **front lps** this row only, ch 1, sc in each st across, turn.

Rows 16-24: Ch 1, sc in each st across, turn. Fasten off at end of last row.

ASSEMBLY

1: Whipstitch plastic canvas arm pieces to plastic canvas back piece according to Diagram No. 1.

2: Whipstitch **back lps** of row 45 on front of Back Cover to 15th bar up from bottom on plastic canvas back.

3: For **back rest**, glue 2" side of 1" x 2" x 8" foam piece to plastic canvas back according to Diagram No. 2. Allow to dry completely. For **seat cushion**, glue 1" x 3½" x 8" piece to back rest piece according to same diagram. Allow to dry completely.

4: Working with Bottom & Back Cover, sew ends of rows 15-18 of inside bottom to rows 19-22 on outer bottom. Sew ends of rows 23-32 to unworked stitches on row 18 of inside bottom.

5: Whipstitch **back lps** of row 36

DIAGRAM #2

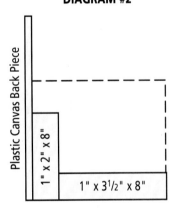

DIAGRAM #3

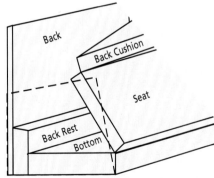

to bottom edge of plastic canvas back piece.

6: Fold back of Back Cover over plastic canvas back piece and sew row 78 to **front lps** of row 36.

7: Fold crocheted Arm Covers over each plastic canvas arm with **back lps** of row 14 on top edge and rows 15-24 on inside towards cushion. Whipstitch rows 24-15 to rows 5-14 on front edge.

8: Sew remaining edges of Bottom & Back Cover together and Whipstitch row 1 of Arm Covers to plastic canvas arms.

9: For **back cushion**, skip first 14 unworked sts on rnd 18; sew **back lps** of next 32 sts on rnd 18 to 32 sts on row 32. Sew ends of rows 19-32 on each side of back cushion to 14 sts on each remaining side of rnd 18, inserting 1" x 3½" x 8" foam piece before closing.

10: For **seat cushion**, repeat Step #9.

11: Sew center seam of 32 sts on back cushion and seat cushion together as shown in Diagram No. 3.☙

GRANDFATHER CLOCK

Designed by Mary K. Perry

PHOTO on page 11
TECHNIQUE: Plastic Canvas
SIZE: 1¼" x 3" x 10⅝" tall.
MATERIALS: One sheet of 7-count plastic canvas; ¼ sheet of 10-count plastic canvas; One 3" plastic canvas circle; 2⅛" x 7⅛" piece clear plastic; ⅛" hole punch; Permanent marker; Small amount of brown embroidery floss; #5 pearl cotton or six-strand embroidery floss (for amount see Color Key on page 14); Medium metallic braid, ⅛" metallic ribbon or metallic cord (for amounts see Color Key); Worsted-weight or plastic canvas yarn (for amount see Color Key).

CUTTING INSTRUCTIONS:

NOTES: Use 10-count canvas for F and G pieces and circle for H.

Graphs and diagrams on page 14.

A: For front, cut one according to graph.

B: For back, cut one according to graph.

C: For sides pieces, cut two each 8 x 30 holes, 8 x 18 holes, 8 x 12 holes, 4 x 8 holes and 2 x 8 holes (no graphs).

D: For top, cut one 8 x 15 holes (no graph).

E: For inner support, cut one 7 x 14 holes (no graph).

F: For face, cut one from 10-count 20 x 20 holes.

G: For weights, cut three from 10-count 5 x 11 holes (no graph).

H: For pendulum, cut one from circle according to graph.

I: For "glass", cut one from plastic 2⅛" square for top piece and one 1½" x 4¾" for bottom piece.

STITCHING INSTRUCTIONS:

NOTE: E piece is unworked.

1: Using dk. brown and stitches indicated, work A and B pieces according to graphs, leaving uncoded areas unworked; Overcast unfinished cutout edges of A. Using dk. brown and Continental Stitch, work C and D pieces. Using gold metallic, French Knot and Straight Stitch, embroider A as indicated on graph.

2: Using metallic braid colors and stitches indicated, work F and H pieces according to graphs; with gold, Overcast unfinished edge of H. Using pearl cotton or six strands floss, Straight Stitch and Cross Stitch, embroider F as indicated.

3: Using gold and Continental Stitch, work G pieces. For each weight, Whipstitch 11-hole edges of one G piece together, forming cylinder; Overcast unfinished edges.

4: Leaving indicated lengths of metallic for "chains," with gold, attach weights and pendulum to center of E according to Mechanism Assembly Diagram. With dk. brown, tack back corners of inner support to wrong side of B as indicated.

5: With dk. brown, attach I pieces to wrong side of front according to "Glass" Assembly Diagram. With brown floss, tack clock face behind upper cutout.

6: For each side, Whipstitch one of each size C piece together according to Side Assembly Diagram.

7: With dk. brown, Whipstitch pieces together according to Grandfather Clock Assembly Diagram; Overcast unfinished edges.☙

Grandfather Clock

Photo on page 11
Instructions on page 13

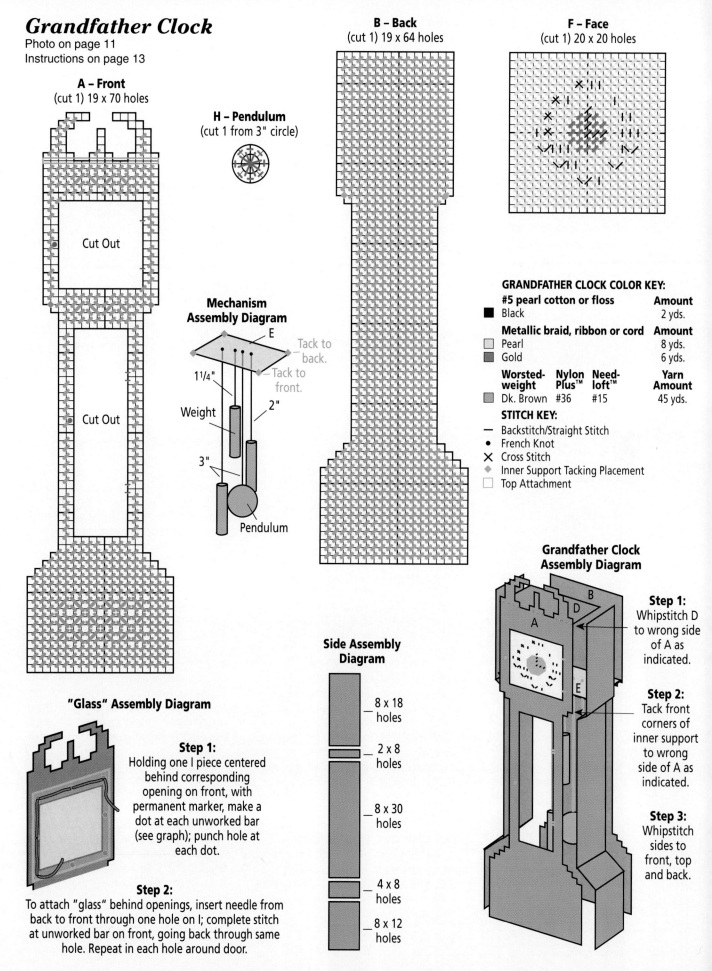

A – Front
(cut 1) 19 x 70 holes

Cut Out

Cut Out

H – Pendulum
(cut 1 from 3" circle)

B – Back
(cut 1) 19 x 64 holes

F – Face
(cut 1) 20 x 20 holes

**Mechanism
Assembly Diagram**

E

Tack to back.

Tack to front.

1¹⁄₄"

2"

Weight

3"

Pendulum

GRANDFATHER CLOCK COLOR KEY:

#5 pearl cotton or floss			Amount
■ Black			2 yds.
Metallic braid, ribbon or cord			**Amount**
▨ Pearl			8 yds.
▨ Gold			6 yds.
Worsted-weight	**Nylon Plus™**	**Need-loft™**	**Yarn Amount**
▨ Dk. Brown	#36	#15	45 yds.

STITCH KEY:
- — Backstitch/Straight Stitch
- • French Knot
- ✕ Cross Stitch
- ◆ Inner Support Tacking Placement
- ☐ Top Attachment

**Grandfather Clock
Assembly Diagram**

B

D

A

E

Step 1:
Whipstitch D to wrong side of A as indicated.

Step 2:
Tack front corners of inner support to wrong side of A as indicated.

Step 3:
Whipstitch sides to front, top and back.

**Side Assembly
Diagram**

8 x 18 holes

2 x 8 holes

8 x 30 holes

4 x 8 holes

8 x 12 holes

"Glass" Assembly Diagram

Step 1:
Holding one I piece centered behind corresponding opening on front, with permanent marker, make a dot at each unworked bar (see graph); punch hole at each dot.

Step 2:
To attach "glass" behind openings, insert needle from back to front through one hole on I; complete stitch at unworked bar on front, going back through same hole. Repeat in each hole around door.

– 14 –

PICTURES

Designed by Rosemarie Walter

TECHNIQUE: Paper Craft
SIZE: 2" x 2½".
MATERIALS: Two 2" x 2½" frames; Two 2½" x 3" pieces of beige perforated paper; Colored pencils in each color — dk. blue, lt. blue, dk. green, lt. green, dk. brown, lt. brown, violet, yellow and red; Scissors; Craft glue or glue gun.

INSTRUCTIONS:
1: Using colored pencils, draw one design onto each piece of perforated paper as indicated on graphs and according to Perforated Paper Illustration.
2: Trim finished designs to fit each frame opening. Position and glue into frames to secure.❧

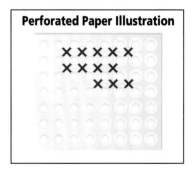

Perforated Paper Illustration

X HOME SWEET HOME COLOR KEY:
- Dk. Green
- Red
- Violet

X SUMMER GARDEN COLOR KEY:
- Dk. Blue
- Lt. Blue
- Dk. Brown
- Lt. Brown
- Dk. Green
- Lt. Green
- Red
- Yellow

Home Sweet Home

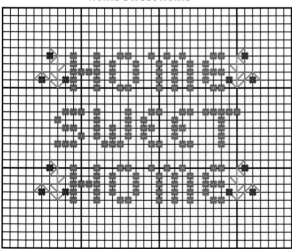

Summer Garden

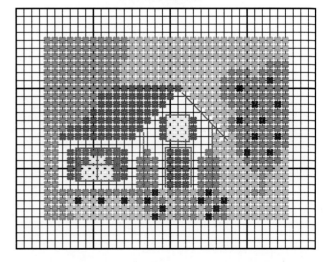

RUG & FLOOR PILLOW

Designed by Michele Wilcox

PHOTO on page 11
TECHNIQUE: Plastic Canvas
SIZE: Rug is 8" x 9¾", not including fringe; Floor Pillow is 5¼" square, not including tassels.
MATERIALS: 1½ sheets of 7-count plastic canvas; Polyester fiberfill; 3" square cardboard; #3 pearl cotton or 2-ply yarn (for amount see Rug Color Key); Worsted-weight or plastic canvas yarn (for amounts see individual Color Keys).

CUTTING INSTRUCTIONS:
A: For Rug, cut one 53 x 65 holes.

B: For Floor Pillow, cut two 35 x 35 holes.

STITCHING INSTRUCTIONS:
1: Using colors and stitches indicated, work A and B pieces according to graphs. Fill in uncoded areas using beige and Continental Stitch; Overcast unfinished edges of A.

NOTE: Wrap pearl cotton around 3" cardboard 54 times; cut wraps at each end.

2: For each fringe, holding two 3" lengths of pearl cotton or 2-ply yarn together, tie a Lark's Head Knot in every other hole across each short end of Rug. Trim ends.
3: For Floor Pillow, holding B

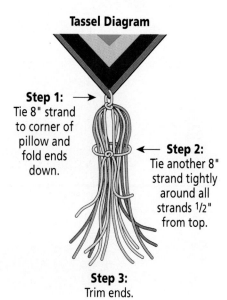

Tassel Diagram

Step 1: → Tie 8" strand to corner of pillow and fold ends down.

Step 2: ← Tie another 8" strand tightly around all strands ½" from top.

Step 3: Trim ends.

RUG COLOR KEY:

#3 pearl cotton or 2-ply yarn			Amount
☐ Ecru			4½ yds.

Worsted-weight	Nylon Plus™	Need-loft™	Yarn Amount
☐ Beige	#43	#40	22 yds.
▨ Green	#58	#28	18 yds.
▨ Denim	#06	#33	15 yds.
■ Burgundy	#13	#03	12 yds.

A – Rug (cut 1) 53 x 65 holes

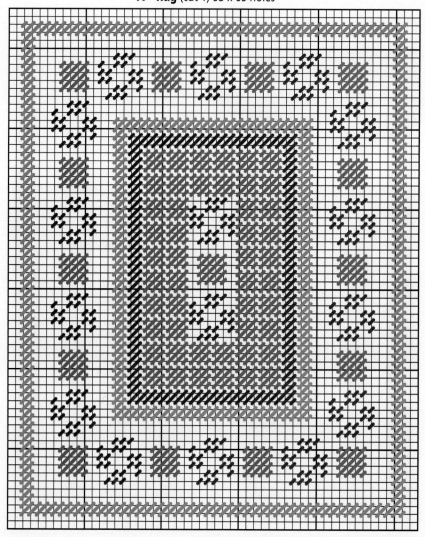

pieces wrong sides together, with denim, Whipstitch together, stuffing with fiberfill before closing.

4: For each tassel, wrap beige around 3" cardboard 13 times. Tie separate 8" strand tightly around loops at one end; cut loops at opposite end. Attach and finish tassel according to Tassel Diagram.❧

B – Floor Pillow
(cut 2)
35 x 35 holes

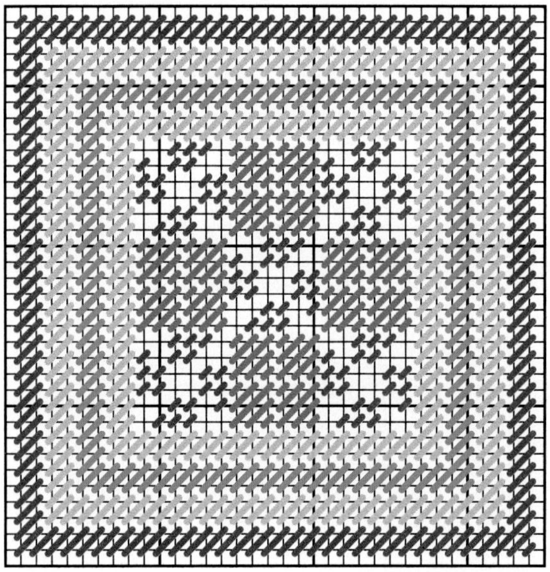

FLOOR PILLOW COLOR KEY:

	Worsted-weight	Nylon Plus™	Need-loft™	Yarn Amount
☐	Beige	#43	#40	26½ yds.
■	Burgundy	#13	#03	15 yds.
▨	Denim	#06	#33	12 yds.
▥	Green	#58	#28	12 yds.

MOCCASINS

Designed by Priscilla Cole

TECHNIQUE: Sewing
SIZE: Fits 11½" fashion doll.
MATERIALS: 2" x 3½" scrap of soft leather (car chamois, old glove, etc.); 3" square piece heavy cardboard; Quilting needle; Thread to match leather.

CUTTING INSTRUCTIONS:

1: From soft leather, cut two Top pieces following Top pattern and two Sole pieces following Sole pattern.

STITCHING INSTRUCTIONS:

1: Lay top and sole pieces on cardboard; using quilting needle, punch indicated holes through the leather (the holes need to be pre-punched to measure the gathering of the sole on the top piece and to help with sewing). Clip heels of sole where indicated on sole pattern.

2: To secure thread in heel, double thread needle and insert in heel pulling thread almost all the way through; then, reach around and insert needle between threads (see Knot Illustration).

3: Assemble Moccasins according to Moccasin Assembly Diagram.❧

Knot Illustration

Heel Overlap Diagram

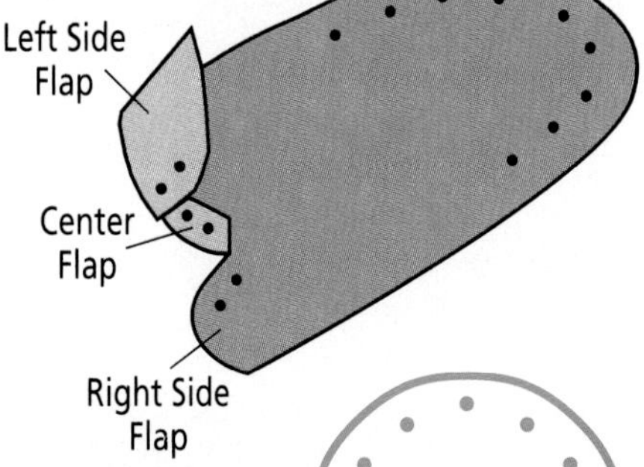

Left Side Flap

Center Flap

Right Side Flap

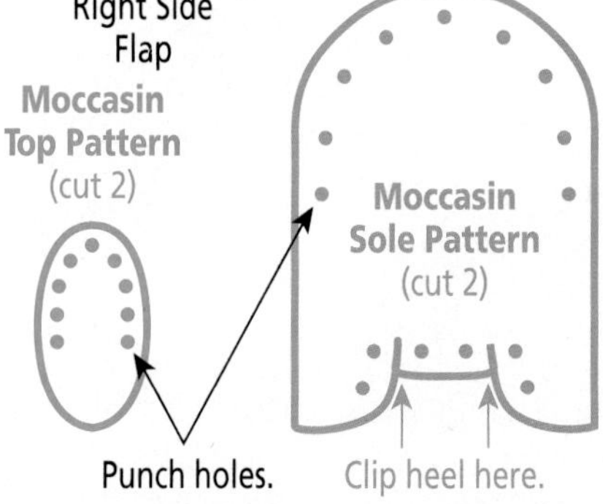

Moccasin Top Pattern
(cut 2)

Moccasin Sole Pattern
(cut 2)

Punch holes.

Clip heel here.

Moccasin Assembly Diagram

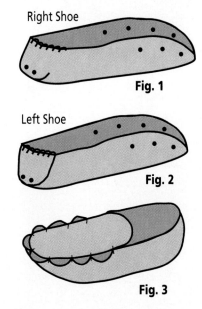

Right Shoe

Fig. 1

Left Shoe

Fig. 2

Fig. 3

Step 1:
For right shoe (see Fig.1), matching punched holes at bottom of heel, fold center flap up (see Heel Overlap Diagram), fold left side flap over center flap and right side flap over left side flap; sewing through all thicknesses, sew through punched holes several times (like sewing on a button). Whipstitch flaps together at top of heel.

Step 2:
For left shoe (see Fig. 2), work same as Step 1 for right shoe, folding left side flap over right side flap.

Step 3:
Matching punched holes, Whipstitch top pieces to soles, easing to fit (soles will pucker as they are eased into place–see Fig. 3).

Make His Comfort First Priority with a Chair that Really Reclines and a Bearskin Rug

His Place

Recliner (page 19); Fish Plaque (page 19);
Bearskin Rug (page 20)

RECLINER

Designed by Trudy Bath Smith

TECHNIQUE: Plastic Canvas
SIZE: 4½" x 6¾" x 8¾" tall when upright.
MATERIALS: Three sheets of 12" x 18" or larger 7-count plastic canvas; Two 30-mm. (¼" shank) plastic doll joints; ⅓ yd. denim print fabric; Sewing needle and matching color thread; Polyester fiberfill; Gravel or marbles; Craft glue or glue gun; Worsted-weight or plastic canvas yarn (for amount see Color Key).

CUTTING INSTRUCTIONS:
NOTE: Graphs and diagrams continued on page 21.
A: For cushion front pieces, cut two according to graph.

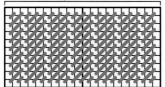

F – Cushion Back Flap
(cut 1) 10 x 20 holes
Whipstitch to B.

FISH PLAQUE

Designed by Brenda R. Wendling

TECHNIQUE: Novelty Craft
SIZE: 3⅜" x 5⅜".
MATERIALS: One 3⅜" x 5⅜" wooden oval plaque; One 3"-long fishing lure; 1½" x 6" scrap of black tulle; Two oblong gold-plated metal nailheads; Fruitwood wood stain; Wire cutters; Craft glue or glue gun.

INSTRUCTIONS:
1: Using wire cutters, cut hooks from lure.
2: Stain wooden plaque with fruitwood stain. Gather tulle and glue to back of fish as shown in photo.
3: Glue fish and nailheads to plaque as shown. ❧

B: For cushion back pieces, cut two according to graph.
C: For cushion top and upper sides, cut one 7 x 93 holes (no graph).
D: For cushion lower side pieces, cut four according to graph.
E: For cushion inner support, cut one 7 x 18 holes (no graph).
F: For cushion back flap, cut one 10 x 20 holes.
G: For seat cushion, cut one 20 x 52 holes (no graph).
H: For seat cushion side pieces, cut four according to graph.

Continued on page 20

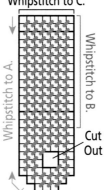

D – Cushion Lower Side Piece
(cut 4) 7 x 22 holes
Whipstitch to C.
Whipstitch to A.
Whipstitch to B.
Cut Out

RECLINER COLOR KEY:
Nylon Plus™ Needloft™ yarn
☐ #07   #48 Dk. Royal – 4 oz.
STITCH KEY:
✦ Footrest Attachment

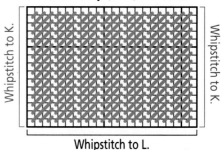

J – Footrest Top (cut 1) 15 x 22 holes
Whipstitch to K.
Whipstitch to K.
Whipstitch to L.

M – Chair Front Piece
(cut 2) 27 x 42 holes
Whipstitch to Q between red arrows.
Whipstitch to Q between red arrows.
Whipstitch to R between green arrows.
Whipstitch to R between green arrows.
Whipstitch to P.

N – Chair Back Piece
(cut 2) 27 x 42 holes
Whipstitch to Q between red arrows.
Whipstitch to Q between red arrows.
Whipstitch to R between green arrows.
Whipstitch to R between green arrows.
Whipstitch to P.

BEARSKIN RUG

Designed by Fran Rohus

PHOTO on page 18
TECHNIQUE: Novelty Craft
SIZE: 8" x 8".
MATERIALS: 9" x 12" piece of white fur fabric; One 5-mm. beige pom-pom; One 1½", one ¾" and two ¼" white pom-poms; Two 6-mm. brown animal eyes; Craft glue or glue gun.

CUTTING INSTRUCTIONS:
1: From white fur fabric, cut one body following Body Pattern.

ASSEMBLY INSTRUCTIONS:
NOTE: Use 5-mm. beige pom-pom for nose, 1½" white pom-pom for head, ¾" pom-pom for muzzle and ¼" pom-poms for ears.
1: Glue muzzle, eyes and ears to head according to Head Assembly Diagram; glue nose to muzzle.
2: Glue head to body as shown in photo.❦

Recliner
Continued from page 19
I: For seat cushion back, cut one 7 x 20 holes (no graph).
J: For footrest top, cut one 15 x 22 holes.
K: For footrest side pieces, cut four according to graph.
L: For footrest bottom, cut one 6 x 22 holes (no graph).
M: For chair front pieces, cut two according to graph.
N: For chair back pieces, cut two according to graph.
O: For chair bottom pieces, cut two 21 x 36 holes (no graph).
P: For seat cushion support pieces, cut two 21 x 22 holes (no graph).
Q: For armrests, cut two 21 x 36 holes (no graph).
R: For chair side pieces, cut four 19 x 21 holes (no graph).
S: For head cushion, cut one from fabric 5" x 10½".
T: For arm cushions, cut two from fabric 4" x 8".

STITCHING INSTRUCTIONS:
NOTE: E, I, O and P pieces are unworked.
1: Using dk. royal and stitches indicated, work F and J pieces according to graph; using Continental Stitch, work C, G, L and Q pieces.
2: Holding two matching pieces together and working through both thicknesses as one, using stitches indicated, work A, B, M and N pieces according to graphs; using Continental Stitch, work R pieces.
3: Working one of each set on opposite side of canvas, work D, H and K pieces as in Step 2.
4: Whipstitch and assemble pieces as indicated on graphs and according to Recliner Assembly Diagram.
5: For each cushion, folding fabric in half crosswise with wrong sides together and using ¼" seams, sew side edges together, leaving one end open. Turn right side out. Stuff half of cushion lightly with fiberfill. Turn unfinished edges ¼" to inside and sew opening closed. If desired, sew across center of backrest to hold fiberfill in place.
6: With fiberfill at bottom front, glue headrest to top of cushion as shown in photo. With fiberfill on top, glue one armrest cushion to each armrest as shown.❦

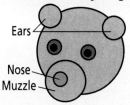

Head Assembly Diagram

Ears

Nose
Muzzle

**Bearskin Rug
Body Pattern**
(cut 1)

A – Cushion Front Piece (cut 2) 34 x 46 holes
Whipstitch to C between arrows.

B – Cushion Back Piece (cut 2) 34 x 39 holes
Whipstitch to C between arrows.

K – Footrest Side Piece
(cut 4) 5 x 16 holes

Whipstitch to J.

Whipstitch to L.

Whipstitch to D between purple arrows.

Whipstitch to D between purple arrows.

Whipstitch to D between green arrows.

Whipstitch to D between green arrows.

Whipstitch to F.

RECLINER COLOR KEY:
Nylon Plus™ Needloft™ yarn
#07   #48 Dk. Royal – 4 oz.
STITCH KEY:
✦ Footrest Attachment

Recliner Assembly Diagram

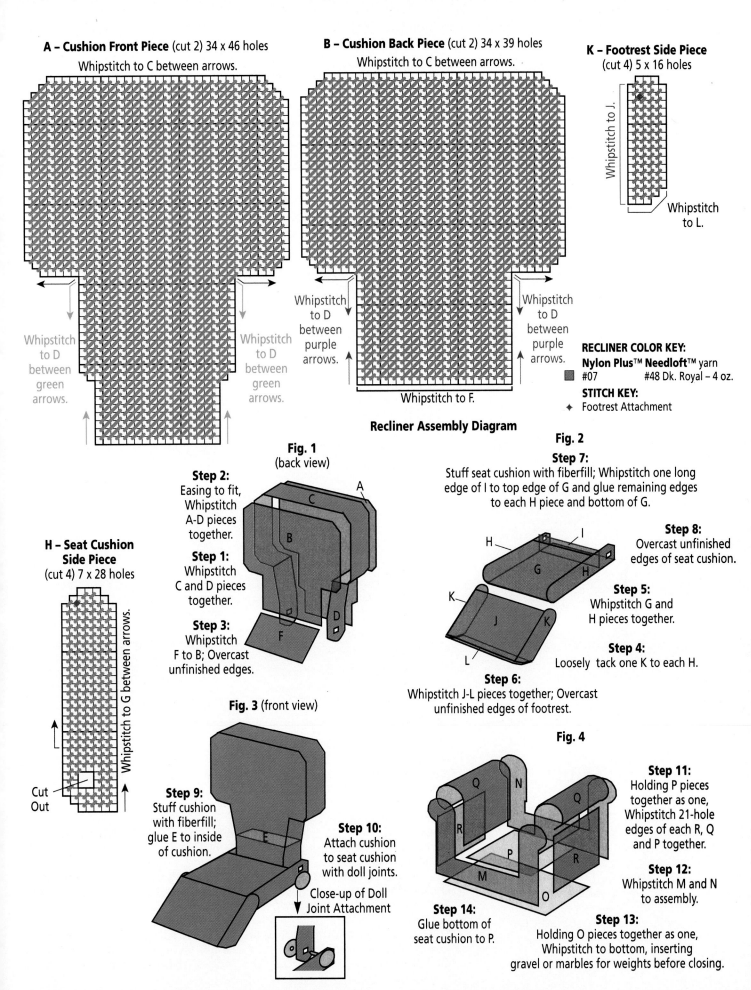

H – Seat Cushion Side Piece
(cut 4) 7 x 28 holes

Whipstitch to G between arrows.

Cut Out

Fig. 1
(back view)

Step 2:
Easing to fit, Whipstitch A-D pieces together.

Step 1:
Whipstitch C and D pieces together.

Step 3:
Whipstitch F to B; Overcast unfinished edges.

Fig. 2
Step 7:
Stuff seat cushion with fiberfill; Whipstitch one long edge of I to top edge of G and glue remaining edges to each H piece and bottom of G.

Step 8:
Overcast unfinished edges of seat cushion.

Step 5:
Whipstitch G and H pieces together.

Step 4:
Loosely tack one K to each H.

Step 6:
Whipstitch J-L pieces together; Overcast unfinished edges of footrest.

Fig. 3 (front view)

Step 9:
Stuff cushion with fiberfill; glue E to inside of cushion.

Step 10:
Attach cushion to seat cushion with doll joints.

Close-up of Doll Joint Attachment

Fig. 4

Step 11:
Holding P pieces together as one, Whipstitch 21-hole edges of each R, Q and P together.

Step 12:
Whipstitch M and N to assembly.

Step 14:
Glue bottom of seat cushion to P.

Step 13:
Holding O pieces together as one, Whipstitch to bottom, inserting gravel or marbles for weights before closing.

Share Giggles & Girl Talk on a Feminine Bunk Bed

Slumber Party

BUNK BED

Designed by Dorothy Tabor

TECHNIQUE: Plastic Canvas
SIZE: 6½" x 13" x 11½" tall.
MATERIALS: Ten sheets of 7-count plastic canvas; Polyester fiberfill; Craft glue or glue gun; Worsted-weight or plastic canvas yarn (for amounts see Color Key).

CUTTING INSTRUCTIONS:

NOTE: B graph, illustration and diagram on page 24.

A: For ends, cut four according to graph.

B: For sides, cut two according to graph.

C: For upper mattress support, cut one 40 x 83 holes (no graph).

D: For bed bottom, cut one 40 x 85 holes (no graph).

E: For mattress tops, cut two 39 x 82 holes.

F: For mattress bottoms, cut two 39 x 82 holes (no graph).

G: For mattress sides, cut four 10 x 82 holes (no graph).

H: For mattress ends, cut four 10 x 39 holes (no graph).

I: For ladder, cut one according to graph.

STITCHING INSTRUCTIONS:

NOTE: C, D and F pieces are unworked.

1: Using colors and stitches indicated (see Smyrna Cross Stitch Illustration), work A, B and E pieces according to graphs, leaving uncoded areas unworked; with eggshell, Overcast unfinished cutout edges of B pieces as indicated on graph. Using eggshell and Slanted Gobelin Stitch over narrow width, work F and G pieces; using Continental Stitch, work I. With pink, Overcast unfinished edges of ladder.

2: With eggshell, Whipstitch bed and mattress pieces together as indicated on graph and according to Bunk Bed Assembly Diagram. Glue ladder to bed as shown in photo.🍎

BUNK BED COLOR KEY:

Worsted-weight	Nylon Plus™	Need-loft™	Yarn Amount
☐ Eggshell	#24	#39	7 oz.
☐ Pink	#11	#07	45 yds.
☐ Green	#58	#28	20 yds.

I – Ladder (cut 1) 18 x 72 holes

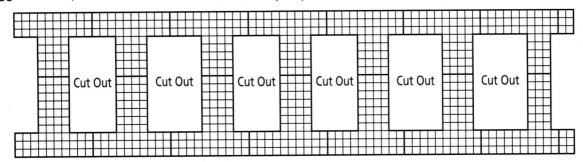

A – End
(cut 4) 40 x 76 holes
Whipstitch between arrows.

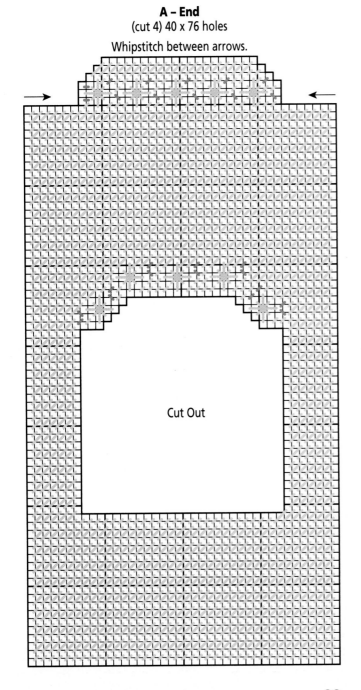

E – Mattress Top (cut 2) 39 x 82 holes

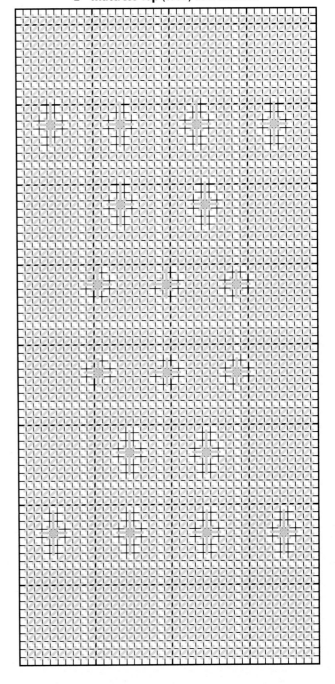

Bunk Bed

Instructions and photo on page 22

Bunk Bed Assembly Diagram

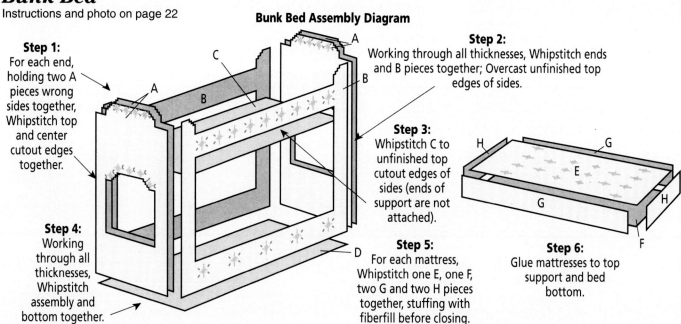

Step 1:
For each end, holding two A pieces wrong sides together, Whipstitch top and center cutout edges together.

Step 2:
Working through all thicknesses, Whipstitch ends and B pieces together; Overcast unfinished top edges of sides.

Step 3:
Whipstitch C to unfinished top cutout edges of sides (ends of support are not attached).

Step 4:
Working through all thicknesses, Whipstitch assembly and bottom together.

Step 5:
For each mattress, Whipstitch one E, one F, two G and two H pieces together, stuffing with fiberfill before closing.

Step 6:
Glue mattresses to top support and bed bottom.

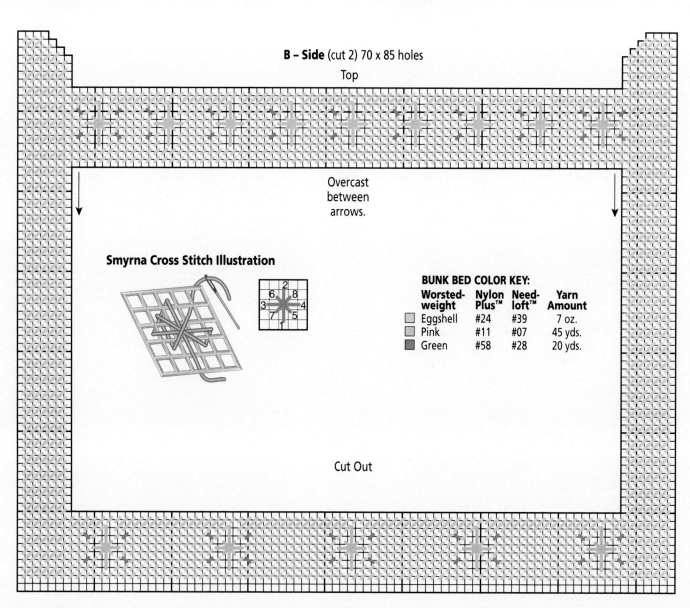

B – Side (cut 2) 70 x 85 holes

Top

Overcast between arrows.

Cut Out

Smyrna Cross Stitch Illustration

BUNK BED COLOR KEY:

	Worsted-weight	Nylon Plus™	Need-loft™	Yarn Amount
☐	Eggshell	#24	#39	7 oz.
☐	Pink	#11	#07	45 yds.
☐	Green	#58	#28	20 yds.

Relax in Luxury with Peach Bathroom Accents Adorned with Perky Bows.

Bathing Beauty

Bath Set (page 26)

BATH SET

Designed by Rosemarie Walter

PHOTO on page 25
TECHNIQUE: Crochet
SIZE: Tissue Cover is ¾" tall; Tissue Roll Cover is ¾" tall; Wastebasket Cover is 1⅛" tall; Rug is 3¼" x 4¼".
MATERIALS FOR ALL FOUR: Size 10 bedspread cotton — 75 yds. peach and small amount mint; Size 30 crochet cotton — 25 yds. ecru; Small amount white worsted-weight yarn; 24" mint 1/16" satin ribbon; 1⅛" tall x ¾" across bottom x ⅞" across top plastic lid (from pump spray bottle) for wastebasket; Craft glue or hot glue; Tapestry needle; No. 9, 6 and 3 steel crochet hooks or sizes needed to obtain gauges.
GAUGES: No. 9 hook, (sc, ch 1) 3 times in each of next 6 sts = 1". No 6 hook, 8 sc sts = 1"; 7 sc rnds = ¾". No. 3 hook, 7 sc sts = 1"; 6 sc rows over cord = 1".

TISSUE COVER

Rnd 1: Starting at top, with peach and No. 6 hook, ch 6, sl st in first ch to form ring, ch 1, 12 sc in ring, join with sl st in first sc (12 sc).

Rnd 2: Ch 1, sc in first st, 3 sc in next st, (sc in each of next 2 sts, 3 sc in next st) 3 times, sc in last st, join (20).

Rnd 3: Working in **back lps** this rnd only, ch 1, sc in each st around, join.

Rnd 4: Ch 1, sc in each st around, join.

NOTE: Fasten off each color when no longer needed.

Rnd 5: Ch 1, sc in each st around changing to mint in last st, join.

Rnd 6: Ch 1, sc in each st around changing to peach in last st, join.

Rnds 7-9: Ch 1, sc in each st around, join. Fasten off at end of last rnd.

Rnd 10: For **ruffle,** working in **front lps** this rnd only, join ecru with sc in first st, (ch 1, sc, ch 1, sc, ch 1) in same st, (sc, ch 1) 3 times in each st around, join, fasten off.

Cut an 8" piece of ribbon. Fold ribbon to form a 1" triple-loop bow; tie a separate piece of mint bedspread cotton around center of bow to secure and glue to rnd 9 on Tissue Cover as shown in photo.

Fold a facial tissue accordian style lengthwise, then crosswise, forming a ¾" square. Insert tissue in cover, pulling a small corner through top opening.

TISSUE ROLL COVER

NOTE: Fasten off each color when no longer needed.

Rnd 1: Starting at top, with peach and No. 6 hook, ch 2, 6 sc in 2nd ch from hook, join with sl st in first sc (6 sc).

Rnd 2: Ch 1, 2 sc in each st around, join (12).

Rnd 3: Ch 1, (2 sc in next st, sc in next st) around, join (18).

Rnd 4: Working in **back lps** this rnd only, ch 1, sc in each st around, join.

Rnd 5: Ch 1, sc in each st around, join.

Rnd 6: Ch 1, sc in each st around changing to mint in last st, join.

Rnd 7: Ch 1, sc in each st around changing to peach in last st, join.

Rnds 8-10: Ch 1, sc in each st around, join. Fasten off at end of last rnd.

Rnd 11: For **ruffle,** working in **front lps** this rnd only, join ecru with sc in first st, (ch 1, sc, ch 1, sc, ch 1) in same st, (sc, ch 1) 3 times in each st around, join, fasten off.

Cut an 8" piece of ribbon. Fold ribbon to form a 1" triple-loop bow; tie a separate piece of mint bedspread cotton around center of bow to secure and glue to top of Tissue Roll Cover as shown in photo.

Fold a facial tissue lengthwise accordian style, forming a ¾" strip. Roll strip to form tissue roll and insert in cover.

WASTEBASKET COVER

NOTE: Fasten off each color when no longer needed.

Rnd 1: Starting at bottom, with peach and No. 6 hook, ch 2, 6 sc in 2nd ch from hook, join with sl st in first sc (6 sc).

Rnd 2: Ch 1, 2 sc in each st around, join (12).

Rnd 3: Ch 1, (2 sc in next st, sc in next st) around, join (18).

Rnd 4: Working in **back lps** this rnd only, ch 1, sc in each st around, join.

Rnds 5-7: Ch 1, sc in each st around, join.

Rnd 8: Ch 1, sc in each st around changing to mint in last st, join.

Rnd 9: Ch 1, sc in each st around changing to peach in last st, join.

Rnds 10-13: Ch 1, sc in each st around, join. Fasten off at end of last rnd.

Rnd 14: For **ruffle,** working in **front lps** this rnd only, join ecru with sc in first st, (ch 1, sc, ch 1, sc, ch 1) in same st, (sc, ch 1) 3 times in each st around, join, fasten off.

Cut an 8" piece of ribbon. Fold ribbon to form a 1" triple-loop bow; tie a separate piece of mint bedspread cotton around center of bow to secure and glue to side of Wastebasket Cover as shown in photo. Slip Cover over plastic cap and glue to secure.

RUG

Row 1: With peach and No. 3 hook, ch 20; working over white worsted-weight yarn for cord (see ill.), sc in 2nd ch from hook, sc in each ch across, turn (19 sc).

WORKING OVER CORD ILL

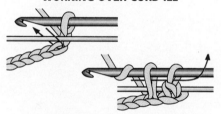

Row 2: Ch 1; working over cord, sc in each st across, turn.

Row 3: Ch 1; working over cord, sc in each st across changing to mint in last st, turn. Fasten off peach.

Row 4: Ch 1; working over cord, sc in each st across changing to peach in last st, turn. Fasten off mint.

Rows 5-7: Ch 1; working over cord, sc in each st across, turn.

Row 8: Ch 1; working over cord, sc in each st across changing to mint in last st, turn. Fasten off peach.

Row 9: Ch 1; working over cord, sc in each st across changing to peach in last st, turn. Fasten off mint.

Rows 10-22: Repeat rows 5-9 consecutively, ending with row 7.

Rnd 24: Working around outer edge and over cord, ch 1, sc in each st and in end of each row around with 3 sc in each corner, join with sl st in first sc, fasten off peach and cut cord.

Rnd 25: With No. 9 hook, join ecru with sc in first st, (ch 1, sc, ch 1, sc, ch 1) in same st, (sc, ch 1) 3 times in each st around, join with sl st in first sc, fasten off.

BATH TOWEL SET

Designed by Rosemarie Walter

TECHNIQUE: Sewing
SIZE: Bath towel is 2½" x 3¾";
Hand towel is 1¾" x 3";
Washcloth is 2½" x 2½".
MATERIALS: One light-weight
rose washcloth; ⅓ yd. off-white
½" flat scalloped lace; ⅓ yd. rose
⅛" satin ribbon; ⅝ yd. off-white
⅛" satin ribbon; Sewing needle
and off-white and rose thread.

CUTTING INSTRUCTIONS:

1: From washcloth, cut one 2½" x
6½" piece for bath towel, one 1¾"
x 5" piece for hand towel and one
1½" x 3" piece for washcloth.

STITCHING INSTRUCTIONS:

1: For towel set, fold each fabric
piece in half crosswise (fold is top
edge), forming a 2½" x 3¼" piece for
bath towel, 1¾" x 2½" piece for hand
towel and a 1½" x 1½" piece for
washcloth. Press each piece. Machine
stitch or Blanket Stitch side and bot-

tom edges of each piece together.

2: Cut lace to fit around outside
edge of washcloth and across bottom
edges of bath towel and hand towel;
stitch in place as shown in photo. Cut
off-white ribbon same as lace; stitch
on top of lace as shown.

3: Cut remaining off-white ribbon
into one 4½" length for bath towel,
one 4" length for hand towel and
one 2¼" length for washcloth; fold
pieces in half, forming small loops at
folds and tack in place as shown.
Repeat with rose ribbon.❦

HANGER STITCH KEY:
✦ Bead/Bow Attachment

Bow Folding Diagram

A – Hanger
(cut 1)
13 x 30 holes

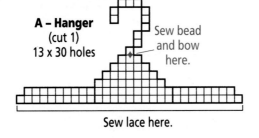

Sew bead
and bow
here.

Sew lace here.

FANCY HANGERS

Designed by Rosemarie Walter

TECHNIQUE: Plastic Canvas
SIZE: 1⅜" x 3", not including
lace.
MATERIALS FOR ONE: Scrap of
colored 10-count plastic canvas;
6" contrasting color ⅛" satin ribbon; One coordinating color
4-mm. pearl bead; 3" white ⅜"
lace; Sewing needle and white
thread.

CUTTING INSTRUCTIONS:

A: For Hanger, cut one according to graph.

ASSEMBLY INSTRUCTIONS:

1: Sew lace to bottom edge of
unworked A as indicated on graph.
Fold ribbon to form bow (see Bow
Folding Diagram); sew bow and
bead to hanger as indicated and as
shown in photo.❦

BEDROOM SET

Designed by Frances Hughes

TECHNIQUE: Crochet, Sewing & Woodcraft
SIZE: Wooden Bed is $8\frac{3}{4}$" wide x $12\frac{1}{2}$" long x $11\frac{3}{8}$" tall; Bedspread is $11\frac{1}{2}$" x 13"; Canopy is 13" x $16\frac{1}{2}$" including edging; Bolster Cover is $7\frac{3}{4}$" long; Pillow Top is $2\frac{1}{2}$" across (point to point); Wooden Table is $3\frac{1}{2}$" across top and $3\frac{1}{2}$" tall; Table Topper is 8" across; Quilt Rack is $2\frac{1}{2}$" x $4\frac{1}{8}$" x $5\frac{1}{2}$" tall; Quilt is $10\frac{1}{2}$" x $12\frac{1}{4}$".
MATERIALS FOR WOODEN FURNITURE: 4 ft. length of white pine 1" x 12" board (see Notes below) or $\frac{1}{2}$ sheet of $\frac{3}{8}$"-thick plywood; Wooden dowel — 12" of $\frac{1}{4}$" and $3\frac{1}{8}$" of $\frac{7}{16}$"; Scroll, band or coping saw; Electric drill with stop collar; $\frac{1}{4}$" and $\frac{7}{16}$" drill bits; Paper and tracing materials; Carpenter's square; Wood glue; Fine grade sand paper; Wood putty (optional — see Note); Two 2" C-clamps and two 18" bar clamps; $\frac{1}{2}$" finishing nails and hammer (optional); Paint brush and white paint.
MATERIALS FOR CROCHETED & FABRIC ACCESSORIES: Size 10 bedspread cotton — 800 yds. white; 2 yds. mauve polished cotton fabric; $\frac{1}{3}$ yd. coordinating striped fabric; Sewing thread to match fabrics; 8 yds. mauve $\frac{1}{8}$" satin ribbon; 20 mauve $\frac{1}{2}$" satin ribbon roses with leaves; Polyester fiberfill; 10" x 12" piece of quilt batting; Craft glue or glue gun; Sewing machine or needle; Tapestry needle; No. 7 steel crochet hook or size needed to obtain gauge.
GAUGE: 9 sc sts = 1"; 5 dc sts and 4 ch-1 sps = 1"; 4 dc rows = 1"; Rnd 1 of Pillow Top is $\frac{3}{4}$" across; Rnds 1-2 of Table Topper are $1\frac{5}{8}$" across.

FURNITURE

NOTES: Bed in photograph was constructed from white pine that had been planed to $\frac{3}{8}$" thick. White pine may be purchased at larger lumber yards as a 1" x 12" x 4' board (actual measurements are $\frac{3}{4}$" x $11\frac{1}{2}$" x 4'). If you do not own a planer, a local cabinet or furniture crafting shop may provide this service to you for a fee.

If you desire, $\frac{3}{8}$" plywood may be substituted for the pine. However, cutting may be more difficult and the edges will not be as smooth. Using a fine-edged saw prevents some splintering that is caused from using a coarse-edged saw. To finish the edges, after the bed is complete, prior to painting, fill the exposed edges with wood putty, allowing to dry according to manufacturer's recommendations. Sand edges smooth, then paint.

When tracing bed pieces, use a carpenter's square to assure perfectly straight pieces.

Instructions are written for gluing wooden pieces together. If desired, you may use finishing nails to assemble, but exercise caution. As bed is intended to be a toy, nails that might protrude from the wood or splinters caused by nails splitting the wood may be hazardous to small children.

Patterns on pages 30-32.

BED

1: For **headboard** and **footboard,** trace pattern pieces (separate at dotted lines as indicated on pattern) onto paper, overlapping pieces as indicated to form one solid piece. Transfer patterns onto wood and cut out with saw. Sand edges as needed, being careful not to harm straight edges and corners which might hamper assembly.

2: For **bed bottom,** cut one $8\frac{5}{8}$" x $11\frac{3}{4}$". For **bed top,** cut one $8\frac{3}{4}$" x $12\frac{1}{2}$". For **rails,** cut two $\frac{3}{4}$" x $11\frac{3}{4}$".

3: Place bed bottom, wrong side up, on a flat surface. Glue one rail, set on edge, to each long edge on wrong side of bed bottom. Secure with small clamps and allow to dry completely following glue manufacturer's recommendations.

4: Securing with bar clamps, glue bottom and rails to headboard and footboard as indicated on pattern piece; allow to dry.

5: Sand remaining rough edges.

Continued on page 30

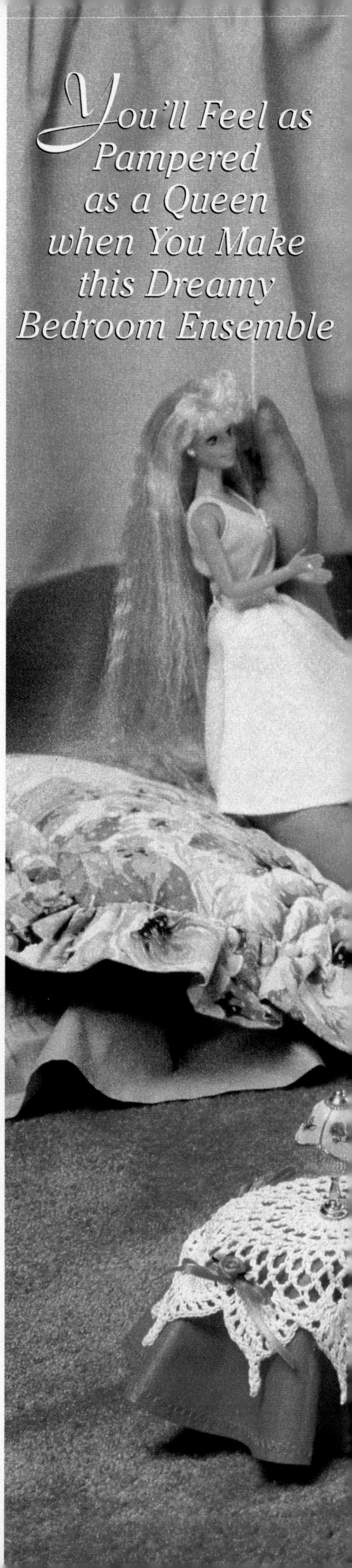
You'll Feel as Pampered as a Queen when You Make this Dreamy Bedroom Ensemble

Victorian Lace

Bedroom Set
Continued from page 28

Continued from page 28

NOTE: Pattern is divided onto two pages. Match lines and overlap while tracing to complete pattern piece.

6: Paint all sides of bed top and assembled bed pieces. Allow to dry overnight.

7: Glue corners of bed top to top of bedposts.

TABLE

1: For **top,** cut one 3½" circle. For **bottom,** cut one 2¼" circle. For **pedestal,** use ⁷⁄₁₆" dowel. Sand edges.

2: Mark center on top and bottom; using ⁷⁄₁₆" bit, drill a ⅛" deep hole in center of each.

3: Glue ends of dowel into holes in top and bottom, forming table. Allow to dry completely.

4: Paint table and let dry.

QUILT STAND

1: For **ends,** trace pattern piece onto paper, marking dowel placements as indicated; cut two from wood. Cut ¼" dowel into three 3⅝" lengths.

2: Mark dowel placements on each end. Using ¼" bit, drill ⅛" deep hole at each placement.

3: Glue dowels in holes on each end, clamping to secure if needed. Allow to dry completely.

4: Paint stand and let dry.

SEWN ACCESSORIES
DUST RUFFLE

1: From mauve fabric, cut 9⅛" x 12¼" piece for top piece and two 4" x 18" pieces for ruffles.

2: With sewing thread and needle, baste along one long edge of each ruffle piece, pull basting thread to fit long edge of top piece. Allowing ¼" for seam, sew basted edges of ruffles to each long edge of top piece.

3: Hem ¼" around bottom edge of entire piece.

MATTRESS

From mauve fabric, cut two 9⅛" x 12¼" pieces. Holding both pieces right sides together, allowing ¼" for seam, sew together leaving 4" opening for turning. Turn right side out and stuff lightly. Sew opening closed.

CANOPY LINING

From mauve fabric, cut 9¼" x 13" piece. Hem outer edge ¼".

Cut away here for footboard.

Optional Cutout

HEADBOARD
(Cut 1)

Cut away here for footboard.

Cut away here for footboard.

Optional Cutout

TABLE UNDERSKIRT

From mauve fabric, cut 10½" circle. Hem edge ¼".

BOLSTER PILLOW

1: From mauve fabric, cut one 5½" x 9½" piece for sides and two 1¼" x 5½" pieces for ends.

2: With wrong sides together, matching 5½" edges and allowing ¼" for seams, sew one end piece to each end of side piece. Folding one end piece lengthwise, with wrong sides together, make first fold by folding end piece in half; make second fold by folding end piece over side piece. Topstitch along second fold ⅛" from edge, catching unfinished edge of end piece in topstitching. Repeat on other end.

3: Fold side piece in half lengthwise, wrong sides together; sew along open edge, forming tube. Turn right side out.

4: Baste across folded edge of one end piece; pull tightly to gather in center. Secure thread.

5: Stuff pillow firmly; repeat Step #4 on open end.

THROW PILLOW

From mauve fabric, cut two 3" circles. Holding circles right sides together, allowing ¼" for seam, sew together leaving 1" open for turning. Turn right side out and stuff. Sew opening closed.

QUILT

1: From striped fabric, cut two 11" x 12¾" pieces. Turn under ¼" on all edges of each piece.

2: Place fabric pieces wrong sides together with batting between; baste or pin together. Whipstitch together around outer edges.

3: Using Running Stitch, quilt lengthwise across fabric every ¾" following stripes.

4: Sew 43" piece of ⅛" mauve ribbon around quilt ¼" from edge, folding corners to keep ribbon flat and overlapping ends.

5: Sew one ribbon rose over ribbon at bottom left corner of Quilt. Sew two more roses to left edge spaced 1" apart above first rose, and another rose 1" to right of corner rose. Sew remaining rose to upper right corner.

6: Cut two 6" pieces of ⅛" ribbon; tie each in knot at center.

Sew to lower right and upper left corners of Quilt over ribbon.

CROCHETED ACCESSORIES
BEDSPREAD

Row 1: Ch 82, dc in 6th ch from hook, (ch 1, skip next ch, dc in next ch) across, turn (40 dc, 39 ch-1 sps).

Row 2: Ch 4, skip next ch sp, dc in next st, (ch 1, skip next st, dc in next st) across with ch 1, dc in 3rd ch of ch-5, turn.

Rows 3-42: Ch 4, skip next ch sp, dc in next st, (ch 1, skip next ch sp, dc in next st) across with ch 1, dc in 3rd ch of ch-4, turn. **Do not** fasten off at end of last row.

Edging

Rnd 1: Working around outer edge, ch 1, sc in each st, in each ch sp and 2 sc in end of each row around with 3 sc in each corner, join with sl st in first sc, **turn** (334 sc).

Row 2: Working in rows, for **first side,** (ch 4, skip next 2 sts, sc in next st) 28 times leaving remaining sts unworked, turn (28 ch sps).

Row 3: Sl st into first ch sp, ch 4, 8 tr in same sp, (sc in next ch sp, ch 3, sc in next ch sp, 9 tr in next ch sp) across, turn.

Row 4: Ch 4, *(dc in next st, ch 1) 3 times, [dc in next st, ch 5, sc in 2nd ch from hook, sc in each of next 3 chs, dc in same st as last dc, (ch 1, dc in next st) 4 times], sc in next ch-3 sp, dc in next tr, ch 1; repeat from * 8 times, (dc in next st, ch 1) 3 times; repeat between [ ], **do not** turn, fasten off.

Row 2: For **second side,** join with sl st in 3rd corner st on opposite side, (ch 4, skip next 2 sts, sc in next st) 28 times, turn (28 ch sps).

Rows 3-4: Repeat rows 3 and 4 of first side.

Finishing

Cut four pieces of ribbon each 12" long. Tie each piece into a bow around each corner st. Glue one ribbon rose to each bow.

CANOPY

Rows 1-2: Repeat same rows of Bedspread (36 dc, 35 ch-1 sps).

Rows 3-48: Repeat row 3 of Bedspread.

Edging

Rnd 1: Working around outer

Continued on page 32

Optional Cutout

Optional Cutout

Cut away here for footboard.

Bed Bottom and Rail Placement

Bedroom Set
Continued from page 31

edge, ch 1, sc in each st, in each ch sp and 2 sc in end of each row around with 3 sc in each corner st, join with sl st in first sc (342 sc).

Rnd 2: Ch 1, (sc in next st, ch 4, skip next 2 sts) around, join, **turn** (114 ch sps).

Rnd 3: Sl st into first ch sp, ch 4, 8 tr in same sp, sc in next ch sp, ch 3, sc in next ch sp, (9 tr in next ch sp, sc in next ch sp, ch 3, sc in next ch sp) around, join with sl st in top of ch-4.

Rnd 4: Ch 4, *(dc in next st, ch 1) 3 times, [dc in next st, ch 5, sc in 2nd ch from hook, sc in each of next 3 chs, dc in same st as last dc, (ch 1, dc in next st) 4 times, sc in next ch-3 sp], dc in next tr, ch 1; repeat from * around to last 8 sts,

QUILT STAND ENDS
(Cut 2)

(dc in next st, ch 1) 3 times; repeat between [ ], join with sl st in 3rd ch of ch-4, fasten off.

Finishing
1: Glue Canopy Lining over Bed top. Place crocheted Canopy over Lining.

2: Gathering slightly, starting at center ch sp of any corner, insert 16" piece of ribbon through ch sp to the right of center ch sp, skipping center ch sp, pull ribbon up through ch sp to the left of center; tie ends into a bow. Glue one ribbon rose to each bow.

3: Repeat Step #2 for each corner.

TABLE TOPPER
Rnd 1: Ch 4, sl st in first ch to form ring, ch 3, 21 dc in ring, join with sl st in top of ch-3 (22 dc).

Rnd 2: Ch 4, (dc in next st, ch 1) around, join with sl st in 3rd ch of ch-4 (22 dc, 22 ch-1 sps).

Rnd 3: Ch 5, (dc in next st, ch 2) around, join with sl st in 3rd ch of ch-5.

Rnd 4: Ch 4, dc in same st, ch 1, dc in next st, ch 1, *(dc, ch 1, dc) in next st, ch 1, dc in next st, ch 1; repeat from * around, join with sl st in 3rd ch of ch-4.

Rnd 5: Sl st into first ch sp, (ch 4, sc in next ch sp) around; to **join,** ch 2, dc in first ch of first ch-4 (33 ch sps).

Rnds 6-7: (Ch 4, sc in next ch sp) around, join as before.

Rnd 8: Ch 4, (sc in next ch sp, ch 4) around, join with sl st in first ch of first ch-4.

Rnds 9-10: Repeat rnds 3 and 4 of Canopy Edging.

Finishing
Cut four pieces of ribbon each 9" long. Tie ribbons into bows around sts on rnd 8 evenly spaced around topper. Glue one ribbon rose to each bow.

BOLSTER COVER
Row 1: Ch 44, dc in 6th ch from hook, (ch 1, skip next ch, dc in next ch) across, turn (21 dc, 20 ch sps).

Row 2: Repeat row 2 of Bedspread.

Rows 3-18: Repeat row 3 of Bedspread. Fasten off at end of last row.

Sew rows 1 and 18 together.

Edging
Rnd 1: Working in ends of rows, join with sl st in any row, ch 4, 6 tr in same row, sc in next row, ch 3, sc in next row, (7 tr in next row, sc in next row, ch 3, sc in next row) around, join with sl st in top of ch-4.

Rnd 2: Ch 4, *(dc in next st, ch 1) 2 times, [dc in next st, ch 5, sc in 2nd ch from hook, sc in each of next 3 chs, dc in same st as last dc, (ch 1, dc in next st) 3 times, sc in next ch-3 sp], dc in next tr, ch 1; repeat from * 4 times, (dc in next st, ch 1) 2 times; repeat between [ ], join with sl st in 3rd ch of ch-4, fasten off.

Repeat edging in ends of rows on opposite side.

Finishing
Cut two pieces of ribbon each 16" long. Weave ribbons in ch sps below each Edging, tie ends into bows. Glue one ribbon rose to each bow.

Slide Bolster Cover over bolster and glue tips of edging to Cover.

PILLOW TOP
Rnd 1: Ch 4, 13 dc in 4th from hook, join with sl st in top of ch-3 (14 dc).

Rnd 2: Ch 4, (dc in next st, ch 1) around, join with sl st in 3rd ch of ch-4.

Rnd 3: Sl st into first ch sp, ch 3, 4 dc in same sp, sc in next ch sp, (5 dc in next ch sp, sc in next ch sp) around, join with sl st in top of ch-3.

Rnd 4: Ch 3, (sc in next st, ch 3) around, join with sl st in first ch of first ch-3, fasten off.

Finishing
Cut 9" piece of ribbon. Tie into a bow around st on rnd 3. Glue one ribbon rose to bow.

Glue Pillow Top to one side of Throw Pillow.❧

Domestic Pleasures

TRAY OF COOKIES

Designed by Connie Folse

TECHNIQUE: Crochet
SIZE: 1¾" x 2½".
MATERIALS: Size 10 bedspread cotton — small amount each blue, brown and ecru; 1¼" x 2" piece of stiff cardboard; Tapestry needle; No. 9 steel crochet hook or size needed to obtain gauge.
GAUGE: 10 sc sts = 1"; 10 sc rows = 1".

TRAY SIDE (make 2)
 Row 1: With blue, ch 21, sc in 2nd ch from hook, sc in each ch across, turn (20 sc).
 Rows 2-12: Ch 1, sc in each st across, turn. Fasten off at end of last row.

Continued on page 35

Kitchen Set (page 34)

Company's Coming, so get Ready to Bake & Serve a Savory Meal

ELEGANT DINNERWARE

Designed by Rosemarie Walter

TECHNIQUE: Crochet
SIZE: Plate is 1⅜" across; Cup is ⅝" tall; Saucer is ⅞" across; Bowl is ⅜" tall.
MATERIALS FOR ALL FOUR:
Size 10 bedspread cotton — small amount white; Small amount gold metallic braid; Liquid fabric stiffener; Craft glue or hot glue; Tapestry needle; No. 9 steel crochet hook or size needed to obtain gauge.
GAUGE: 7 sc sts = 1".

PLATE

Rnd 1: With white, ch 2, 6 sc in 2nd ch from hook, join with sl st in first sc (6 sc).

Rnd 2: Ch 1, 2 sc in each st around, join (12).

Rnd 3: Ch 1, (2 sc in next st, sc in next st) around, join (18).

Rnd 4: Ch 1, (2 sc in next st, sc in next 2 sts) around, join (24).

Rnd 5: Ch 1, (2 sc in next st, sc in each of next 3 sts) around, join (30).

Rnd 6: Ch 1, (2 sc in next st, sc in next 4 sts) around, join (36).

Rnd 7: Ch 1, (2 sc in next st, sc in next 5 sts) around, join, fasten off (42).

Rnd 8: Working in **back lps** this rnd only, join metallic braid with sl st in first st, sl st in each st around, join with sl st in first st, fasten off.

Apply liquid fabric stiffener to Plate following manufacturer's stiffening instructions. Shape and allow to dry completely.

CUP

Rnd 1: With white, ch 2, 6 sc in 2nd ch from hook, join with sl st in first sc (6 sc).

Rnd 2: Ch 1, 2 sc in each st around, join (12).

Rnd 3: Working in **back lps** this rnd only, ch 1, sc in each st around, join.

Rnd 4: Ch 1, (2 sc in next st, sc in each of next 2 sts) around, join (16).

Rnds 5-6: Ch 1, sc in each st around, join. Fasten off at end of last rnd.

Rnd 7: Join metallic braid with sl st in first st, sl st in each st around, join, fasten off.

Rnd 8: For **base,** working in **front** lps of rnd 2, with top of Cup facing you, join white with sc in first st, sc in each st around, join, fasten off (12).

Rnd 9: Join metallic braid with sl st in first st, ch 1, (sl st in next st, ch 1) around, join with sl st in first st, fasten off.

For **handle,** with white, ch 6, fasten off; join metallic braid with sl st in first ch, sl st in each ch across, fasten off (6 sl sts).

Glue ends of handle to side of Cup as shown in photo. Allow glue to dry completely.

Apply liquid fabric stiffener to Cup following manufacturer's stiffening instructions. Shape and allow to dry completely.

SAUCER

Rnd 1: With white, ch 2, 6 sc in 2nd ch from hook, join with sl st in first sc (6 sc).

Rnd 2: Ch 1, 2 sc in each st around, join (12).

Rnd 3: Ch 1, (2 sc in next st, sc in next st) around, join (18).

Rnd 4: Ch 1, (2 sc in next st, sc in each of next 2 sts) around, join (24).

Rnd 5: Working in **back lps** this rnd only, join metallic braid with sl st in first st, sl st in each st around, join with sl st in first st, fasten off.

Apply liquid fabric stiffener to Saucer following manufacturer's stiffening instructions. Shape and allow to dry completely.

BOWL

Rnd 1: With white, ch 2, 6 sc in 2nd ch from hook, join with sl st in first sc (6 sc).

Rnd 2: Ch 1, 2 sc in each st around, join (12).

Rnd 3: Working in **back lps** this rnd only, ch 1, sc in each st around, join.

Rnd 4: Ch 1, (2 sc in next st, sc in next st) around, join (18).

Rnd 5: Ch 1, sc in each st around, join, fasten off.

Rnd 6: Working in **back lps** this rnd only, join metallic braid with sl st in first st, sl st in each st around, join with sl st in first st, fasten off.

Rnd 7: For **base,** working in **front lps** of rnd 2, with top of Saucer facing you, join white with sc in first st, sc in each st around, join, fasten off (12).

Rnd 8: Join metallic braid with sl st in first st, ch 1, (sl st in next st, ch 1) around, join with sl st in first st, fasten off.

Apply liquid fabric stiffener to Bowl following manufacturer's stiffening instructions. Shape and allow to dry completely. ❧

KITCHEN SET

Designed by Rosemarie Walter

PHOTO on page 33
TECHNIQUE: Crochet
SIZE: Apron is 3" x 3¾"; Dishtowel is 1⅞" x 3½"; Pot Holders are 1⅜" square.
MATERIALS FOR ALL FOUR:
Size 10 bedspread cotton — small amount variegated green; Embroidery floss — 2½ yds. rose, 1 yd. each yellow and green; White washcloth; 16" of 1/16" satin ribbon; 3-mm. pearl bead; White sewing thread; Sewing needle; No. 9 steel crochet hook or size needed to obtain gauge.
GAUGE: 7 sc sts = 1".

APRON

Cut a 3" x 4" piece from washcloth; turn edges under ¼" and baste in place.

Rnd 1: With right side of work facing you and 4" edge up, working over folded edges, using variegated green, with lp on hook, push hook through cloth ⅛" from edge at top right hand corner, yo, draw lp through, complete as sc, 3 sc in same corner, (evenly space 20 sc across to next corner, 4 sc in corner, evenly space 16 sc across to next corner), 4 sc in corner; repeat between ( ), join with sl st in first sc (88 sc).

Rnd 2: Sl st in next 2 sts; for

waistband casing, ch 3, dc in next 23 sts; for **edging**, (ch 3, sc in next st) around to first ch-3, join with sl st in first ch of first ch-3, fasten off.

Using rose, green and Lazy Daisy Stitch for flower and leaves and yellow and French Knot for flower center, embroider detail on Apron as shown in photo.

Weave ribbon through waistband casing.

DISHTOWEL

Cut a 2" x 3" piece from washcloth; turn edges under ¼" and baste in place.

Rnd 1: With right side of work facing you and 2" edge up, working over folded edges in same manner as rnd 1 of Apron, join variegated green with sc in top right-hand corner, 3 sc in same corner, evenly space 11 sc across to next corner, 4 sc in corner, evenly space 14 sc across to next corner, 4 sc in corner, evenly space 11 sc across to next corner, 4 sc in corner, evenly space 14 sc across to next corner, join with sl st in first sc (66 sc).

Rnd 2: Ch 1, sc first 2 sts tog, (sc next 2 sts tog) 8 times, (ch 1, sc in next st) 17 times, (ch 3, sc in next st) 16 times, (ch 1, sc in next st) 15 times, ch 1, join with sl st in first sc (57 sc).

Row 3: Ch 1, sc in first 9 sts leaving remaining sts unworked, turn (9).

Row 4: Ch 1, sc in each st across, turn.

Rows 5-7: Ch 1, sc first 2 sts tog, sc in each st across to last 2 sts, sc last 2 sts tog, turn (7, 5, 3).

Rows 8-18: Ch 1, sc in each st across, turn.

Row 19: For **bead loop**, ch 1, sc in first st, ch 4, skip next st, sc in last st, fasten off.

Using rose, green and Lazy Daisy Stitch for flower and leaves and yellow and French Knot for flower center, embroider detail on Dishtowel as shown in photo.

Sew bead to center of row 5. Slip bead loop over bead.

POT HOLDER (make 2)

Cut a 1" x 2" piece from washcloth; fold in half to form 1" square.

Rnd 1: Working around outer edge, in same manner as rnd 1 of Apron, join variegated green with sc in any corner, 3 sc in same corner, evenly space 4 sc across to next corner, (4 sc in corner, evenly space 4 sc across to next corner) around, join with sl st in first sc (32 sc).

Rnd 2: Ch 1; for **hanging loop**, sc in first st, ch 10, sc in next st); ch 1, (sc in next st, ch 1) around, join with sl st in first sc, fasten off.

Using rose and Lazy Daisy Stitch for flower and yellow and French Knot for flower center, embroider detail on Pot Holder as shown in photo.🍂

Tray of Cookies
Continued from page 33

Edging

Rnd 1: Holding both pieces wrong sides together, matching sts, working through both thicknesses, join blue with sc in any st, sc in each st around with 3 sc in each corner and inserting cardboard before closing, join with sl st in first sc.

Rnd 2: Ch 1, (hdc in each of next 2 sts, sl st in next st) around, join with sl st in top of first hdc, fasten off.

COOKIE (make 12)

Rnd 1: With ecru, ch 2, 6 sc in 2nd ch from hook, join with sl st in first sc (6 sc). (Wrong side of stitches is top of each Cookie.)

Rnd 2: Ch 1, (sc in next st, 2 sc in next st) around, join, fasten off leaving 8" for sewing.

Using brown and Straight Stitch, embroider chocolate chips randomly on top of each Cookie.

Sew Cookies to Tray in three rows of four Cookies each.🍂

Designed by Nancy Marshall

TECHNIQUE: Cross Stitch
SIZE: Place mat is 2" x 4"; Bread cover is 3¼" x 3¼".
MATERIALS: 5" x 7" piece of light blue 16-count Aida; 1½"-diameter x 1" deep basket (without handles); Fray preventer.

CUTTING INSTRUCTIONS:

A: From light blue Aida, cut one 2" x 4" piece for place mat and one 3¼" x 3¼" piece for bread cover.

STITCHING INSTRUCTIONS:

1: For place mat, stitch design in each corner, positioning design two squares from 4" edges and four squares from 2" edges, using two strands floss for Cross Stitch. Stay stitch two squares from 2" edges; pull out crosswise threads to fray edges. Apply fray preventer to 4" edges.

2: For bread cover, stitch design in each corner, positioning design four squares from edges, using two strands floss for Cross

Stitch. Stay stitch two squares from edges; pull out crosswise threads to fray edges. Place into basket as shown in photo.🍂

Table Set

PLACE MAT & BREAD COVER COLOR KEY:

X	DMC	ANCHOR	J.&P. COATS	COLORS
☐	#726	#295	#2295	Golden Yellow
▨	#899	#52	#3282	Rose Med.
▨	#911	#205	#6205	Emerald Green

Warm & Cozy

Spend a Rainy Afternoon Curled up under an Afghan Sipping Tea by the Fire

FIRE SCREEN

Designed by Mary K. Perry

TECHNIQUE: Plastic Canvas
SIZE: 3⅞" x 2¾" tall.
MATERIALS: Scrap of 7-count plastic canvas; Three 4½" plastic canvas quartered radial circles; ¾" brass machine bolt (⅛" diameter) and nut; Heavy metallic braid, ⅛" metallic ribbon or metallic cord (for amount see Color Key).

CUTTING INSTRUCTIONS:

A: For holder sides, cut two from circles according to graph.
B: For screen sections, cut five from circles according to graph.
C: For handle, cut one 2 x 10 holes.

STITCHING INSTRUCTIONS:

1: Using gold and stitches indicated, work A-C pieces according to graphs. Overcast unfinished cutout edges of A pieces and outer edges of B and C pieces as indicated on graphs.
2: Whipstitch and assemble

Fire Screen Assembly Diagram

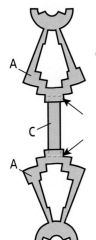

Step 1:
Overlapping pieces and working through both thicknesses to join ends of handle, Whipstitch outer edges of A pieces and C together.

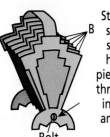

Step 2:
Stacking screen sections right sides up, fold holder over B pieces; insert bolt through pieces at indicated holes and secure with nut.

pieces as indicated and according to Fire Screen Assembly Diagram. Spread screen sections to stand. ❧

C – Handle
(cut 1) 2 x 10 holes

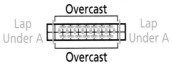

Overcast

Lap Under A   Lap Under A

Overcast

FIRE SCREEN COLOR KEY:

	Metallic braid, ribbon or cord	Amount
▨	Gold	15 yds.

STITCH KEY:
◆ Screw Attachment

A – Holder Side
(cut 2 from circles – only 1 can be cut per circle)

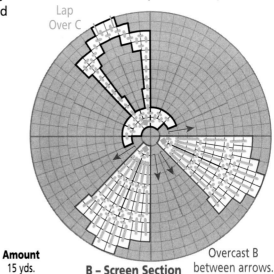

Lap Over C

Overcast B between arrows.

B – Screen Section
(cut 5 from circles – 2 can be cut from each circle)

FLORAL AFGHAN

Designed by Michele Wilcox

TECHNIQUE: Crochet
SIZE: 9½" x 11½".
MATERIALS: Sport yarn — 2 oz. off-white, small amount each purple, lavender, lt. blue, rose and green; Tapestry needle; E crochet hook or size needed to obtain gauge.
GAUGE: 9 sts = 2"; 3 hdc rows = 1".

AFGHAN

Row 1: With off-white, ch 41, sc in 2nd ch from hook, sc in each ch across, turn (40 sc).
Row 2: Ch 1, sc in first st, hdc in next st, dc in next st, hdc in next st, sc in next st, (sc in next st, hdc in next st, dc in next st, hdc in next st, sc in next st) across, turn (16 sc, 16 hdc, 8 dc).
NOTE: Fasten off each color when no longer needed.
Row 3: Repeat row 2 changing to lavender in last st.
Row 4: Ch 3, hdc in next st, (sc in next st, hdc in next st, dc in each of next 2 sts, hdc in next st) across to last 3 sts, sc in next st, hdc in next st, dc in last st, turn (16 dc, 16 hdc, 8 sc).
Row 5: Repeat row 4 changing to rose in last st.

Rows 6-7: Repeat row 2 changing to lt. blue in last st of last row.
Rows 8-9: Repeat row 4 changing to off-white in last st of last row.
Row 10: Repeat row 2.
Rows 11-27: Ch 2, hdc in each st across, turn.
Row 28: Repeat row 2 changing to lt. blue in last st.
Rows 29-30: Repeat row 4 changing to rose in last st of last row.
Rows 31-32: Repeat row 2 changing to lavender in last st of last row.
Rows 33-34: Repeat row 4 changing to off-white in last st of last row.
Rows 35-36: Repeat row 2.
Row 37: Ch 1, sc in each st across, turn.
Rnd 38: Working around outer edge, in sts and in ends of rows, ch 1, 3 sc in same st, sc in next 38 sts, 3 sc in next st, *(sc in each of next 2 sc rows, 2 sc in each of next 2 dc rows) 2 times, sc in next sc row; evenly space 23 sc across next 17 hdc rows, sc in next sc row, (2 sc in each of next 2 dc rows, sc in each of next 2 sc rows) 2 times*; working on opposite side of starting ch, 3 sc in first ch, sc in next 38 chs, 3 sc in next ch; repeat between **, join with sl st in first sc, fasten off (186 sc).
Rnd 39: Join lt. blue with sl st in first st, ch 3, skip next st, (sl st in next
Continued on page 38

Floral Afghan

Continued from page 37

st, ch 3, skip next st) around, join with sl st in first st, fasten off.

Flower (make 2 lt. blue, 2 rose, 2 purple, 2 lavender)

Ch 4, dc in 4th ch from hook, ch 3, sl st in same ch as first dc, *ch 3, (dc, ch 3, sl st) in same ch as first dc; repeat from * 2 more times, fasten off.

Leaves (make 4)

With green, (ch 6, sc in 2nd ch from hook, hdc in next ch, dc in next ch, hdc in next ch, sl st in last ch) 2 times, fasten off.

Finishing

Sew flowers and leaves on Afghan as shown in photo.❦

TRAY

Designed by Michele Wilcox

TECHNIQUE: Plastic Canvas
SIZE: ¾" x 2¼" x 3¼".
MATERIALS: ¼ sheet of 10-count plastic canvas; #3 pearl cotton or six-strand embroidery floss (for amounts see Color Key).

B – Side (cut 2) 6 x 30 holes

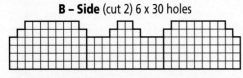

A – Bottom (cut 1) 21 x 30 holes

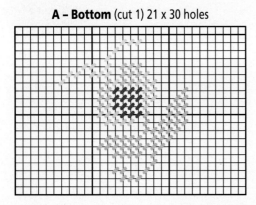

CUTTING INSTRUCTIONS:

A: For bottom, cut one 21 x 30 holes.
B: For sides, cut two according to graph.
C: For ends, cut two according to graph.

STITCHING INSTRUCTIONS:

1: Using pearl cotton or six strands floss in colors indicated and Continental Stitch, work A according to graph. Fill in uncoded areas and work B and C pieces using lt. green and Continental Stitch.

2: With lt. green, Overcast unfinished cutout edges of C pieces. Holding A-C pieces right sides together, Whipstitch together according to Tray Assembly Diagram; Overcast unfinished edges.❦

TRAY COLOR KEY:

#3 pearl cotton or floss	Amount
☐ Lt. Green	15 yds.
▨ Dk. Green	2 yds.
■ Red	1 yd.
▨ Lt. Pink	½ yd.
▨ Dk. Pink	½ yd.
▨ Yellow	¼ yd.

Tray Assembly Diagram

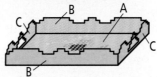

C – End (cut 2) 6 x 21 holes
Cut out gray area carefully.

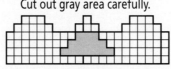

BASKET OF FLOWERS

Designed by Sue Childress

TECHNIQUE: Crochet
SIZE: Each Flower is ½" across. Each Bud is ¼" across.
MATERIALS: Pompadour baby yarn — small amount each pink and blue; 1½ yds. pink ⅛" satin ribbon; 1" plastic ring; 1¾" tall x 3" across opening wicker basket; 2½" Styrofoam® ball; Artificial leaves; Four 24-gauge floral wires; Floral tape; Craft glue or hot glue gun; F crochet hook or size needed to obtain gauge.

FLOWER (make 17)

With pink, (ch 4, sc in 4th ch from hook) 3 times, fasten off.

BUD (make 12)

With blue, ch 4, sc in 4th ch from hook, fasten off.

FINISHING

1: Cut 29 pieces of floral wire each 2" in length.
2: Secure Flowers and Buds to ends of wires with floral tape.
3: Glue foam ball in basket.
4: Bend and shape Flowers, Buds and leaves as desired; arrange and insert wire ends into foam.
5: Cut 2" piece of floral wire; fold ribbon into a 5-loop bow and wrap wire around center of bow; twist ends to secure and insert into foam.
6: Glue plastic ring to center bottom of basket.❦

Create Fairy Tale Magic with Mythical Beasts and Raven-haired Maidens

Twilight Evening

Black Beaded Ball Gown (page 40); Ruffled Slip (page 41);
Crown & Septer (page 41); Winged Horse (page 51)

BLACK BEADED BALL GOWN

Designed by Jean Carpenter

PHOTO on page 39 with Ruffled Slip (page 41) beneath
TECHNIQUE: Crochet
SIZE: Fits 11"-11½" fashion doll.
MATERIALS: Size 10 bedspread cotton — 325 yds. black; Size 3/0 snap; 425 silver seed beads; Black sewing thread; Sewing and beading needles; No. 1 steel crochet hook or size needed to obtain gauge.
GAUGE: 6 sts = 1"; 2 tr rows = 1".

SKIRT

Row 1: Starting with **waistband,** ch 21, sc in 2nd ch from hook, sc in each ch across, turn (20 sc).

Row 2: Ch 1, sc in each st across, turn.

NOTES: Ch-3 at beginning of each tr row is not used or counted as a stitch.

Sl sts are not used or counted as stitches.

Row 3: For **skirt,** sl st in first 3 sts, ch 43, tr in 4th ch from hook, tr in next 37 chs, hdc in last ch, sl st in next sc on waistband, turn (40 sts).

Row 4: Hdc in first hdc, tr in each tr across, turn.

Row 5: Ch 3, tr in each tr across with hdc in last hdc, sl st in same st as last sl st on waistband, sl st in next st on waistband, turn.

Row 6: Hdc in first hdc, tr in each tr across, turn.

Row 7: Ch 3, tr in each tr across with hdc in last hdc, sl st in same st as last st on waistband, turn.

Row 8: Hdc in first hdc, tr in each tr across, turn.

Row 9: Ch 3, tr in each tr across with hdc in last hdc, sl st in same st as last st on waistband, sl st in next st on waistband, turn.

Row 10: Hdc in first hdc, tr in each tr across, turn.

Row 11: Ch 3, tr in each tr across with hdc in last hdc, sl st in same st as last sl st on waistband, sl st in next st on waistband, turn.

Rows 12-54: Repeat rows 6-11 consecutively, ending with row 10.

Rows 55-56: Repeat rows 9 and 10.

Rows 57-58: Repeat rows 7 and 8.

Rows 59-60: Repeat rows 9 and 10.

Row 61: Holding rows 1 and 60 together, matching sts; working through both thicknesses, sc in first 30 sts; sc in each remaining st on row 60 across to waistband, sl st in next st on waistband, fasten off. (This is wrong side of gown).

BODICE

Row 1: With right side facing you, working in opposite side of starting ch on row 1 of waistband; for **snap flap,** skip first 2 chs; join with sc in next ch, hdc in next 16 chs, sc in last ch, turn (18 sts).

NOTE: Ch-1 at beginning of each hdc row is not used or counted as a stitch.

Row 2: Ch 1, skip first st; for **hdc dec,** (yo, insert hook in next st, yo, draw lp through) 2 times, yo, draw through all 5 lps on hook; hdc in each of next 2 sts, 2 hdc in next st, hdc in next 6 sts, 2 hdc in next st, hdc in each of next 2 sts, hdc dec leaving last st unworked, turn (16 sts).

Rows 3-4: Ch 1, hdc dec, hdc in each of next 2 sts, 2 hdc in next st, hdc in next 6 sts, 2 hdc in next st, hdc in each of next 2 sts, hdc dec, turn (16 sts).

Row 5: Ch 1, hdc in each st across, turn.

Row 6: Ch 1, hdc first 5 sts, 2 hdc in each of next 2 sts, hdc in each of next 2 sts, 2 hdc in each of next 2 sts, hdc in last 5 sts, turn (20).

Row 7: Ch 1, hdc in each st across, turn.

Row 8: For **right shoulder,** ch 1, hdc in first 8 sts, hdc dec leaving last 10 sts unworked, turn (9).

Row 9: Ch 1, hdc dec, hdc in next 6 sts leaving last st unworked, turn (7).

Row 10: Ch 1, hdc in first 5 sts, hdc dec, turn (6).

Row 11: Ch 1, (hdc dec) 3 times, turn (3).

Row 12: Ch 1, hdc in first st, hdc dec, turn (2).

Row 13: Ch 1, hdc dec; for **strap,** ch 40, fasten off.

Row 8: For **left shoulder,** with wrong side of work facing you, join with sl st in next unworked st on row 7, ch 1, hdc dec, hdc in last 8 sts, turn (9).

Row 9: Ch 1, skip first st, hdc in next 6 sts, hdc dec, turn (7).

Row 10: Ch 1, hdc dec, hdc in last 5 sts, turn (6).

Row 11: Ch 1, (hdc dec) 3 times, turn (3).

Row 12: Ch 1, hdc dec, hdc in last st, turn (2).

Row 13: Ch 2, hdc dec; for **strap,** ch 40, fasten off.

FINISHING

1: Sew half of snap to snap flap; sew other half to stitches on rows 1 and 2 of Skirt.

2: Thread beading needle with 24" strand of beading thread; double and knot ends together.

3: Secure end of thread at top of one shoulder. Run 3¼" of beads onto thread. Sew strand to inside edge of shoulders.

4: Beginning with starting ch on Skirt, secure single strand of thread on first ch, run needle through bead and secure to ch. *(Weave needle through next 7 chs, run needle through bead and secure to ch) 5 times*.

5: Weave needle through stitch across to next row, skipping first 7 stitches, weave needle down to 8th stitch. Run needle through bead and secure to stitch. (Weave needle through next 7 stitches, run needle through bead and secure to stitch) 4 times. Weave needle through last 4 sts and across to next row.

6: Secure bead to first stitch. Repeat between ** in Step #4.

7: Repeat Steps #5 and #6 alternately across Skirt.

8: Place gown on doll. Cross straps and thread through 3rd row down from top of each shoulder; tie straps into a bow at center back.❧

RUFFLED SLIP

Designed by Dolores Franks

PHOTOGRAPHED under Black Beaded Ball Gown.
TECHNIQUE: Sewing
SIZE: Fits 11½" fashion doll.
MATERIALS: 22½" x 72" piece of white nylon net; 6" white seam saver; 4" of ½" invisible elastic; Tracing paper; Sewing needle and white thread.

CUTTING INSTRUCTIONS:

1: For pattern, trace Slip A-1; matching dotted lines (see Tracing Illustration), trace Slip A-2.

2: From white nylon net, cut one Slip piece following Slip pattern (placing one side edge on fold according to Slip A-2 tracing pattern), and two 6½" x 72" strips for ruffle.

Slip A-1
Tracing Pattern

Match to A-1.

Tracing Illustration

Slip A-2
Tracing Pattern

Match to A-2.

Place on fold.

STITCHING INSTRUCTIONS:

1: Stitch one edge of seam saver to waist edge of slip; stitch ends of elastic to side edges below seam saver. Fold seam saver down over elastic and stitch remaining edge to slip, being careful not to catch elastic in seam. With right sides together and with ¼" seams, stitch side edges together for backseam. Turn right side out.

2: With ¼" seams, stitch short edges of 6½" x 72" strips together, forming ring; fold in half lengthwise with wrong sides together. Run a row of gathering stitches ¼" from folded edge. Pull gathers to fit slip 3¼" from bottom edge. Being sure bottom edges of ruffle and slip are even, overlapping ends, stitch ruffle to slip over gathered stitches.❦

CROWN & SCEPTER

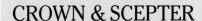

Designed by Alice Heim

PHOTO on page 40
TECHNIQUE: Crochet
SIZE: Crown fits 11"-11½" fashion doll. Scepter is about 3¼" tall.
MATERIALS FOR BOTH: Medium metallic braid or size 10 bedspread cotton — 12 yds. black; 13 crystal 5-mm. gemstones; Fabric stiffener; Round toothpick; Silver glitter paint; Craft glue or hot glue; Tapestry needle; No. 7 steel crochet hook or size needed to obtain gauge.
GAUGE: 11 sc sts = 2".

CROWN

Rnd 1: Ch 24, sl st in first ch to form ring, ch 1, sc in each ch around, join with sl st in first sc (24 sc).

NOTE: For **picot,** ch 5, sl st in 4th ch from hook.

Rnd 2: Ch 1, sc in first st, picot, skip next st, (sc in next st, picot, skip next st) around, join with sl st in first sc, fasten off.

SCEPTER

For **first point,** ch 7, sl st in first ch; (for **next point,** ch 6, sl st in first ch of first point) 4 times, fasten off.

FINISHING

1: Apply liquid fabric stiffener to Crown and Scepter following manufacturer's stiffening instructions. Shape as shown in photo and allow to dry completely.

2: Glue one gemstone to center of Scepter and one to each picot on Crown as shown.

3: Apply glitter paint to toothpick following manufacturer's instructions and allow to dry completely.

4: Glue Scepter to toothpick as shown.❦

Dress in Royal Robes and Ride a Mystic Unicorn through Fluffy Dream Clouds

Fantasy

SNOW PRINCESS

Designed by Dolores Franks

TECHNIQUE: Sewing
SIZE: Fits 11½" fashion doll.
MATERIALS: ⅜ yd. of white denim fabric; ⅛ yd. of white fur; ½" of white ¾" Velcro®; 1¾" piece of silver chain; Two ⅛" jewelry jump rings; One 7-mm. silver jewelry spring ring clasp; Two ⅜" pearl teardrops; Two white irridescent chenille stems; Tracing paper; Sewing needle and white thread.

CUTTING INSTRUCTIONS:

NOTE: Patterns continued on pages 44 and 45.

1: For Coat Back pattern, trace Coat Back A-1; matching dotted lines (see Coat Back Tracing Illustration), trace Coat Back A-2.

2: For Coat Front pattern, trace Coat Front B-1; matching dotted lines (see Coat Front Tracing Illustration), trace Coat Front B-2.

3: From white denim fabric, cut one Coat Back piece following Coat Back pattern (placing one side edge on fold according to Coat Back A tracing pattern), cut two Coat Front pieces following Coat Front pattern.

4: From remaining white denim fabric, cut one Gown Front piece following Gown Front pattern and two Gown Back pieces following Gown Back pattern.

5: From white fur, cut one 1" x 8" piece for gown hem, one 1" x 4" piece for gown bodice front, two 1" x 2" pieces for gown bodice back, two 1" x 3" pieces for coat sleeves and one 1" x 35" piece for coat edging.

STITCHING INSTRUCTIONS:

1: For gown, with right sides together, stitch darts on gown front where indicated on pattern. Position right side of fur pieces against wrong side of gown piece along top bodice edges; stitch in place. Turn fur to right side and stitch fur down to finish edges. With right sides together and with ¼" seams, stitch side seams together. Turn right side out.

2: Stitch fur along hem of gown in same manner as above. With right sides together and with ¼" seams together, leaving back seam open where indicated. Turn right side out. Cut two ¼" x ¾" Velcro® pieces; tack in place at back opening (one close to the top edge of gown and one at bottom edge of opening).

3: For coat, with right sides together, stitch darts on coat front where indicated. With right sides together and with ¼" seams, stitch front and back together along shoulder and sleeve seams. Stitch fur trim

on sleeve hems in same manner as gown.

4: With right sides together and with ¼" seams, stitch side and under sleeve seams. Turn right side out. Stitch fur trim on coat outside edges in same manner as above.

5: For necklace, attach one jump ring at each end of chain; attach clasp to one jump ring and teardrop to center of chain.

NOTE: Cut chenille stems into four 6" pieces.

6: For crown, assemble according to Crown Assembly Diagram.

7: Bend crown to form circle; twist ends together to secure. ❦

**Coat Back
Tracing Illustration**

**Coat Front
Tracing Illustration**

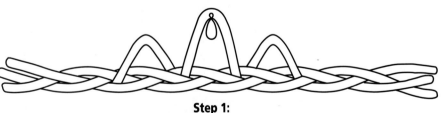

Snow Princess Crown Assembly Diagram

Step 1:
Braid three chenille stem pieces together.

Step 2:
Bend remaining chenille stem piece in half, forming a V-shape and insert ends through braided section (from front to back) being sure to center the middle "V"; bend each end to form a V-shape and insert ends through braided section; twist ends to secure.

Step 3:
Tack pearl teardrop to center of middle "V".

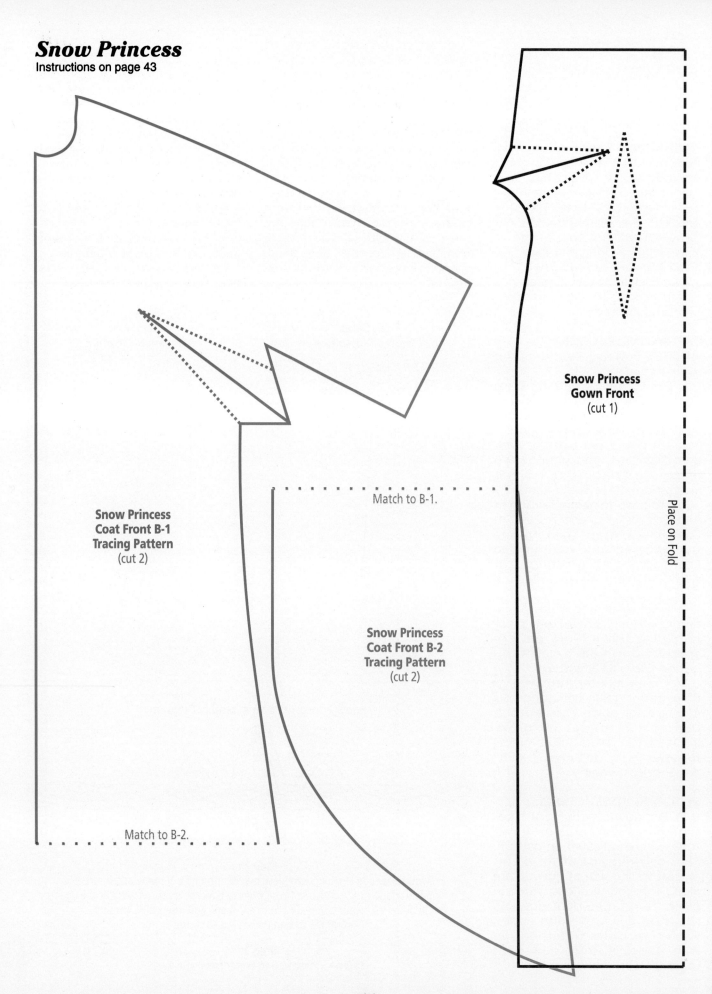

Snow Princess
Instructions on page 43

**Snow Princess
Gown Front**
(cut 1)

Place on Fold

Match to B-1.

**Snow Princess
Coat Front B-1
Tracing Pattern**
(cut 2)

**Snow Princess
Coat Front B-2
Tracing Pattern**
(cut 2)

Match to B-2.

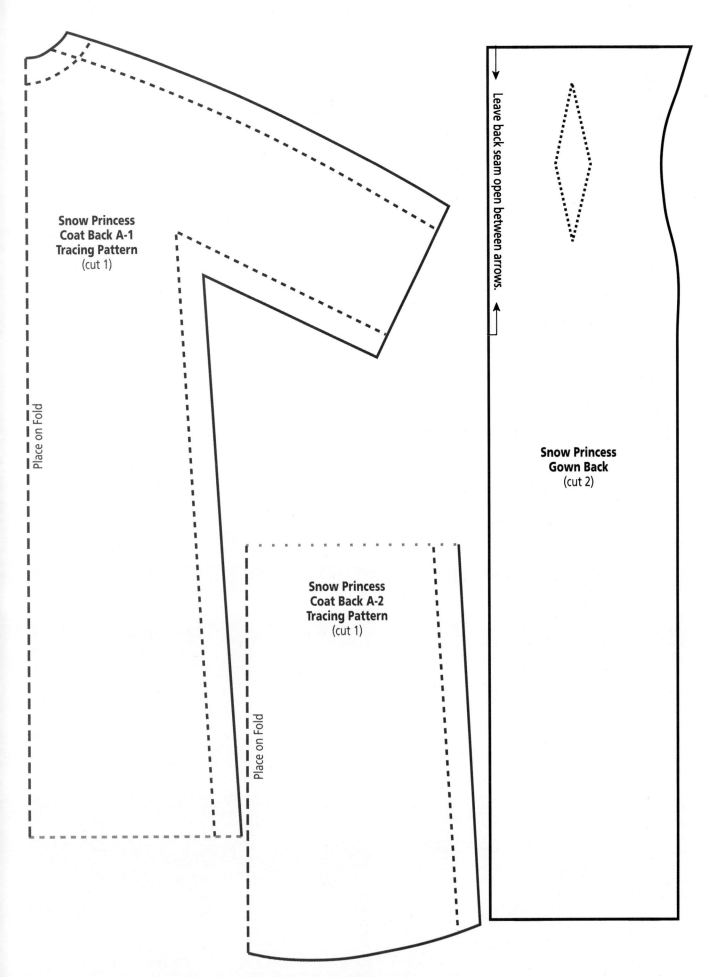

**Snow Princess
Coat Back A-1
Tracing Pattern**
(cut 1)

Place on Fold

**Snow Princess
Coat Back A-2
Tracing Pattern**
(cut 1)

Place on Fold

Leave back seam open between arrows.

**Snow Princess
Gown Back**
(cut 2)

Westward Ho!

BANDANA DRESS

Designed by Minette Smith

TECHNIQUE: Sewing
SIZE: Fits 11½" fashion doll.
MATERIALS: Two red bandanas; 1½" x 4¼" piece denim fabric; 2" strip of Velcro®; Sewing needle and red thread.

CUTTING INSTRUCTIONS:

NOTE: Pattern and diagrams on page 49.

1: From one bandana, cut a 5¼" square out of each corner for skirt front, back and sides. Cut curve at top corner of each square following Curve Diagram.

2: From remaining bandana, cut two Top pieces following Top pattern.

STITCHING INSTRUCTIONS:

1: With right sides together and with ¼" seams, stitch front, back and sides together according to Skirt Diagram. For back opening, cut a 1¼" slit in the center back; machine stitch or Blanket Stitch around opening to finish edge.

2: For waistband, machine stitch or Blanket Stitch across 1½" edges of denim fabric.

3: Run a row of gathering stitches ⅛" from top edge of skirt; pull gathers to fit 4¼" edge of waistband. With right sides together and with ¼" seam, stitch waistband to skirt, extending waistband past skirt ½" on left side; fold waistband to inside of skirt and hem. Trim Velcro® to fit waistband ends; stitch in place.

4: For top, with right sides together and with ¼" seam, stitch

Continued on page 49

Round up the Ponies for a Hay Ride & Sing Along

WESTERN HAT & BOOTS

Designed by Joan Drost

TECHNIQUE: Plastic Canvas
SIZE: Hat is 2¾" across brim; Boots are 2¼" tall and fit female 11½" fashion doll.
MATERIALS: One sheet of 10-count plastic canvas; Scraps of brown and beige felt; Two 1"-long feathers; Six-strand embroidery floss (for amounts see Color Key).

CUTTING INSTRUCTIONS:

A: For Hat crown, cut one according to graph.
B: For Hat crown top, cut one according to graph.
C: For Hat brim, cut one according to graph.
D: For Boot sides, cut two according to graph.
E: For Boot vamp, cut two according to graph.
F: For Boot sole, cut two according to graph.

STITCHING INSTRUCTIONS:

1: Using colors indicated and Continental Stitch, work A-F pieces according to graphs. Using beige, Backstitch and Straight Stitch, embroider D pieces as indicated on graph, reversing design on second piece.
NOTE: Cut two ⅛" x 2" strips from beige felt and one ⅛" x 5½" strip from brown felt.
2: For Hat, with beige, Whipstitch and assemble A-C pieces as indicated and according to Hat Assembly Diagram.

3: For each Boot, with brown, Whipstitch and assemble one of each D-F piece as indicated and according to Boot Assembly Diagram. ❧

B – Hat Crown Top
(cut 1) 4 x 9 holes

A – Hat Crown
(cut 1) 15 x 32 holes

Whipstitch   Whipstitch

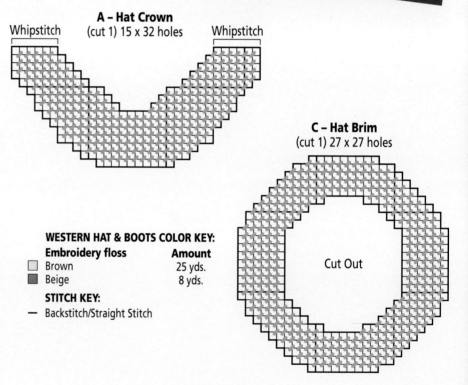

C – Hat Brim
(cut 1) 27 x 27 holes

Cut Out

WESTERN HAT & BOOTS COLOR KEY:

Embroidery floss	Amount
☐ Brown	25 yds.
■ Beige	8 yds.

STITCH KEY:
— Backstitch/Straight Stitch

Hat Assembly Diagram

Step 1:
Whipstitch short edges of A together.

Step 2:
Whipstitch B to top edge and C to bottom edge of A.

Step 3:
Overcast unfinished edges of C.

Step 4:
Glue brown felt strip and feathers to brim as shown in photo.

Felt

B

A

C

F – Boot Sole
(cut 2) 6 x13 holes

Whipstitch to D
between green arrows.

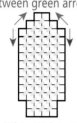

Whipstitch to E
between pink arrows.

D – Boot Sides (cut 2) 21 x 22 holes

Whipstitch

Whipstitch

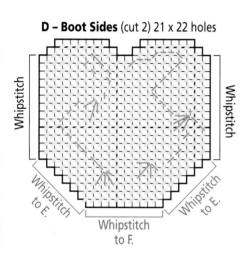

Whipstitch to E.

Whipstitch to E.

Whipstitch to F.

E – Boot Vamp (cut 2) 9 x 17 holes

Whipstitch to D.

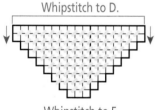

Whipstitch to F
between pink arrows.

Boot Assembly Diagram

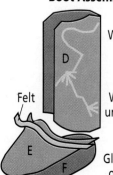

Felt

Step 1:
Whipstitch D-F pieces
together.

Step 2:
With beige, Overcast
unfinished edges of D.

Step 3:
Glue beige felt strips
over front seam as
shown in photo.

Bandana Dress
Continued from page 46

center front beginning at bottom
edge and stitching to dot. Stitch
darts. Finish all unfinished edges.
Trim Velcro® to fit neck straps and
back; stitch in place.❦

Skirt Diagram

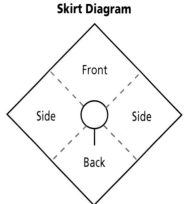

Front

Side

Side

Back

Curve Diagram

1½"

1½"

Cut curve
along
dotted line.

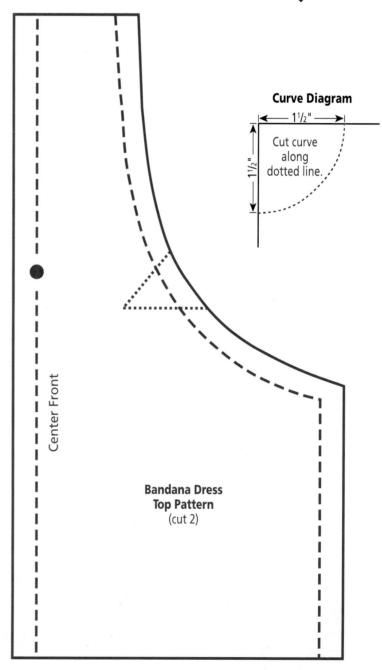

Center Front

Bandana Dress
Top Pattern
(cut 2)

ACOUSTIC GUITAR

Designed by Terry A. Ricioli

TECHNIQUE: Plastic Canvas
SIZE: 2¼" x 6⅛".
MATERIALS: ½ sheet of 10-count plastic canvas; 1 yd. of monofilament fishing line; Craft glue or glue gun; Six-strand embroidery floss (for amounts see Color Key).

CUTTING INSTRUCTIONS:

A: For front, cut one according to graph.
B: For back, cut one according to graph.
C: For side, cut one 4 x 96 holes (no graph).
D: For fingerboard back, cut one according to graph.
E: For bridge, cut one 2 x 8 holes.

STITCHING INSTRUCTIONS:

1: Using colors indicated and Continental Stitch, work A according to graph; with brown, Overcast unfinished cutout edges. Using brown and Continental Stitch, work B, D and E pieces; Overcast unfinished edges of E and bottom edge of D as indicated on graph. Overlapping two holes at ends and working through both thicknesses at overlap area to join, using brown and Continental Stitch, work C.

NOTE: Cut fishing line into four 9" lengths.

2: Whipstitch and assemble pieces as indicated and according to Guitar Assembly Diagram.

ACOUSTIC GUITAR COLOR KEY:

Embroidery floss	Amount
▨ Brown	30 yds.
▨ Gold	15 yds.

STITCH KEY:
□ Bridge Attachment
I String Attachment

E – Bridge
(cut 1) 2 x 8 holes

B – Back
(cut 1) 22 x 32 holes

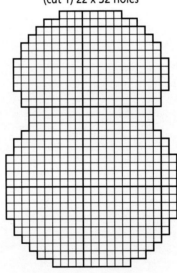

A – Front
(cut 1) 22 x 60 holes

Cut Out

D – Fingerboard Back
(cut 1) 6 x 28 holes

Overcast

Guitar Assembly Diagram

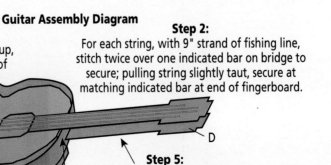

Step 1:
Holding bridge and front right sides up, with brown, tack together at ends of bridge.

Step 2:
For each string, with 9" strand of fishing line, stitch twice over one indicated bar on bridge to secure; pulling string slightly taut, secure at matching indicated bar at end of fingerboard.

Step 5:
Holding D to wrong side of front, Whipstitch unfinished edges together; secure Overcast end with small amount of glue.

Step 4:
Whipstitch side and back together.

Step 3:
Centering seam under fingerboard and easing to fit, Whipstitch side to front, leaving area under fingerboard unjoined.

EQUESTRIAN BEAUTIES

Designed by Trudy Bath Smith

PHOTO of Winged Horse on page 39; Unicorn on page 42; Fancy Horse on pages 46 & 47
TECHNIQUE: Plastic Canvas
SIZE: Each is 10½" tall.
MATERIALS FOR ONE: Two sheets of 7-count plastic canvas; ½ sheet of black 7-count plastic canvas (for Winged Horse); Two 12-mm. animal eyes with washers; Wavy doll hair; Polyester fiberfill; Three snaps; Sewing needle and matching color thread; Craft glue or glue gun; Fine metallic braid or metallic thread (for amount see Unicorn Color Key on page 53); Metallic cord (for amount see individual Color Keys on pages 52 & 53); Worsted-weight or plastic canvas yarn (for amounts see individual Color Keys).

FANCY HORSE
CUTTING INSTRUCTIONS:
NOTE: Graphs on pages 52 & 53.
A: For body, cut two according to graph.
B: For back legs, cut four according to graph.
C: For front legs, cut four according to graph.
D: For stomach gusset, cut one according to graph.
E: For back gusset, cut one according to graph.
F: For head gusset, cut one according to graph.
G: For hoof bottoms, cut four according to graph.
H: For ears, cut two according to graph.
I: For snap bases, cut three 2 x 2 holes (no graph).

STITCHING INSTRUCTIONS:
NOTE: I pieces are unworked.
1: Using colors and stitches indicated, work B and C (two each on opposite side of canvas), F and G pieces according to graphs. Fill in uncoded areas of B, C and F pieces and work A (one on opposite side of canvas), D, E and H pieces using camel and Continental Stitch. Overcast unfinished edges of H and

I pieces, cutout edges of E and indicated edge of each A.
2: With matching colors, Whipstitch and assemble pieces as indicated on graphs and according to Equestrian Beauties Assembly Diagram on page 53.
NOTE: Cut twenty 15" lengths of brown.
3: For each section of hair, holding two strands of brown together, tie together in knot at center point, keeping ends even. For mane, glue knots of six hair sections evenly spaced inside opening at back of neck.
4: For tail, glue knots of remaining hair sections into cutout on back gusset.
5: Separate plys of hair sections and brush to fluff.
NOTE: Cut wavy hair braid into three 8" lengths.
6: With thread, sew socket half of one snap to each I piece; glue one end of each braid to each I on side opposite snap. Snap braids to body.
7: Using royal, watermelon and yellow, tie one strand into a bow around end of each braid as shown in photo. Trim bows, mane and tail as desired.

UNICORN
CUTTING INSTRUCTIONS:
NOTE: Graphs on pages 52 & 53.
A-I: Follow Steps A-I of Fancy Horse.
J: For horn, cut one according to graph.

STITCHING INSTRUCTIONS:
NOTE: I pieces are unworked.
1: Using white in place of camel for body pieces and white/gold metallic cord in place of black for hooves, follow Steps 1 and 2 of Fancy Horse.
2: Folding edges wrong sides together, with metallic cord, Whipstitch long edges of J together as indicated; Overcast unfinished edge. Glue to head gusset as shown in photo.
NOTES: Cut eighteen 15" lengths of white. Cut wavy hair braid into one 16" and three 8" lengths.
3: For each section of white hair, holding two strands of white together, tie together in knot at center point, keeping ends even. For mane, glue knots of five hair

sections and 8" braids evenly spaced inside opening at back of neck. Using metallic cord, tie one strand into a bow around opposite end of each braid as shown.
4: For tail, glue knots of remaining hair sections and each end of 16" braid into cutout on back gusset as shown.
5: Separate plys of hair sections and brush to fluff.
NOTES: Cut two 15" lengths each of lt. pink, lt. blue and lavender. Cut three 15" lengths of metallic braid or thread.
6: For each section of colored hair, holding two strands of matching color yarn and one strand of metallic braid or thread together, tie together in knot at center point, keeping ends even. With thread, sew socket half of one snap to each I piece; glue knot of one colored hair section to each I on side opposite snap. Snap hair sections to body. Trim mane and tail as desired.

WINGED HORSE
CUTTING INSTRUCTIONS:
NOTE: Graphs on pages 52 & 53.
A-I: Follow Steps A-I of Fancy Horse.
J: For wings, cut two according to graph.

STITCHING INSTRUCTIONS:
NOTE: I pieces are unworked.
1: Using black in place of camel for body pieces and multi-black metallic cord in place of black for hooves, follow Steps 1 and 2 of Fancy Horse.
2: With metallic cord and stitches indicated, work each side of each J piece. Glue to each side of body as shown.
NOTES: Cut eighteen 15" lengths of black. Cut wavy hair braid into one 16" and three 8" lengths.
3: For mane, using black in place of white for hair sections and watermelon for metallic cord, follow Step 3 of Unicorn.
4: For tail, glue knots of remaining hair sections and center of 16" braid into cutout on back gusset as shown. Using watermelon, tie one strand into a bow around end of each braid as shown.
5: Separate plys of hair sections

Continued on page 52

Equestrian Beauties

Continued from page 51

and brush to fluff.

NOTE: Cut six 15" lengths watermelon.

6: Using watermelon in place of lt. pink, lt. blue and lavender and omitting metallic braid or thread, follow Step 6 of Unicorn on page 51.

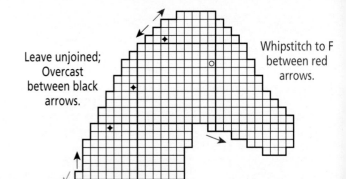

A – Body
(cut 2) 44 x 60 holes

Leave unjoined; Overcast between black arrows.

Whipstitch to F between red arrows.

Whipstitch to E between green arrows.

C – Front Leg
(cut 4)
15 x 41 holes
Whipstitch between arrows.

Whipstitch to D between blue arrows.

B – Back Leg
(cut 4)
20 x 42 holes
Whipstitch between arrows.

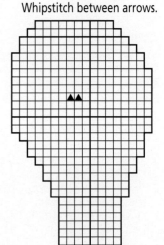

FANCY HORSE COLOR KEY:

	Worsted-weight	Nylon Plus™	Need-loft™	Yarn Amount
☐	Camel	#34	#43	3 1/2 oz.
☐	Dk. Brown	#36	#15	10 yds.
■	Black	#02	#00	6 yds.
▨	White	#01	#41	1/2 yd.
☐	Royal	#09	#32	1/4 yd.
☐	Watermelon	#54	#55	1/4 yd.
☐	Yellow	#26	#57	1/4 yd.

STITCH KEY:
○ Eye Attachment
◆ Snap Attachment
▲ Leg Attachment

E – Back Gusset
(cut 1) 7 x 38 holes
Whipstitch to A between arrows.
Cut out gray area carefully.

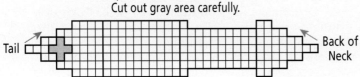

Tail

Back of Neck

D – Stomach Gusset
(cut 1) 9 x 64 holes
Whipstitch to A between arrows.

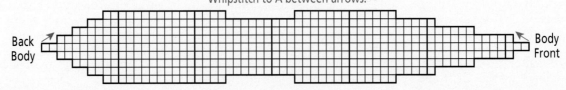

Back Body

Body Front

F – Head Gusset
(cut 1) 5 x 41 holes
Whipstitch to A between arrows.

Under Chin → ← Top of Head

H – Ear
(cut 2)
5 x 5 holes

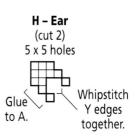

Glue to A.

Whipstitch Y edges together.

J – Unicorn Horn
(cut 1)
11 x 15 holes

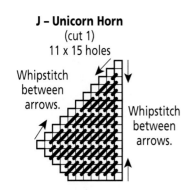

Whipstitch between arrows.

Whipstitch between arrows.

G – Hoof Bottom
(cut 4)
3 x 7 holes

WINGED HORSE COLOR KEY:

Metallic cord			Amount
■ Multi-Black			14 yds.

Worsted-weight	Nylon Plus™	Need-loft™	Yarn Amount
☐ Black	#02	#00	3½ oz.
☐ Watermelon	#54	#55	3½ yds.

STITCH KEY:
○ Eye Attachment
✦ Snap Attachment
▲ Leg Attachment

UNICORN COLOR KEY:

Fine metallic braid or metallic thread	Amount
☐ Gold	1¼ yds.

Metallic cord	Amount
■ White/Gold	8 yds.

Worsted-weight	Nylon Plus™	Need-loft™	Yarn Amount
☐ White	#01	#41	3½ oz.
☐ Red	#19	#02	1 yd.
☐ Royal	#09	#32	1 yd.
☐ Yellow	#26	#57	1 yd.

STITCH KEY:
○ Eye Attachment
✦ Snap Attachment
▲ Leg Attachment

J – Winged Horse Wing
(cut 2)
27 x 39 holes
Overcast between arrows.

Equestrian Beauties Assembly Diagram

Step 1:
For each leg, holding two matching pieces wrong sides together, Whipstitch together, leaving bottom edges unjoined.

Step 2:
Whipstitch one G to open bottom edges of each leg.

Fig. 1

Step 7:
Whipstitch E to each A.

Step 6:
With thread, sew ball half of each snap to one A.

Step 5:
For each ear, Whipstitch open edges of one H together and glue to A.

Step 4:
Attach one eye to each A; secure on wrong side with washer.

Step 3:
Loosely tack one back leg and one front leg to each A.

Step 8:
Whipstitch F to each A.

Step 10:
Whipstitch unfinished edges of each A together, leaving Overcast edges on back of neck unjoined.

Step 9:
Whipstitch D to each A, stuffing with fiberfill before closing.

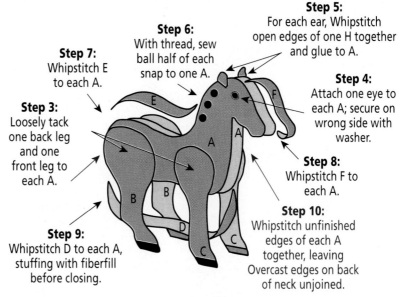

Fig. 2

Splash in the Surf and Walk Along the Beach in a New Swimwear Wardrobe

Black & White Beach Set (page 55); Ice Chest (page 57);
Swim Fins & Mask (page 58); Turquoise Beach Set
(pages 58 & 59); Blue & White Beach Set (page 60)

Fun in the Sun

BLACK & WHITE BEACH SET

Designed by Jean Carpenter

TECHNIQUE: Crochet
SIZE: Fits 11"-11½" fashion doll.
MATERIALS FOR ALL: Size 10 bedspread cotton — 100 yds. white and 70 yds. black; Spray starch; Tapestry needle; No. 1 steel crochet hook or size needed to obtain gauge.
GAUGE: 13 sc sts = 2"; 17 sc rows = 2".

COVER-UP
Back
   Row 1: Starting at shoulders, with white, ch 24, 2 dc in 4th ch from hook, skip next ch, sc in next ch, skip next ch, (5 dc in next ch, skip next ch, sc in next ch, skip next ch) across to last ch, 3 dc in last ch, turn (26 dc, 5 sc).
   Row 2: Ch 3, 2 dc in same st, dc in next sc, (skip next 2 sts, 5 dc in next st, dc in next sc) across to last st, dc in last st, turn (31 dc).
   Rows 3-13: Ch 3, 2 dc in same st, skip next 2 sts, dc in next st, skip next 2 sts, (5 dc in next st, skip next 2 sts, dc in next st, skip next 2 sts) across to last st, 3 dc in last st, turn (31 dc). Fasten off at end of last row.

Right Front
   Row 1: Working on opposite side of starting ch on Back, with wrong side of row 1 facing you, join white with sl st in first ch, ch 3, 2 dc in same ch, skip next ch, sc in next ch, skip next ch, 5 dc in next ch, skip next ch, sc in next ch, skip next ch, 3 dc in next ch leaving remaining chs unworked, turn (11 dc, 2 sc).
   Row 2: Ch 3, 2 dc in same st, skip next 2 sts, dc in next sc, skip next 2 sts, 5 dc in next st, skip next 2 sts, dc in next sc, skip next 2 sts, 3 dc in last st, turn (13 dc).
   Row 3: Ch 3, 2 dc in same st, (skip next 2 sts, dc in next st, skip next 2 sts, 5 dc in next st) 2 times, turn (15).
   Row 4: Ch 3, skip next st, (5 dc in next st, skip next 2 sts, dc in next st, skip next 2 sts) 2 times, 3 dc in last st, turn (16).

Continued on page 56

Black & White Beach Set

Continued from page 55

Row 5: Ch 3, 2 dc in same st, skip next 2 sts, dc in next st, (skip next 2 sts, 5 dc in next st, skip next 2 sts, dc in next st) 2 times, turn.

Row 6: Ch 3, skip next 2 sts, (5 dc in next st, skip next 2 sts, dc in next st, skip next 2 sts) 2 times, 3 dc in last st, turn.

Rows 7-13: Repeat rows 5 and 6 alternately, ending with row 5. Fasten off at end of last row.

Left Front

Row 1: With right side of row 1 on Back facing you, repeat row 1 of Right Front (11 dc, 2 sc).

Rows 2-13: Repeat same rows of Right Front.

WHITE SWIM SUIT

Row 1: Starting at back waist, with white, ch 15, sc in 2nd ch from hook, sc in each ch across, turn (14 sc).

Rows 2-4: Ch 1, sc in each st across, turn.

Rows 5-12: Ch 1, skip first st, sc in each st across, turn, ending with 6 sts in last row.

Row 13: Ch 1, sc first 2 sts tog, sc in each of next 2 sts, sc last 2 sts tog, turn (4).

Row 14: For **crotch,** ch 1, (sc next 2 sts tog) 2 times, turn (2).

Row 15: Repeat row 2.

Row 16: Ch 1, 2 sc in each st across, turn (4).

Row 17: Repeat row 2.

Rows 18-19: Ch 1, 2 sc in first st, sc in each st across with 2 sc in last st, turn (6, 8).

Row 20: Repeat row 2.

Row 21: Repeat row 18 (10).

Row 22: Repeat row 2.

Row 23: Ch 1, 2 sc in first st, sc in each st across with 2 sc in last st; **to join front to back,** fold at crotch, dc in end of row 4, turn.

Row 24: Ch 1, skip first dc, sc in each sc across, dc in opposite end of row 4, turn.

Row 25: Ch 1, skip first dc, sc in each sc across, turn.

Row 26: For **first waist tie loop,** ch 3, sc in first sc, sc in each st across, turn (12 sc, 1 ch-3 lp).

Row 27: For **second waist tie loop,** ch 3, sc in first sc, sc in each st across leaving last ch-3 lp unworked, turn.

Row 28: Ch 1, sc in each st across leaving last ch-3 lp unworked, turn (12 sc).

Rows 29-35: Ch 1, sc in each st across, turn.

Row 36: For **right front,** ch 1, sc in each of first 2 sts, 2 sc in each of next 2 sts, sc in each of next 2 sts leaving remaining sts unworked, turn (8).

Rows 37-41: Ch 1, sc in each st across, turn.

Row 42: Ch 4, *yo 2 times, skip next st, insert hook in next st, yo, draw lp through, (yo, draw through 2 lps on hook) 2 times*, skip next 2 sts; repeat between ** 2 times, yo, draw through all 4 lps on hook; for **tie,** ch 20, **do not** turn, fasten off.

Row 36: For **left front,** join with sl st in same st as last st on row 36 of right front, sc in each of next 2 sts, 2 sc in each of next 2 sts, sc in each of last 2 sts, turn (8 sc).

Rows 37-42: Repeat same rows of right front.

For **waist ties,** ch 40; working on opposite of starting ch, join with sl st in first ch, skip next ch, (sl st in next 4 chs, skip next ch) 2 times, sl st in next ch leaving last ch unworked, ch 40, fasten off. Pull ties through corresponding ch-3 lps on front and tie in back.

BLACK BATHING SUIT

Row 1: Starting at back waist, with black, ch 13, sc in 2nd ch from hook, sc in each ch across, turn (12 sc).

Rows 2-3: Ch 1, sc in each st across, turn.

Row 4: Ch 1, sl st in first st, sc in each st across leaving last st unworked, turn (10).

Rows 5-12: Ch 1, skip first st, sc in each st across, turn, ending with 2 sts in last row.

Rows 13-15: Ch 1, sc in each st across, turn.

Row 16: Ch 1, 2 sc in each st across, turn (4).

Rows 17-20: Ch 1, 2 sc in first st, sc in each st across with 2 sc in last st, turn (12).

Rows 21-24: Ch 1, sc in each st across, turn.

Row 25: For **left front,** ch 1, sc in first 6 sts leaving remaining sts unworked, turn (6).

Rows 26-35: Ch 1, sc in each st across, turn.

Row 36: Ch 4, *yo 2 times, insert hook in next st, yo, draw lp through, (yo, draw through 2 lps on hook) 2 times*, skip next 2 sts; repeat between ** 2 times, yo, draw through all 4 lps on hook; for **tie,** ch 30, turn, fasten off.

Row 25: For **right front,** join with sc in next unworked st on row 24, sc in each st across, turn (6).

Rows 26-36: Repeat same rows of left front.

For **waist ties,** ch 30; working on opposite side of starting ch, join with sc in first ch, sc in each ch across, ch 30, fasten off.

TOTE BAG

Rnd 1: With white, ch 2, 6 sc in 2nd ch from hook, join with sl st in first sc (6 sc).

Rnd 2: Ch 1, (3 sc in next st, sc in each of next 2 sts) 2 times, join (10).

Rnd 3: Ch 1, sc in first st, 3 sc in next st, sc in next 4 sts, 3 sc in next st, sc in each of last 3 sts, join (14).

Rnd 4: Ch 1, sc in each of first 2 sts, 3 sc in next st, sc in next 6 sts, 3 sc in next st, sc in last 4 sts, join (18).

Rnd 5: Ch 1, sc in each of first 3 sts, 3 sc in next st, sc in next 8 sts, 3 sc in next st, sc in last 5 sts, join (22).

Rnd 6: Ch 1, sc in first 4 sts, 4 sc in next st, sc in next 10 sts, 4 sc in next st, sc in last 6 sts, join (28).

Rnd 7: Working in **back lps** this rnd only, ch 1, sc in each st around, join.

Rnd 8: Ch 1, sc in each st around, join, fasten off.

Rnd 9: Join black with sc in first st, sc in each st around, join.

Rnd 10: Repeat rnd 8.

Rnds 11-12: Repeat rnds 9 and 8.

Rnds 13-18: Repeat rnds 9-12 consecutively, ending with rnd 10. **Do not** fasten off at end of last rnd.

Rnd 19: Ch 4, skip next st, (dc in next st, ch 1, skip next st) around, join with sl st in 3rd ch of ch-4, fasten off.

For **drawstring,** with one strand each black and white held together, sl st around first st on rnd 19, ch 50, remove loop from hook, cut ends 4" from loop. Carefully weave drawstring through ch sps on rnd 19, insert hook in lp, sl st around same st as first sl st, pull ends through. Clip ends ½" from joining.

HAT

Rnd 1: With white, ch 2, 6 sc in 2nd ch from hook, join with sl st in first sc (6).

Rnd 2: Ch 1, (sc in next st, 2 sc in next st) around, join (9).

Rnd 3: Ch 1, 2 sc in each st around, join (18).

Rnds 4-6: Ch 1, sc in each st around, join.

Rnd 7: Working in **front lps** this rnd only, ch 1, sc in each st around, join.

Rnd 8: Repeat rnd 3 (36).

Rnd 9: Repeat rnd 4.

Rnd 10: Ch 1, (sc in each of next 2 sts, 2 sc in next st) around, join (48).

Rnds 11-12: Repeat rnd 4.
Rnd 13: Repeat rnd 10 (64).
Rnd 14: Repeat rnd 4, fasten off.
Rnd 15: Join black with sc in first st, sc in each st around, join.
Rnd 16: Repeat rnd 4.
Rnd 17: Ch 1, (sc in next st, ch 1) around, join, fasten off.

For **hat band**, with black, ch 15, join with sc around post of any st on rnd 7, ch 1, (sc around post of next st on same rnd, ch 1) around, join, ch 15, fasten off.

Spray Hat with spray starch. Shape according to photo during drying time.

BEACH TOWEL

Row 1: With white, ch 52, sc in 4th ch from hook, sc in each ch across, turn (49 sc, 1 ch-3 lp).

Row 2: Ch 3, sc in first sc, sc in each st across leaving last ch-3 lp unworked, turn, fasten off.

Row 3: Join black with sl st in first sc, ch 3, sc in same st, sc in each st across leaving last ch-3 lp unworked, turn.

Row 4: Repeat row 2.
Row 5: With white, repeat row 3.
Row 6: Repeat row 2.
Rows 7-18: Repeat rows 3-6 consecutively. **Do not** fasten off at end of last row.

Row 19: Ch 3, sc in first sc, sc in each st across leaving last ch-3 lp unworked, turn.

Rows 20-36: Repeat rows 2-18.✿

ICE CHEST

Designed by Maria Berenger

PHOTO on page 55
TECHNIQUE: Plastic Canvas
SIZE: 1¾" x 3¼" x 1¾" tall.
MATERIALS: Scraps of 7-count plastic canvas; Worsted-weight or plastic canvas yarn (for amounts see Color Key).

CUTTING INSTRUCTIONS:

A: For sides, cut two according to graph.

B: For ends, cut two according to graph.

C: For bottom, cut one 8 x 15 holes (no graph).

D: For lid, cut one 11 x 18 holes.

E: For lid lip pieces, cut two 2 x 15 holes and two 2 x 8 holes (no graphs).

F: For handles, cut two according to graph.

STITCHING INSTRUCTIONS:

1: Using colors and stitches indicated, work A, B and D pieces according to graphs, leaving indicated areas of D unworked. Using yellow for bottom, white for lid lip pieces and Continental Stitch, work C and E pieces.

2: With yellow, Overcast unfin-ished edges of F pieces. With colors indicated, Whipstitch and as-semble pieces as indicated on graphs and according to Ice Chest Assembly Diagram.✿

B – Ice Chest End
(cut 2) 10 x 10 holes

D – Ice Chest Lid
(cut 1) 11 x 18 holes

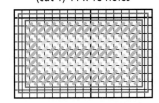

A – Ice Chest Side
(cut 2) 10 x 17 holes

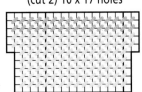

Step 2:
With matching colors, Whipstitch A-C pieces together; with white, Overcast unfinished edges.

Ice Chest Assembly Diagram

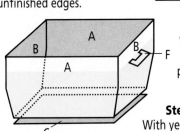

Step 1:
(underside view)
With yellow at unworked areas of D and with white, Whipstitch D and E pieces together; with white, Overcast unfinished edges.

Step 3:
With yellow, tack one F to each end.

F – Ice Chest Handle
(cut 2) 2 x 5 holes

ICE CHEST COLOR KEY:

	Worsted-weight	Nylon Plus™	Need-loft™	Yarn Amount
☐	Yellow	#26	#57	10 yds.
☐	White	#01	#41	8 yds.

STITCH KEY:
☐ Unworked Area/Lid Lip Attachment
◆ Handle Attachment

SWIM FINS & MASK

Designed by Terry A. Ricioli

PHOTO on pages 54 and 55
TECHNIQUE: Plastic Canvas
SIZE: Each "Her" Fin is 1⅛" x 1¾", not including strap; each "His" Fin is 1⅜" x 1¾", not including strap; each Mask is ⅞" 1⅜" x 1⅞", including strap.
MATERIALS: ½ sheet of 10-count plastic canvas; 1¼" x 2" piece of clear vinyl plastic; ½ yd. black ¼" elastic; Craft glue or glue gun; Six-strand embroidery floss (for amount see Color Key).

CUTTING INSTRUCTIONS:
A: For "Her" Fins, cut four according to graph.

C – Fin Gusset
(cut 8) 3 x 6 holes

B: For "His" Fins, cut four according to graph.
C: For Fin gussets, cut eight according to graph.
D: For Mask

SWIM FINS & MASKS COLOR KEY:

Embroidery floss	Amount
■ Black	50 yds.

STITCH KEY:
☐ Elastic Placement

seals, cut two according to graph.
E: For Mask fronts, cut two according to graph.
F: For Mask shields, using one E as a pattern, cut two from vinyl ⅛" smaller at all edges.

STITCHING INSTRUCTIONS:
1: Using six strands floss and Continental Stitch, work A-D pieces according to graphs. Overcast unfinished cutout edges of E pieces.
2: For each "Her" Fin, Whipstitch two A and two C pieces together according to Fin Assembly Diagram; Overcast unfinished edges. For each "His" Fin, substituting B pieces for A pieces, repeat as for "Her" Fin. For each mask, Whipstitch and assemble D-F pieces according to Mask Assembly Diagram.

E – Mask Front
(cut 2) 6 x 12 holes

Cut Out

Fin Assembly Diagram

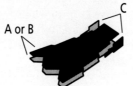

A or B
C

NOTE: Cut elastic into two 3½", two 2½" and two 1¾" lengths.
4: Using 3½" elastic lengths for Masks, 2½" lengths for "His" Fins and remaining lengths for "Her" Fins, glue ends inside fins and masks as indicated on graphs.

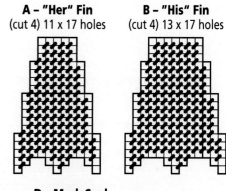

A – "Her" Fin
(cut 4) 11 x 17 holes

B – "His" Fin
(cut 4) 13 x 17 holes

D – Mask Seal
(cut 2)
6 x 36 holes

Lap Over
Lap Under

Mask Assembly Diagram

Step 1:
Whipstitch one D and one E piece together; Overcast unfinished edges.

Step 2:
Glue one F to inside Mask front.

D
E
Seal Seam
1-hole Overlap
F

TURQUOISE BEACH SET

Designed by Rosemarie Walter

PHOTO on page 54
TECHNIQUE: Crochet
SIZE: Cover-up fits 11"-11½" fashion doll. Beach Bag is 1¾" tall not including handles. Beach Towel is 5¾" x 11½".
MATERIALS FOR ALL THREE: Size 10 bedspread cotton — 75 yds. each black, pink and yellow; One turquoise terry washcloth and matching sewing thread; 25 green sequins, 13 pink sequins and 12 yellow sequins; Two 5-mm. wiggle eyes; Craft glue; Sewing and tapestry needles; No. 9 steel crochet hook or size needed to obtain gauge.
GAUGE: 7 sc and 7 ch-3 sps = 3".

BEACH TOWEL
Cut 6" x 11½" piece from washcloth. Fold edges under ¼". Press with warm iron if necessary.
Rnd 1: With black, starting at corner of one long side, with lp on hook, push hook through washcloth ⅛" from edge, yo, draw lp through, complete as sc, ch 3; spacing sts approximately ⅜" apart, *(ch 3, sc) 25 times across to next corner, ch 3, sc in same corner, (ch 3, sc) 11 times across to next corner*, ch 3, sc in same corner; repeat between ** with last sc in same corner as first sc, ch 3, join with sl st in first sc, fasten off (77 sc, 77 ch-3 sps).
Rnd 2: Working over ch-3 sps, join pink with sc on right side of first sc on last rnd, ch 3, (sc on right side of next sc, ch 3) around, join, fasten off.
Rnd 3: Working over ch-3 lps on last 2 rnds, join yellow with sc in first ch sp on rnd 1, ch 3, (sc in next

ch sp, ch 3) around, join, fasten off.

Fish (make one yellow and one pink)
Row 1: Ch 2, 3 sc in 2nd ch from hook, turn (3 sc).
Rows 2-3: Ch 1, 2 sc in first st, sc in each st across with 2 sc in last st, turn (5, 7).
Rows 4-7: Ch 1, sc in each st across, turn.
Rows 8-9: Ch 1, sc first 2 sts tog, sc in each st to last 2 sts, sc last 2 sts tog, turn (5, 3).
Row 10: For **tail**, ch 4, 3 tr in same st, ch 4, sl st in next st, ch 4, (3 tr, ch 4, sl st) in last st, fasten off.

Finishing
Glue one wiggle eye over rows 2-4 on each Fish.
Glue Fishes, eight yellow sequins, nine pink sequins and 17 green sequins to Beach Towel according

to Beach Towel Diagram.

COVER-UP

Cut piece from washcloth according to Cover-Up Diagram. Fold edges under ¼". Press with warm iron if necessary.

Rnd 1: Working sts in same manner as rnd 1 of Beach Towel, join black with sc in bottom right corner of left front, (ch 3, sc) 26 times across to next corner, ch 3, sc in same corner, (ch 3, sc) 9 times across to next corner, ch 3, sc in same corner, (ch 3, sc) 26 times across to next corner, ch 3, sc in same corner, (ch 3, sc) 4 times across to next corner, ch 3, sc in same corner, (ch 3, sc) 32 times across to next corner, ch 3, sc in same corner, (ch 3, sc) 4 times across to next corner with last sc in same corner as first sc, ch 3, join with sl st in first sc, fasten off.

Rnd 2: Repeat same rnd of Beach Towel.

Rnd 3: Working over ch-3 lps on last 2 rnds, join yellow with sc in ch sp of rnd 1 to right side of first sc on last rnd, (ch 3, sc in next ch sp) 19 times; to **join back to front,** (ch 1, sc in corresponding ch-3 sp on front, ch 1, sc in next ch sp on back) 6 times, (ch 3, sc in next ch sp on back) 29 times; to **join front to back,** (ch 1, sc in corresponding ch-3 sp on back, ch 1, sc in next ch sp on front) 6 times, ch 3, (sc in next ch sp, ch 3) around, join, fasten off.

Finishing

To **gather waist,** with sewing needle and thread, baste across one front 2¼" from bottom edge,

pull basting thread slightly to gather. Repeat on back and other front.

Glue sequins on front according to Cover-Up Diagram.

BEACH BAG

Cut 2" x 3" oval. Fold edges under ¼". Press with warm iron if necessary.

Rnd 1: Working sts in same manner as rnd 1 of Beach Towel, spacing sts ¼" apart, join with sc in oval piece, ch 3, (sc, ch 3) 20 more times evenly spaced around, join with sl st in first sc (21 sc, 21 ch-3 sps).

Rnds 2-3: Repeat same rnds of Beach Towel.

Rnd 4: With black, repeat rnd 3 of Beach Towel.

Rnd 5: With pink, repeat rnd 3 of Beach Towel.

Rnd 6: Repeat rnd 3 of Beach Towel.

Rnds 7-18: Repeat rnds 4-6 consecutively. **Do not** fasten off at end of last rnd.

Rnd 19: Sl st into first ch sp, ch 1, 4 sc in same sp, 4 sc in each ch sp to center ch sp on side; (for **handle,** sl st in next ch sp, ch 15, sl st in next ch sp, **turn,** ch 7, sc in center of ch-15, ch 7, sl st in

same sp as first sl st); 4 sc in same sp, 4 sc in each ch sp to center ch sp on opposite side; repeat between ( ); 4 sc in each ch sp around, join, fasten off.❦

COVER-UP DIAGRAM

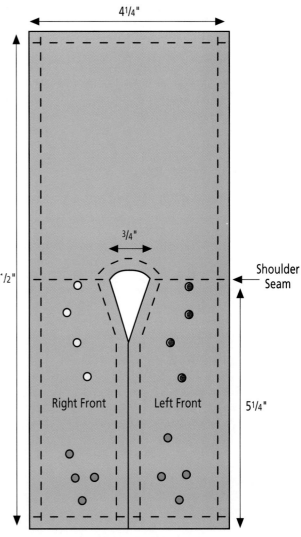

BEACH TOWEL DIAGRAM

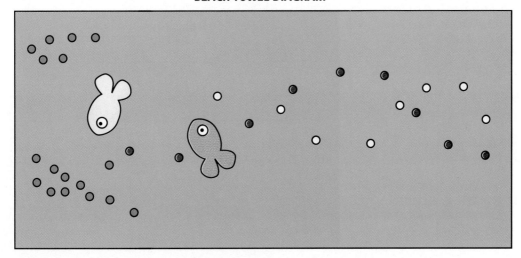

BLUE & WHITE BEACH SET

Designed by Angela J. Tate

TECHNIQUE: Crochet
SIZE: Two-piece Swimsuit and Cover-up fit 11"-11½" fashion doll; Tote is 2" x 2½" not including handles.
MATERIALS FOR ALL THREE: Size 5 pearl cotton — 50 yds. each blue and white; tapestry needle; No. 5 steel crochet hook or size needed to obtain gauge.
GAUGE: 8 dc sts = 1", 7 dc rows = 2".

SWIMSUIT
TOP

Row 1: For **front,** with blue, ch 25, dc in 4th ch from hook, dc in each ch across, turn (23 dc).

Row 2: Ch 3, dc in each st across, turn.

Row 3: Ch 1, sc in first 5 sts, dc in next 13 sts, sc in last 5 sts, turn.

Row 4: Ch 1, sc in first 5 sts, (hdc in next st, dc in next st, tr in each of next 2 sts, dc in next st, hdc in next st), sc in next st; repeat between ( ), sc in last 5 sts, **do not** turn.

Row 5: For **first side,** ch 3, 5 dc evenly spaced across ends of rows 4-1, turn (6).

Row 6: Ch 3, (dc next 2 sts tog) 2 times, dc in last st, turn (4).

Row 7: Ch 3, dc next 2 sts tog, dc in last st, turn (3).

Row 8: Ch 1, skip first st, sl st in next st; for **tie,** ch 30 leaving last st unworked, fasten off.

Row 5: For **second side,** with wrong side of row 1 facing you, join blue with sl st in end of row 1 on opposite side of front, ch 3, 5 dc evenly spaced across ends of rows, turn (6).

Rows 6-8: Repeat same rows of first side.

BOTTOM

Row 1: Beginning at top of leg opening, with blue, ch 32; for **front,** dc in 4th ch from hook, dc in next 8 chs; for **crotch,** sl st in next 5 chs; for **back,** tr in last 15 chs, turn (30 sts).

Row 2: Ch 4, tr in next 9 sts, sl st in next 10 sts, dc in last 10 sts, turn.

Row 3: Ch 3, dc in next 9 sts, sl st in next 5 sts, tr in last 15 sts, fasten off.

For **back ties,** with blue, ch 30; working in ends of rows across back, with right side of row 8 facing you, 12 sc evenly spaced across; ch 30, fasten off.

For **front ties,** working 9 sc evenly spaced across front, work same as back ties.

COVER-UP

Row 1: Working from side to side, with white, ch 74, dc in 6th ch from hook, (ch 1, skip next ch, dc in next ch) across, turn (35 ch sps, 36 dc).

Row 2: Ch 4, skip next ch, dc in next dc, (ch 1, skip next ch, dc in next dc) across to ch-5, ch 1, skip next ch, dc in next ch, turn (35 ch sps).

Rows 3-5: Ch 4, (dc in next dc, ch 1) across with last dc in 3rd ch of ch-4, turn.

Row 6: For **back,** ch 4, dc in next dc, (ch 1, dc in next dc) 17 times leaving remaining sts unworked, turn (17 ch sps).

Rows 7-8: Repeat row 3.

Row 9: For **second side,** ch 39, dc in 6th ch from hook, (ch 1, skip next ch, dc in next ch or in next dc) across, turn (35 ch sps).

Rows 10-13: Repeat row 3. Fasten off at end of last row.

Fold narrow sides in half; leaving 1" open for armholes, sew opposite side of row 1 together. Repeat on row 13.

TOTE

Rnd 1: With blue, ch 24, dc in 6th ch from hook, (ch 1, skip next ch, dc in next ch) 9 times, (ch 1, dc in same ch as last dc) 3 times; working on opposite side of ch, (ch 1, skip next ch, dc in next ch) 9 times, ch 1, dc in same ch as last dc, ch 1, join with sl st in 4th ch of ch-5 (24 ch sps).

Rnds 2-8: Ch 4, skip next ch, (dc in next dc, ch 1, skip next ch) around, join with sl st in 3rd ch of ch-4.

Rnd 9: Ch 4, dc in next dc, (ch 1, dc in next dc) 3 times; *for **handle,** ch 15; skip next ch, next dc and next ch, dc in next dc*, (ch 1, dc in next dc) 10 times; repeat between **, ch 1, (dc in next dc, ch 1) 5 times, join.

Rnd 10: Ch 1, sc in each ch-1 sp and in each dc around with 20 sc in each ch-15 lp, join with sl st in first sc, fasten off.

Sip Cold Lemonade While your Backyard Chef does the Grilling

Patio Party

BARBECUE GRILL

Designed by Sandra Miller-Maxfield

PHOTO on page 61
TECHNIQUE: Novelty Craft
SIZE: 5¼" x 8½" x 11⅛ " tall.
MATERIALS: 1lb. 10 oz. size salt box; 60" of 3/16" dowel; One drinking straw; Scrap of thin cardboard; 20 x 35 hole piece of black 7-count plastic canvas; Craft glue or glue gun; Black and silver paint; Paint brush.

CUTTING INSTRUCTIONS:

1: Remove spout from salt box; cut hole at one end and opening for lid according to Lid Cutting Illustration.

2: Cut ¼" x 2" piece of cardboard for handle.

3: From drinking straw, cut one 1⅛" piece; cut open according to Straw Cutting Illustration.

4: From 3/16" dowel, cut four 7⅝" pieces, two 7" pieces, one 5¼" piece, one 3¾" piece, one 2¾" piece and one 1" piece.

5: From plastic canvas, cut two 17 x 20 hole pieces for grates.

ASSEMBLY INSTRUCTIONS:

1: Paint salt box and handle black; let dry.

2: Fold handle according to Handle Diagram. Place one dot of glue on each folded end; let dry. Paint glue dots black; let dry. Glue handle to box as shown in Barbecue Grill Assembly Diagram.

3: Sand ends of each dowel piece.

4: Paint dowel pieces and drinking straw piece silver; let dry.

5: Assemble Barbecue Grill according to Barbecue Grill Assembly Diagram.

6: Place grates inside grill.❦

Straw Cutting Illustration

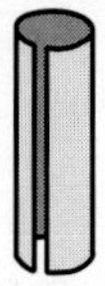

Handle Diagram

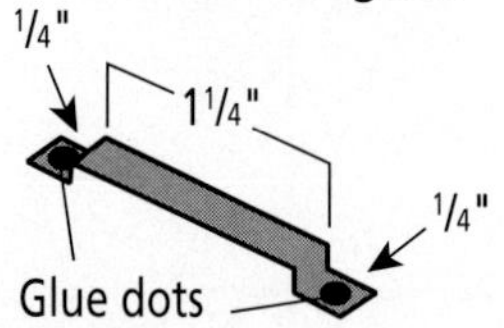
¼"
1¼"
¼"
Glue dots

Lid Cutting Illustration

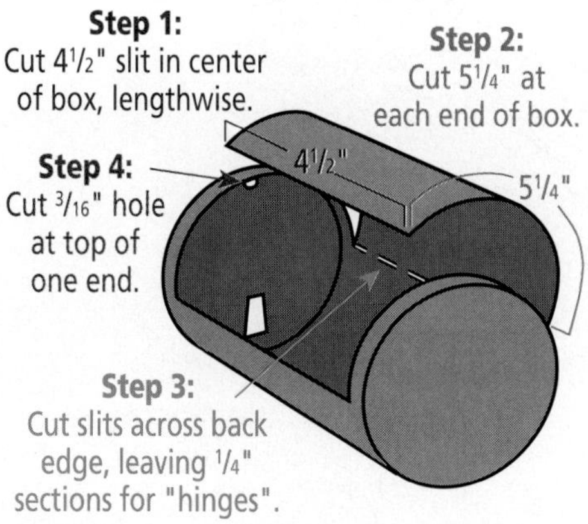
Step 1:
Cut 4½" slit in center of box, lengthwise.
Step 2:
Cut 5¼" at each end of box.
Step 4:
Cut 3/16" hole at top of one end.
4½"
5¼"
Step 3:
Cut slits across back edge, leaving ¼" sections for "hinges".

Barbeque Grill Assembly Diagram

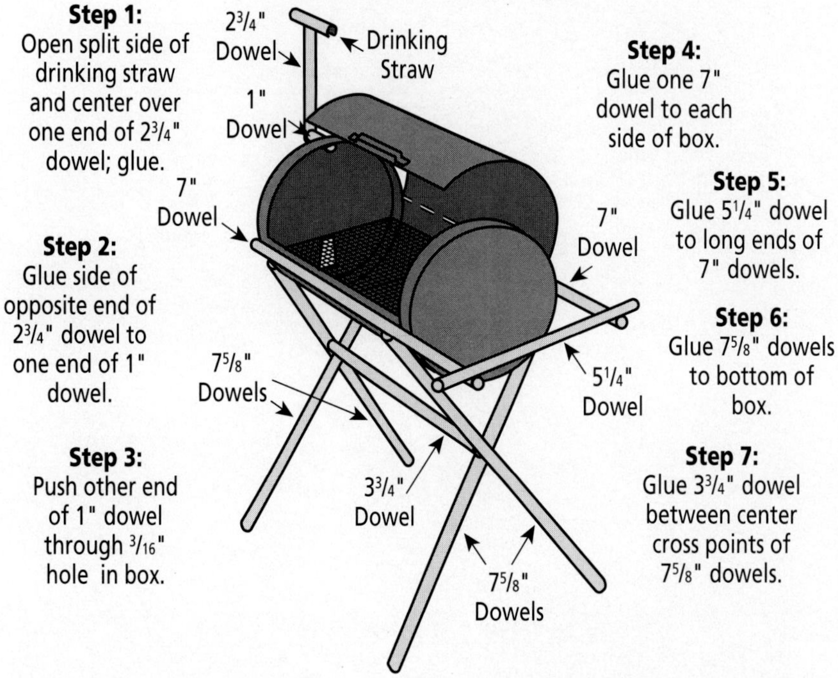
Step 1:
Open split side of drinking straw and center over one end of 2¾" dowel; glue.
2¾" Dowel
Drinking Straw
1" Dowel
7" Dowel
Step 2:
Glue side of opposite end of 2¾" dowel to one end of 1" dowel.
7⅝" Dowels
Step 3:
Push other end of 1" dowel through 3/16" hole in box.
3¾" Dowel
7⅝" Dowels
Step 4:
Glue one 7" dowel to each side of box.
7" Dowel
Step 5:
Glue 5¼" dowel to long ends of 7" dowels.
Step 6:
Glue 7⅝" dowels to bottom of box.
5¼" Dowel
Step 7:
Glue 3¾" dowel between center cross points of 7⅝" dowels.

WATERMELON SUMMER OUTFIT

Designed by Minette Collins Smith

PHOTO on page 61
TECHNIQUE: Plastic Canvas & Sewing
SIZE: Fits an 11½" fashion doll.
MATERIALS: Three 4½" plastic canvas radial circles; Scraps of 7-count plastic canvas; ¼ yd. pink and white polka dot fabric; 7½" pink ⅜" grosgrain ribbon; 6" of ⅛" elastic; One hook and eye set; Craft glue or glue gun; Sewing needle and thread to match fabric; Raffia straw (for amounts see Color Key on page 64).

HAT, BAG & BELT CUTTING INSTRUCTIONS:

NOTE: Graphs and diagrams on page 64.

A: For Hat, cut one canvas circle according to graph.

B: For Bag sides, cut one from each remaining canvas circle according to graph.

C: For Bag bottom, cut one 5 x 35 holes.

D: For Belt, cut one 3 x 35 holes.

STITCHING INSTRUCTIONS:

NOTES: Use a doubled strand of raffia throughout. Use raffia lengths no longer than 24"; longer lengths may split. Use shorter lengths for Overcast. Untwist and flatten raffia strands before stitching.

1: With pink, Overcast unfinished cutout center of A according to Hat Wrapping Diagram; with lt. green, Overcast unfinished outside edge, working over bars to fill in uncoded areas.

2: Using colors and stitches indicated, work B-D pieces according to graphs, leaving uncoded areas of B and D pieces unworked. Using black and Straight Stitch, embroider seeds as indicated on B graph.

3: With lt. green, Whipstitch and assemble pieces as indicated and according to corresponding assembly diagrams.

DRESS CUTTING INSTRUCTIONS:

1: From fabric, cut two Dress

Continued on page 64

BARBECUE ACCESSORIES

Designed by Sandra Miller-Maxfield

PHOTO on page 61
TECHNIQUE: Sewing
SIZE: Fits 11½" fashion doll.
MATERIALS: ⅛ yd. white fabric; ⅞ yd. white bias tape; Small amount of duct tape; Heavy cardboard; Black acrylic paint; Black marker; Sewing needle and white thread.

CUTTING INSTRUCTIONS:

1: From white fabric, cut one Apron following Apron Pattern, one Hat Crown following Hat Crown Pattern, and one 4" x 4½" piece for hat brim.

2: From heavy cardboard, cut one Spatula following Spatula Pattern.

STITCHING INSTRUCTIONS:

1: For apron, encase outer edges with bias tape according to Encasement Diagram.

2: For hat, fold brim in half matching 4½" edges; fold in half again matching 2" edges. With ⅛" seam, stitch 2" edges together; do not turn. Run gathering thread ⅛" from outside edge of crown; pull gathers to fit one edge of brim. Stitch crown to edge of brim opposite folded edge. Turn right side out. Fold brim up, forming cuff as shown in photo.

3: For spatula, finish according to Spatula Diagram.

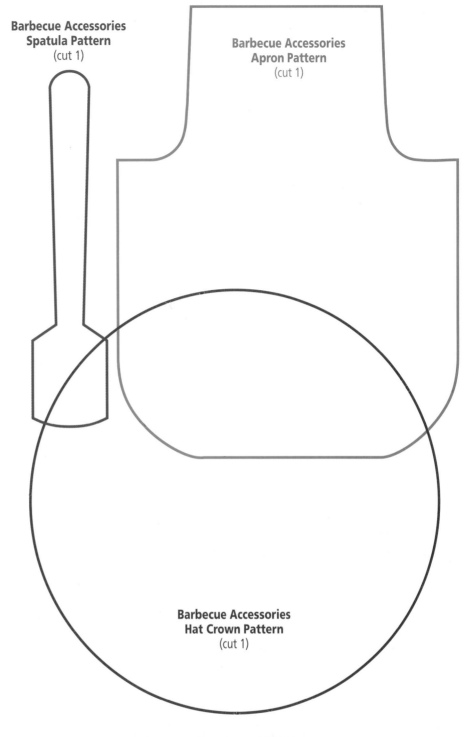

Barbecue Accessories
Spatula Pattern
(cut 1)

Barbecue Accessories
Apron Pattern
(cut 1)

Barbecue Accessories
Hat Crown Pattern
(cut 1)

Spatula Diagram

Step 1:
Paint handle with black acrylic paint. Let dry.

Step 2:
Cover metal end with duct tape, trimming to fit. Bend to shape at red dotted line.

Step 3:
With black marker, draw slots.

Encasement Diagram

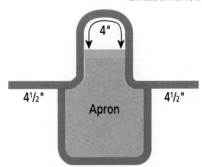

4"

4½" 4½"

Apron

Step 1:
Encase top edge.

Step 2:
Encase bottom edge below armholes.

Step 3:
Leaving 4" extending above top edge for neck and 4½" extending beyond each armhole, encase armholes.

Watermelon Summer Outfit

Continued from page 62

pieces following Dress pattern and one 4½" x 12" piece for bodice.

STITCHING INSTRUCTIONS:

1: With wrong sides together and with ¼" seam, stitch one side seam of dress.

2: Fold bodice in half lengthwise; stitch top casing ⅛" from folded edge.

3: For waist, with wrong sides together and with ¼" seam, stitch bodice to dress, easing to fit.

4: For waist casing, topstitch ⁵⁄₁₆" from waist seam.

NOTE: Cut elastic in half.

5: Run elastic through each casing; with wrong sides together and with ¼" seam, stitch remaining side seam.

6: Fold bottom edge of dress under ½" and hem. ❧

Waist

Place on fold.

Belt Assembly Diagram

Step 1: Overcast unfinished edges of D.

D

Hook

Eye

Step 2: Sew hook to wrong side and eye to right side of D.

Watermelon Outfit Dress Pattern
(cut 2)

Hat Wrapping Diagram

C – Bag Bottom
(cut 1)
5 x 35 holes

D – Belt
(cut 1)
3 x 35 holes

Overcast between arrows.

Bag Assembly Diagram

Step 3: With matching colors, Overcast unfinished edges; Whipstitch loosely across "rind" ends.

Ribbon

Step 2: Glue ends of ribbon inside ends of bag.

B

B

C

Step 1: Whipstitch B and C pieces together, working over bars on sides to fill in uncoded areas.

WATERMELON SUMMER OUTFIT COLOR KEY:

Raffia straw	Amount
▨ Pink	10 yds.
▨ Lt. Green	7 yds.
■ Black	1 yd.

STITCH KEY:
— Backstitch/Straight Stitch
◆ Hook & Eye Attachment

A – Hat
(use 4½" circle)
Cut out gray center.

Continue wrapping from 2nd row over center cutout according to Hat Wrapping Diagram.

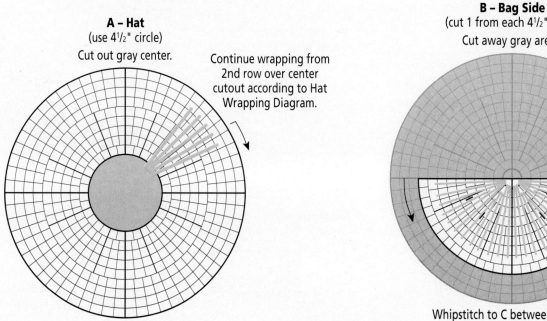

B – Bag Side
(cut 1 from each 4½" circle)
Cut away gray areas.

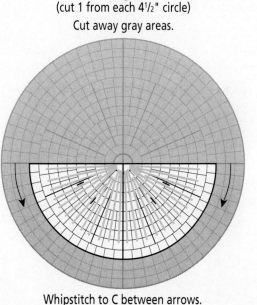

Whipstitch to C between arrows.

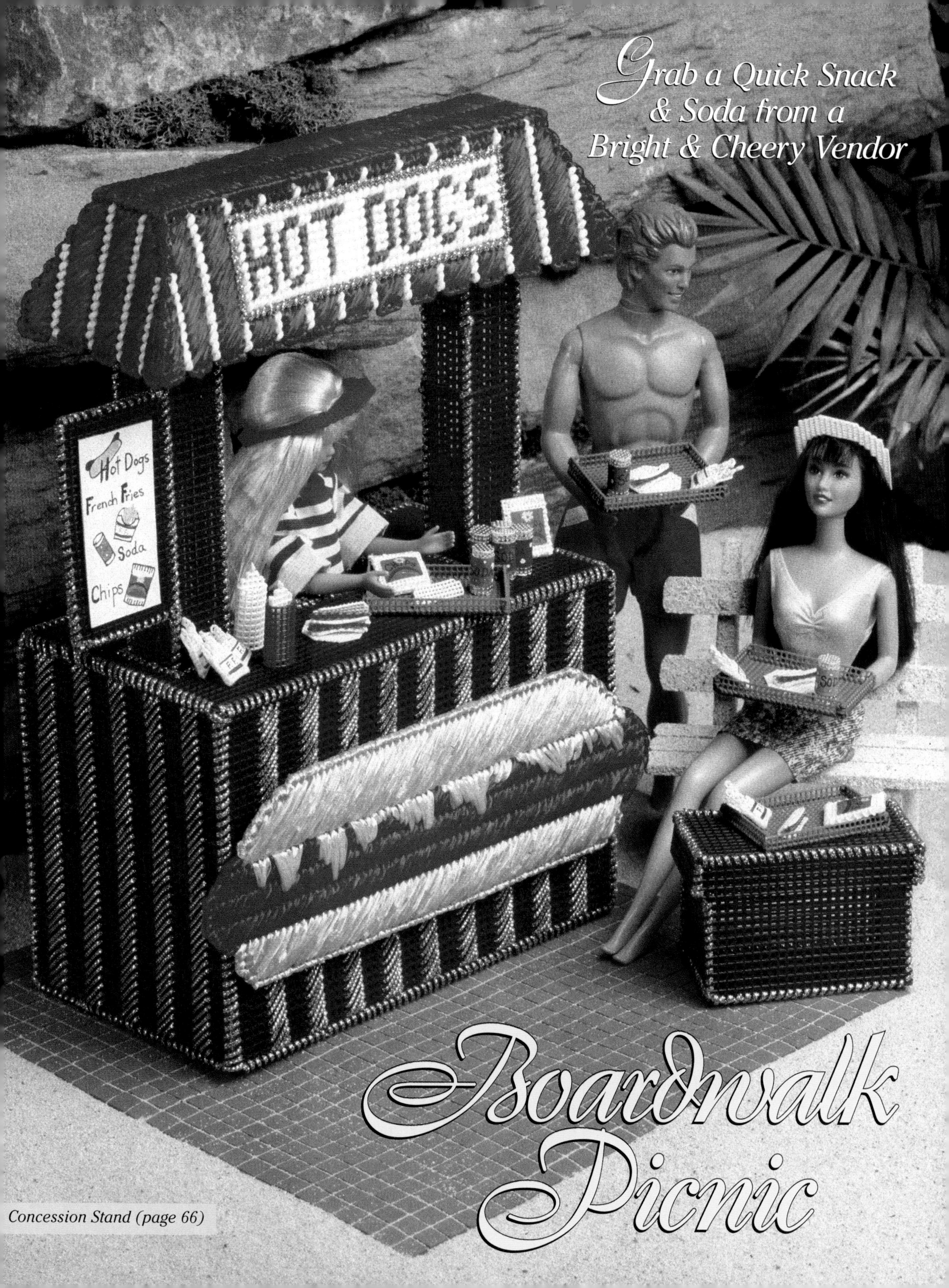

HOT DOGS
Hot Dogs
French Fries
Soda
Chips

Grab a Quick Snack & Soda from a Bright & Cheery Vendor

Boardwalk Picnic

Concession Stand (page 66)

CONCESSION STAND

Designed by Trudy Bath Smith

PHOTO on page 65
TECHNIQUE: Plastic Canvas
SIZE: 5½" x 10½" x about 14⅛" tall.
MATERIALS: Four sheets of dk. blue 7-count plastic canvas; Two sheets of clear 7-count plastic canvas; ¼ sheet of dk. green and scraps of white, red and yellow 10-count plastic canvas; Scraps of white and beige 14-count plastic canvas; ¼ sheet of silver 14-count perforated paper; Polyester fiberfill; Scraps of drawing paper; Colored felt tip markers; 1½" x 3" piece of poster board; Craft glue or glue gun; Six-strand embroidery floss (for amounts see Color Key); Raffia straw (for amounts see Color Key); Metallic cord (for amount see Color Key); Worsted-weight or plastic canvas yarn (for amounts see Color Key).

STAND
CUTTING INSTRUCTIONS:
NOTES: Use blue canvas for A-F, K and L pieces and clear canvas for remaining pieces. Diagrams on page 68.
A: For front, cut two 40 x 60 holes.
B: For outer sides, cut four 32 x 40 holes.

CONCESSION STAND COLOR KEY:

Embroidery floss			Amount
☐ Green			5 yds.
☐ White			5 yds.
☐ Red			½ yd.
☐ Yellow			½ yd.

Raffia straw			Amount
▨ Red			55 yds.
▨ Yellow			15 yds.
▨ Tan			5 yds.

Metallic cord			Amount
☐ Blue/Silver			65 yds.

Worsted-weight	Nylon Plus™	Need-loft™	Yarn Amount
☐ White	#01	#41	20 yds.
■ Royal	#09	#32	5 yds.

STITCH KEY:
− Backstitch/Straight Stitch
☐ Door Support Attachment
···· Fold Lines

C: For inner side and back pieces, cut eight 16 x 40 holes (no graph).
D: For top and bottom, cut four (two for top and two for bottom) according to graph.
E: For doors, cut four 13 x 40 holes (no graph).
F: For door support, cut one 4 x 28 holes (no graph).
G: For awning support pieces, cut eight 7 x 90 holes (no graph).
H: For awning front and back, cut two (one for front and one for back) according to graph.
I: For awning sides, cut two according to graph.
J: For awning top, cut one 11 x 56 holes (no graph).
K: For menu board, cut two 14 x 24 holes (no graph).
L: For display straps, cut four 1 x 7 holes (no graph).
M: For motif, cut two according to graph.

STITCHING INSTRUCTIONS:
NOTES: Use raffia lengths no longer than 24"; longer lengths may split. Use shorter strands for Whipstitch and Overcast. Untwist and flatten raffia strands before stitching.

C-G, K and L pieces are unworked.

1: Using colors and stitches indicated, work A, B (hold matching A and B pieces together and work through both thicknesses as one), H (omit sign on back H and fill in background areas following established pattern), I and M (hold

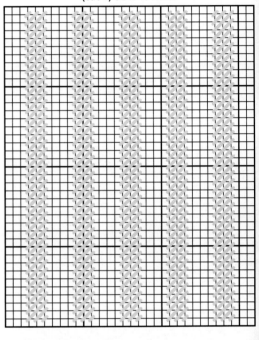

I – Awning Side
(cut 2) 16 x 23 holes

B – Outer Side
(cut 4) 32 x 40 holes

A – Front (cut 2) 40 x 60 holes

pieces together and work through both thicknesses as one) pieces according to graphs. Using red raffia and Slanted Gobelin Stitch over five bars, work J.

2: With matching colors, Whipstitch unfinished edges of M pieces together. Using yellow raffia and Straight Stitch, embroider mustard as indicated on graph.

3: For each awing support, with metallic cord, Whipstitch G and bottom D pieces together according to Awning Support Assembly Diagram on page 68.

4: With matching colors, Whipstitch and assemble pieces as indicated and according to Stand Assembly Diagram. For menu, draw and color poster board as shown in photo; glue to menu board.

ACCESSORIES
CUTTING INSTRUCTIONS:

NOTE: Graphs and diagrams on pages 68 and 69.

A: For Box sides, cut two from blue 7-count 16 x 23 holes (no graph).

B: For Box ends, cut two from blue 7-count 13 x 16 holes (no graph).

C: For Box bottom, cut one from blue 7-count 13 x 23 holes (no graph).

D: For Lid top, cut one from blue 7-count 14 x 25 holes (no graph).

E: For Lid lip pieces, cut one from blue 7-count 4 x 25 holes and two from blue 7-count 4 x 14 holes (no graphs).

F: For Tray sides, cut eight from green 10-count 2 x 23 holes (no graph).

G: For Tray ends, cut eight from green 10-count 2 x 16 holes (no graph).

H: For Tray bottoms, cut four from green 10-count 16 x 23 holes (no graph).

I: For Visors, cut two from 10-count (one from white canvas and one from red canvas) according to graph.

J: For condiment bottle, cut two from 10-count (one from red canvas and one from yellow canvas) 10 x 14 holes (no graph).

K: For condiment nozzle pieces, cut four from white 10-count according to graph.

L: For Plates, cut three from white 14-count according to graph.

M: For Hot Dogs, cut six from red 10-count according to graph.

N: For Hot Dog buns, cut six
Continued on page 68

H – Awning Front & Back
(cut 1 each) 16 x 68 holes

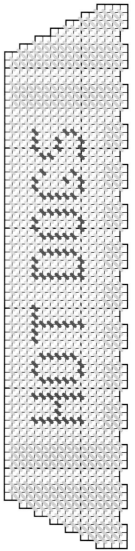

M – Motif
(cut 1) 22 x 69 holes

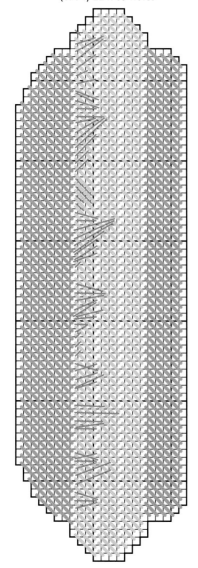

D – Top & Bottom (cut 2 each) 32 x 60 holes

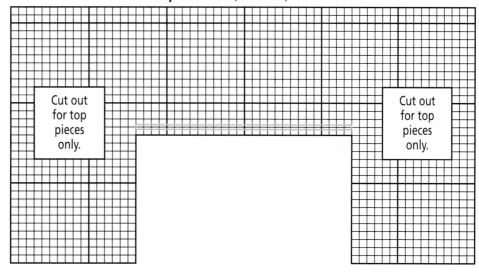

Cut out for top pieces only.

Cut out for top pieces only.

Concession Stand

Continued from page 67

from beige 14-count according to graph.

O: For French Fry bags, cut six from white 14-count according to graph.

P: For French Fries, cut thirty from yellow 10-count according to graph.

Q: For Chip Bag sides, cut eight from white 14-count 11 x 14 holes (no graph).

R: For Soda Can sides, cut seven from silver perforated paper 10 x 16 holes (no graph).

S: For Soda Can top and bottom, cut fourteen (seven for top and seven for bottom) from silver perforated paper according to graph.

ASSEMBLY INSTRUCTIONS:

NOTE: All pieces are unworked;

do not Overcast unfinished edges.

1: For Box, Condiment Bottles, Hot Dogs, French Fries and Soda Cans, with six strands floss and metallic cord in colors indicated, Whipstitch and assemble pieces as indicated and according to corresponding assembly diagrams.

2: For each Tray, with six strands green floss, Whipstitch F-H pieces together according to Tray Assembly Diagram.

3: For each Chip Bag, holding two Q pieces together, with six strands white floss, Whipstitch together (stuff lightly with fiberfill before closing), working in every other hole on long edges and over two bars on short edges.

4: For French Fries, Soda Can and Chip Bag labels, draw and color drawing paper as shown in photo; glue labels to corresponding pieces. 🐾

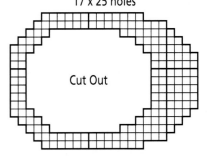

I – Visor
(cut 1 each from red & white 10-count)
17 x 25 holes

Cut Out

K – Condiment Nozzle Piece
(cut 4 from white 10-count)
4 x 13 holes

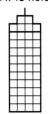

Stand Assembly Diagram
(Pieces are shown in different colors for contrast.)

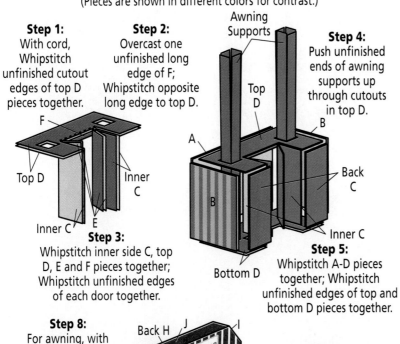

Step 1:
With cord, Whipstitch unfinished cutout edges of top D pieces together.

Step 2:
Overcast one unfinished long edge of F; Whipstitch opposite long edge to top D.

Step 4:
Push unfinished ends of awning supports up through cutouts in top D.

Step 3:
Whipstitch inner side C, top D, E and F pieces together; Whipstitch unfinished edges of each door together.

Step 5:
Whipstitch A-D pieces together; Whipstitch unfinished edges of top and bottom D pieces together.

Step 6:
Whipstitch remaining unfinished edges of awning support pieces together, catching one long edge of each K and ends of each L to supports as you work; do not Overcast unfinished top edges of supports.

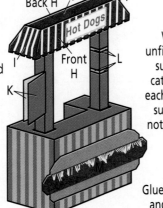

Step 8:
For awning, with matching colors, Whipstitch H-J pieces together; Overcast unfinished bottom edges.

Step 7:
Whipstitch unfinished edges of K pieces together.

Step 9:
Glue awning to supports and M to stand front.

Condiment Bottle Assembly Diagram

Step 2:
Insert two K pieces into each bottle; if desired, glue to secure.

J (red or yellow)

1-hole overlap

Step 1:
For each bottle, with matching color floss, Whipstitch short ends of J together.

Awning Support Assembly Diagram
(Pieces are shown in different colors for contrast.)

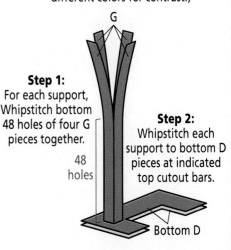

Step 1:
For each support, Whipstitch bottom 48 holes of four G pieces together.

48 holes

Step 2:
Whipstitch each support to bottom D pieces at indicated top cutout bars.

Bottom D

M – Hot Dog
(cut 6 from
red 10-count)
7 x 7 holes

N – Hot Dog Bun
(cut 6 from
beige 14-count)
8 x 13 holes

Hot Dog Assembly Diagram
Step 1:
For each Hot Dog, fold
one N in half lengthwise.

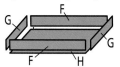

Step 2:
Glue folded bun and
one M together.

Tray Assembly Diagram

L – Plate
(cut 3 from
white 14-count)
14 x 14 holes

P – French Fry
(cut 30 from
yellow 10-count)
5 x 5 holes

S – Soda Can
Top & Bottom
(cut 14 from
silver paper)
5 x 5 holes

O – French Fries Bag
(cut 6 from
white 14-count)
8 x 18 holes

Whipstitch between arrows.

Whipstitch between arrows.

French Fries
Assembly Diagram
Step 2:
Glue five P pieces
to inside of bag.

Whipstitch

Whipstitch

Step 1:
For each bag, fold one O in
half; with white floss,
Whipstitch side edges together.

CONCESSION STAND COLOR KEY:

Embroidery floss	Amount
☐ Green	5 yds.
☐ White	5 yds.
☐ Red	½ yd.
☐ Yellow	½ yd.

Raffia straw	Amount
▨ Red	55 yds.
▨ Yellow	15 yds.
▨ Tan	5 yds.

Metallic cord	Amount
▨ Blue/Silver	65 yds.

Worsted-weight	Nylon Plus™	Need-loft™	Yarn Amount
☐ White	#01	#41	20 yds.
■ Royal	#09	#32	5 yds.

STITCH KEY:
– Backstitch/Straight Stitch
☐ Door Support Attachment
···· Fold Lines

Soda Can Assembly Diagram
Step 2:
Glue one of each top
and bottom S to side.

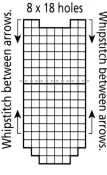

Step 1:
For each can, glue ends of
one R together, forming side.

Box Assembly Diagram
Step 2:
Whipstitch D and E pieces
together, forming lid.

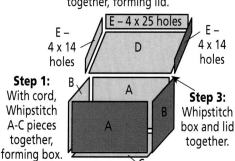

E – 4 x 25 holes

E –
4 x 14
holes

E –
4 x 14
holes

Step 1:
With cord,
Whipstitch
A-C pieces
together,
forming box.

Step 3:
Whipstitch
box and lid
together.

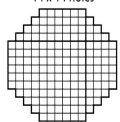

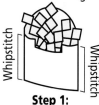

Bon Voyage

Set Sail for Adventure on a Luxurious Cruise Ship

PURPLE & WHITE LUGGAGE

Designed by Maria Berenger

TECHNIQUE: Plastic Canvas
SIZE: Makeup Case is 1¼" x 2⅛" x 1⅜" tall, not including handle; Suitcase is 1¼" x 4⅝" x 2⅞" tall, not including handle.
MATERIALS: ½ sheet of 7-count plastic canvas; Round white Velcro® closure; 1" x 1¾" piece of poster board; 1" x 1¾" piece of aluminum or craft foil; Sewing needle and off-white thread; Craft glue or glue gun; Worsted-weight or plastic canvas yarn (for amounts see Color Key).

CUTTING INSTRUCTIONS:

NOTE: Graphs and diagrams continued on page 75.

A: For Suitcase front and back, cut two (one for front and one for back) 18 x 30 holes.

B: For Suitcase ends, cut two 7 x 18 holes.

STRAPLESS WHITE DRESS & HAT

Designed by Elizabeth Flaim

TECHNIQUE: Sewing
SIZE: Fits 11½" fashion doll.
MATERIALS: 6½" x 7" piece of white fabric; One small red ribbon rose; Two size 1 snaps; ⅞ yd. white ⅜" satin ribbon; Fashion doll size straw hat; Sewing needle and white thread.

C: For Suitcase top and bottom, cut one according to graph and one 7 x 30 holes.

D: For Suitcase handle, cut one 1 x 10 holes (no graph).

E: For Suitcase latch, cut one according to graph.

F: For Makeup Case front and back, cut two (one for front and one for back) 8 x 13 holes.

G: For Makeup Case ends, cut two 8 x 8 holes.

H: For Makeup Case lid and bottom, cut one according to graph and one 8 x 13 holes (no bottom graph).

I: For Makeup Case handle, cut one 1 x 16 holes (no graph).

J: For Makeup Case latch, cut one according to graph.

STITCHING INSTRUCTIONS:

NOTE: Bottom H is unworked.

1: Using lavender and stitches indicated, work A, C, F, G and lid H pieces according to graphs. Fill in uncoded areas and work B, E and J pieces using eggshell and Continental Stitch. With eggshell, Overcast E and J as indicated on

STITCHING INSTRUCTIONS:

1: For dress, press fabric under ½" along all edges; stitch in place. For back seam, fold side edges back so edges lay side-by-side (see Folding Diagram. Fig. 1), press; slip stitch edges together, leaving ½" at bottom edge and 2" from top edge unsewn (see Folding Diagram Fig. 2). Sew one snap at top edge of dress.

2: For belt, cut a 5" length from ⅜" satin ribbon. Stitch ribbon rose to center of belt and sew remaining snap at ends.

3: Glue remaining ribbon to top of hat as shown in photo; let dry. ❦

graphs. With lavender, Overcast unfinished edges of D and I pieces. Using lavender and Backstitch, embroider B pieces as indicated; catching ends of D at indicated holes as you work, embroider top C.

NOTE: Cut closure in half.

2: With eggshell for latch and with lavender, Whipstitch A, B, C and E pieces together as indicated and according to Suitcase Assembly Diagram. Sew closure pieces to wrong side of latch and to corresponding area on front.

NOTE: For mirror, glue foil to poster board.

3: With eggshell for latch and with lavender, Whipstitch F-J pieces together as indicated and according to Makeup Case Assembly Diagram. Trimming to fit, sew remaining closure pieces to wrong side of latch and corresponding area on front. Glue mirror inside lid. ❦

**PURPLE & WHITE
LUGGAGE COLOR KEY:**

	Worsted-weight	Nylon Plus™	Need-loft™	Yarn Amount
☐	Eggshell	#24	#39	23 yds.
■	Lavender	#22	#45	11 yds.

STITCH KEY:
— Backstitch/Straight Stitch
◆ Suitcase Handle Attachment

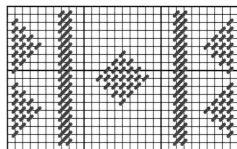

A – Suitcase Front & Back
(cut 1 each) 18 x 30 holes

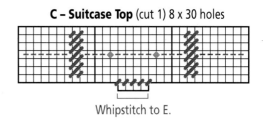

C – Suitcase Top (cut 1) 8 x 30 holes

Whipstitch to E.

C – Suitcase Bottom (cut 1) 7 x 30 holes

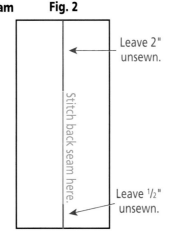

Fig. 1   Folding Diagram   Fig. 2

Side Edge

Fold

(Side edges should meet here.)

Fold

Side Edge

Stitch back seam here.

Leave 2" unsewn.

Leave ½" unsewn.

EYELET SUIT

Designed by Ginger Kean Berk

PHOTO of skirt set and wrist corsage on page 70
TECHNIQUE: Sewing
SIZE: Fits 11½" fashion doll.
MATERIALS: 4" x 12" scrap of white fabric; 1¾ yds. white 5"-wide flat eyelet with scalloped edge; ¼ yd. white 3"-wide flat eyelet with scalloped edge; ⅝ yd. white 1½"-wide flat eyelet with scalloped edge; 1 yd. pink ⅜" satin ribbon; 7" of pink ⅝" satin ribbon; Two small pink ribbon roses; Small flower bouquet on wire; ⅓ yd. ⅛"-wide elastic; Three size 0 snaps; Tacky glue; ¼" x ½" piece Velcro®; Sewing needle; pink and white sewing thread.

CUTTING INSTRUCTIONS:

1: From 5"-wide eyelet, cut 1½"-wide x 8" long piece for jacket bottom; with bottom edges of pattern pieces on scalloped edge of eyelet, cut one piece following Jacket Back pattern and two pieces (reversing pattern for second piece) following Jacket Front pattern.

2: From white fabric, cut two pieces following Split Skirt Top Piece pattern and two Panty Side pieces following Panty Side pattern.

ASSEMBLY INSTRUCTIONS:

NOTE: All seams are ¼" unless otherwise noted.

1: For jacket, with right sides together, stitch darts on jacket front where indicated on pattern; press. With right sides together, fold facing on each front where indicated; stitch along neckline. Clip curves and trim seams. Turn facing to

wrong side; press. With right sides together stitch shoulder, sleeve and side seams. Clip curves where indicated. Hem sleeves. Turn jacket right side out. With wrong sides together, fold back facing, clipping where necessary; glue in place.

2: Turn short edges of jacket bottom ⅜" to wrong side; press. Glue jacket bottom to jacket according to Jacket Illustration.

3: For belt, from ⅜" satin ribbon, cut one 4¼" length and one 15" length. Cut one ¼" x ½" Velcro® piece; tack to ends of 4¼" ribbon. Tie 15" ribbon in a bow; glue to one end of belt. Trim ends.

4: For short skirt, fold under ¼" along unfinished edge of 3"-wide eyelet; press. Cut a 4" length of ⅛" elastic and stitch along cut edge of pressed fold, stretching to fit (fabric will gather as you stitch). With right sides together, stitch back seam. Turn right side out.

5: For panties, with right sides together, stitch front and back seams of panty sides. Press under ⅜" along top edge. Cut 3½" length of elastic and stitch in same manner as short skirt. Press under ¼" along bottom of each side for hem, clipping where necessary; stitch over cut edge and along fold. With right sides together, matching front and back seams, stitch across bottom edge, forming legs.

6: For split skirt, with right sides together, stitch front seam of top pieces. Press under ¼" along top edge. Cut remaining 5"-wide eyelet into two 12" lengths. Run a row of gathering stitches along unfinished top edge of each eyelet piece. With right sides together, pull gathers to fit leg openings of top pieces; adjust gathers evenly and stitch in place.

7: Cut 4" length of ⅛" elastic and stitch in same manner as short skirt. With right sides together, stitch back seam of top pieces. Stitch inseam.

8: For hat, gather 1½"-wide eyelet along unfinished edge to 5½" length. With right sides together, stitch 7" length of ⅝" pink satin ribbon along gathered edge. Fold ribbon over, encasing gathered edge; glue in place. Stitch short edges of eyelet together, forming ring. Tie remaining ⅜" ribbon in a bow; Trim ends. Glue to right side of hat at seam. Glue ribbon rose to center of bow.

9: For wrist corsage, shape bouquet to fit wrist of fashion doll.🌿

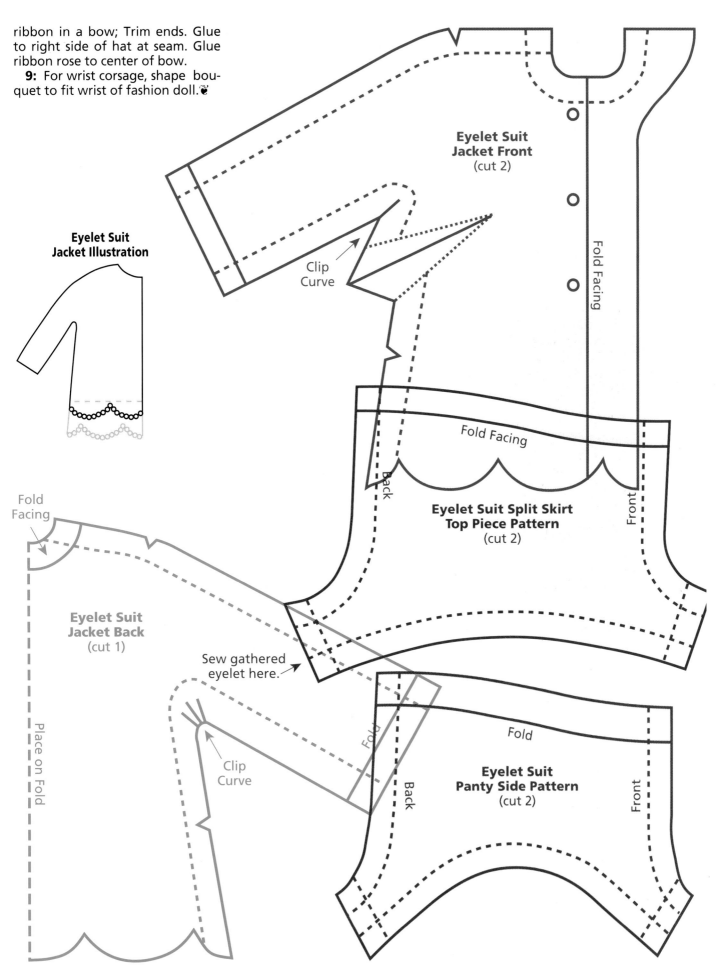

Eyelet Suit Jacket Illustration

Eyelet Suit Jacket Front
(cut 2)

Fold Facing

Clip Curve

Fold Facing

Back

Eyelet Suit Split Skirt Top Piece Pattern
(cut 2)

Front

Fold Facing

Eyelet Suit Jacket Back
(cut 1)

Place on Fold

Sew gathered eyelet here.

Clip Curve

Fold

Back

Fold

Eyelet Suit Panty Side Pattern
(cut 2)

Front

HEARTS TRAVEL CASES

Designed by Diane T. Ray

PHOTO on page 70
TECHNIQUE: Plastic Canvas
SIZE: Garment Bag is 1½" x 3⅞"x 4½" tall, not including handle; Cosmetic Case is 1½" x 2¾" x 1⅞" tall, not including handle; Tote is ¾" x 1¾" x 3" tall, including handle; each Hanger is 1¾" x 2⅞".
MATERIALS: One sheet each of bright blue and bright pink 7-count plastic canvas; Scrap each of bright green, bright yellow and bright purple 7-count plastic canvas; Worsted-weight or plastic canvas yarn (for amounts see Color Key).

GARMENT BAG
CUTTING INSTRUCTIONS:
NOTES: Use pink for B, H and one J piece and blue canvas for remaining pieces.
A: For sides, cut two 25 x 29 holes.
B: For side panels, cut two ac-

cording to graph.
C: For outer top, cut one according to graph.
D: For outer ends, cut two from blue 9 x 29 holes (no graph).
E: For inner top, cut one 9 x 23 holes.
F: For inner ends, cut two from blue 9 x 28 holes (no graph).
G: For bottom, cut one from blue 9 x 25 holes (no graph).
H: For handle, cut one from pink 2 x 13 holes (no graph).
I: For hanger holder, cut one according to graph.
J: For hangers (see photo above right), cut one from each color according to graph.

STITCHING INSTRUCTIONS:
NOTE: C-J pieces are unworked.
1: With bright blue, Whipstitch I to one A as indicated on graphs. Holding one B to side of A opposite holder as indicated and working through both thicknesses as one, using bright pink and Continental Stitch, work according to A graph, leaving uncoded areas unworked; repeat with remaining A and B pieces.
2: With matching colors, Whipstitch A-H pieces together as in-

dicated and according to Garment Bag Assembly Diagram; do not Overcast unfinished edges.
3: Hook hangers over center bar of holder inside garment bag. Fold garment bag sides up and pull handle through cutout on outer top to close.

COSMETIC CASE
CUTTING INSTRUCTIONS:
NOTE: Use pink for B and F pieces and blue canvas for remaining pieces. Graphs and diagram on page 78.

J – Garment Bag Hanger
(cut 1 from each color)
11 x 19 holes

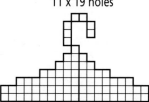

B – Garment Bag Side Panel
(cut 2 from pink)
21 x 26 holes
Cut out gray areas carefully.

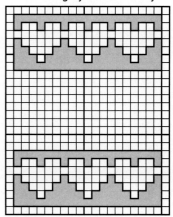

A – Garment Bag Side
(cut 2 from blue) 25 x 29 holes

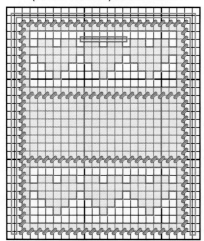

I – Garment Bag Hanger Holder
(cut 1 from blue)
7 x 9 holes

Whipstitch to one A.

E – Garment Bag Inner Top
(cut 1 from blue) 9 x 23 holes

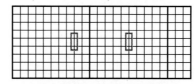

C – Garment Bag Outer Top
(cut 1 from blue) 9 x 25 holes

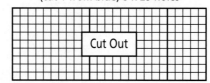

Cut Out

Garment Bag Assembly Diagram

Step 3:
Whipstitch remaining bag side, C and D pieces together.

Step 4:
Whipstitch sides and G together.

Sides

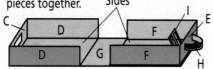

Step 2:
Whipstitch E and F pieces together; Whipstitch to bag side with hanger holder as indicated.

Step 1:
Whipstitch ends of H to E.

HEARTS TRAVEL CASES COLOR KEY:

	Worsted-weight	Nylon Plus™	Need-loft™	Yarn Amount
☐	Bt. Blue		#60	10 yds.
▨	Bt. Pink		#62	10 yds.

STITCH KEY:
☐ Hanger Holder Attachment
☐ Side Panel Placement
☐ Inner Top & End Attachment
☐ Handle Attachment

A: For sides, cut two 11 x 17 holes.

B: For side panels, cut two according to graph.

C: For ends, cut two from blue 9 x 11 holes (no graph).

D: For inner top, cut one 8 x 17 holes.

E: For outer top and bottom, cut one according to graph and one from blue 9 x 17 holes (no bottom graph).

F: For handle, cut one from pink 2 x 13 holes (no graph).

STITCHING INSTRUCTIONS:

NOTE: C-F pieces are unworked.

1: For each side, holding one A and one B together as indicated on graph and working through both thicknesses as one, using bright pink and Continental Stitch, work according to A graph.

2: With bright pink, tack short ends of F to D as indicated. With bright blue, Whipstitch pieces together as indicated and according to Cosmetic Case Assembly Diagram; do not Overcast unfinished edges.

TOTE BAG
CUTTING INSTRUCTIONS:

NOTES: Use pink for B and D pieces and blue canvas for A and C pieces. Graphs and diagram on page 78.

A: For sides, cut two 11 x 11 holes.

B: For side panels, cut two according to graph.

C: For ends and bottom, cut three from blue 4 x 11 holes (no graph).

D: For handles, cut two from pink 1 x 23 holes (no graph).

STITCHING INSTRUCTIONS:

NOTE: C and D pieces are unworked.

1: For each side, holding one A and one B together as indicated on graph and working through both thicknesses as one, using bright pink and Continental Stitch, work according to A graph, catching ends of one D (overlap two holes on opposite side of canvas as indicated) as you work (see Tote Bag Assembly Diagram).

2: With bright blue, Whipstitch pieces together according to diagram; do not Overcast unfinished edges. ❧

Purple & White Luggage
Instructions on page 71

E – Suitcase Latch
(cut 1) 4 x 4 holes

Do not Overcast; Whipstitch to top C.

J – Makeup Case Latch
(cut 1) 3 x 4 holes

Do not Overcast; Whipstitch to H.

G – Makeup Case Ends
(cut 2) 8 x 8 holes

F – Makeup Case Front & Back
(cut 1 each) 8 x 13 holes

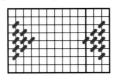

B – Suitcase Ends
(cut 2) 7 x 18 holes

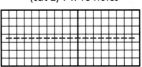

H – Makeup Case Lid
(cut 1) 9 x13 holes

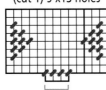

Whipstitch to J.

PURPLE & WHITE LUGGAGE COLOR KEY:

	Worsted-weight	Nylon Plus™	Need-loft™	Yarn Amount
☐	Eggshell	#24	#39	23 yds.
■	Lavender	#22	#45	11 yds.

STITCH KEY:
— Backstitch/Straight Stitch
◆ Suitcase Handle Attachment

Suitcase Assembly Diagram

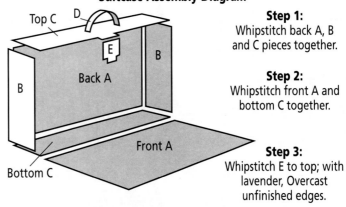

Top C D
E
B
Back A
B
Front A
Bottom C

Step 1:
Whipstitch back A, B and C pieces together.

Step 2:
Whipstitch front A and bottom C together.

Step 3:
Whipstitch E to top; with lavender, Overcast unfinished edges.

Makeup Case Assembly Diagram

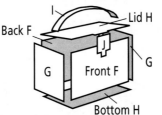

I Lid H
Back F
J
G Front F G
G
Bottom H

Step 1:
Whipstitch F-H pieces together.

Step 2:
Whipstitch lid H to back F and J to lid.

Step 3:
With lavender, Overcast unfinished edges, catching ends of handle on each side of lid as you work.

Girls' Day Out

GARDEN PARTY

Designed by Barbara Tipton

TECHNIQUE: Plastic Canvas
SIZE: Straw Hat is 3" across; Garden Hat is 4" across; Basket is 1¼" across x ¾" tall, not including handle; Purse is ⅜" x 1" x 1½", not including handle.
MATERIALS FOR ONE OF EACH: Scraps of 7-count plastic canvas; One 3" and one 4½" plastic canvas radial circle; ½ yd. peach ⅜" satin ribbon, 1 yd. purple ⅛" satin ribbon; 1 yd. violet ¹⁄₁₆" satin ribbon; 1½" scrap of ecru ¾" scalloped lace; 3" scrap of ⅛" elastic cord; Four peach ½" ribbon roses; Several small silk flowers; Sewing needle and matching color thread; Raffia straw (for amount see Straw Hat & Purse Color Key on page 79); 2-ply yarn (for amount see Garden Hat Color Key).

STRAW HAT & PURSE CUTTING INSTRUCTIONS:

NOTE: Graphs and diagam on page 79.

A: For brim, cut one from 3" circle according to graph.
B: For top, cut one from 3" circle according to graph.
C: For side, cut one 4 x 36 holes.
D: For Purse, cut one 10 x 13 holes.

STITCHING INSTRUCTIONS:

1: Using lt. brown and stitches indicated, work A and B pieces according to graphs; Overcast unfinished outside edges of A. Overlapping four holes as indicated on graph and working through both thicknesses at overlap area to join, work C according to graph; Whipstitch A-C pieces together according to Straw Hat Assembly Diagram.

2: Leaving about 1" for handle, attach a strand of raffia to one end of D as indicated. Fold D wrong sides

together; Whipstitch together as indicated. Overcast unfinished edges.

3: Tie ⅜" peach ribbon into a bow around brim; trim ends. Glue bow and one trimmed scrap of ribbon to Purse and ribbon roses to Hat and Purse as shown in photo.

GARDEN HAT & BASKET CUTTING INSTRUCTIONS:

NOTE: Graphs and diagram on page 79.

A: For Hat, cut one from 4½" circle according to graph.
B: For Basket side, cut one 4 x 28 holes.

C: For Basket bottom, cut one from 4½" circle according to graph.
D: For Basket handle, cut one 1 x 18 holes (no graph).

STITCHING INSTRUCTIONS:

1: Using orchid, wrap each separate ring on A according to Garden Hat Wrapping Diagram. Overlapping two holes as indicated on B graph and working through both thicknesses at overlap area to join, using stitches indicated, work B and C pieces according to graphs.

2: For Basket, Whipstitch B and

Dress up for a Day of Shopping and Sight-Seeing

C pieces together; Overcast unfinished edges of Basket and D. Tack ends of handle to each side of Basket.

NOTE: Cut $1/8$" ribbon into 9" lengths; cut three 9" lengths of $1/16$" ribbon.

3: Tie 9" ribbons into bows. Glue remaining $1/16$" ribbon across length of handle and around top edge of Basket side. Glue bows, lace and flowers to Basket and Hat as shown in photo.

FLOPPY BRIM HAT

Designed by Michele Wilcox

TECHNIQUE: Crochet
SIZE: Fits 11"-11½" fashion doll.
MATERIALS: Worsted-weight yarn — small amount yellow; 1 yd. pink 1" satin ribbon; Three small silk flowers; Craft glue or hot glue; Tapestry needle; F crochet hook or size needed to obtain gauge.
GAUGE: 9 sc sts = 2"; 9 sc rnds = 2".

HAT
Rnd 1: Ch 2, 6 sc in 2nd ch from hook (6 sc).
Rnd 2: 2 sc in each st around (12).
Rnd 3: (Sc in next st, 2 sc in next st) around (18).
Rnds 4-7: Sc in each st around.
Rnd 8: (Sc in each of next 2 sts, 2 sc in next st) around (24).
Rnd 9: Working in **front lps** this rnd only, (sc in next st, 2 sc in next st) around (36).
Rnd 10: Sc in each st around.
Rnd 11: (Sc in each of next 2 sts, 2 sc in next st) around (48).
Rnd 12: Sc in each st around, join with sl st in first sc.
Rnd 13: Ch 3, skip next st, (sl st in next st, ch 3, skip next st) around, join with sl st in joining sl st of last rnd, fasten off.
Fold center 5" of ribbon in half crosswise; place around brim of hat and tie into a bow at back, leaving long ends for streamers. Glue knot to crown of Hat.
Turn up front of Hat and glue in place as shown in photo.
Glue flowers to front of Hat as shown.

Top Off a Shorts Set with a Fun & Floppy Hat & Tote

WHITE TOTE

Designed by Linda Mershon

TECHNIQUE: Crochet
SIZE: 2½" tall.
MATERIALS: Size 10 bedspread cotton — 35 yds. white and small amount lavender; Tapestry needle; No. 5 steel crochet hook or size needed to obtain gauge.
GAUGE: 10 sc sts = 1"; 10 sc rnds = 1".

TOTE
NOTE: Do not join rnds unless otherwise stated. Mark first st of each rnd.
Rnd 1: With white, ch 2, 8 sc in 2nd ch from hook (8 sc).
Rnd 2: 2 sc in each st around (16).
Rnd 3: (Sc in next st, 2 sc in next st) around (24).
Rnd 4: (Sc in each of next 2 sts, 2 sc in next st) around (32).
Rnd 5: (Sc in each of next 3 sts, 2 sc in next st) around, join with sl st in first sc (40).
Rnd 6: Working in **back lps** this rnd only, ch 1, sc in each st around, join.
Rnd 7: Ch 1, sc in each st around.
Rnds 8-24: Sc in each st

Continued on page 79

FLORAL TOTE

Designed by Rosemarie Walter

TECHNIQUE: Plastic Canvas
SIZE: ⅜" x 1¾" x 2⅞" tall.
MATERIALS: ¼ sheet of white 10-count plastic canvas; Scraps of pink, lavender, rose and green 10-count plastic canvas; Six-strand embroidery floss (for amounts see Color Key).

CUTTING INSTRUCTIONS:

A: For Tote front and back, cut one each from white according to graph.

B: For Tote side, cut one from white 3 x 48 holes (no graph).

C: For flowers, cut three from rose, two from pink and two from lavender according to graph.

D: For leaves, cut five from green according to graph.

STITCHING INSTRUCTIONS:

NOTE: A and B pieces are un-worked.

1: Positioning leaves on front A as shown in photo and working through both thicknesses to join, using six strands green and Back-stitch, work D pieces according to graph; using yellow and Cross Stitch, repeat with C pieces.

2: With white, Whipstitch A and B pieces together as indicated on graph, leaving remaining edges unfinished.❧

A – Tote Front & Back
(cut 1 each from white) 16 x 27 holes

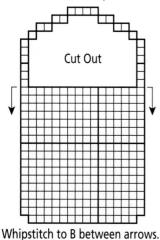

Cut Out

Whipstitch to B between arrows.

C – Flower
(cut 3 from rose, 2 from pink, 2 from lavender)
4 x 4 holes

D – Leaf
(cut 5 from green)
3 x 3 holes

FLORAL TOTE COLOR KEY:

Embroidery floss	Amount
☐ White	2 yds.
■ Green	¼ yd.
▨ Yellow	¼ yd.

STITCH KEY:
- – Backstitch/Straight Stitch
- ✕ Cross Stitch

Hearts Travel Cases

Instructions on page 74

Cosmetic Case Assembly Diagram

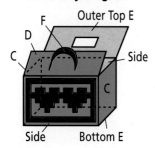

HEARTS TRAVEL CASES COLOR KEY:

Worsted-weight	Nylon Plus™	Need-loft™	Yarn Amount
☐ Bt. Blue	#60		10 yds.
▨ Bt. Pink	#62		10 yds.

STITCH KEY:
- ☐ Hanger Holder Attachment
- ☐ Side Panel Placement
- ☐ Inner Top & End Attachment
- ☐ Handle Attachment

A – Cosmetic Case Side
(cut 2 from blue) 11 x 17 holes

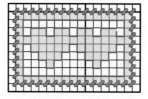

B – Cosmetic Case Side Panel
(cut 2 from pink) 9 x 15 holes
Cut out gray areas carefully.

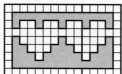

A – Tote Side
(cut 2 from blue)
11 x 11 holes

Tote Bag Assembly Diagram

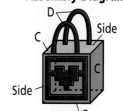

D – Cosmetic Case Inner Top
(cut 1 from blue) 8 x 17 holes

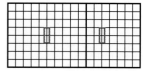

E – Cosmetic Case Outer Top
(cut 1 from blue) 9 x 17 holes

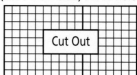

Cut Out

B – Tote Side Panel
(cut 2 from pink) 9 x 9 holes
Cut out gray areas carefully.

Garden Party
Instructions on page 76

Garden Hat
Wrapping Diagram

A – Garden Hat
(cut 1 from
4½" circle)

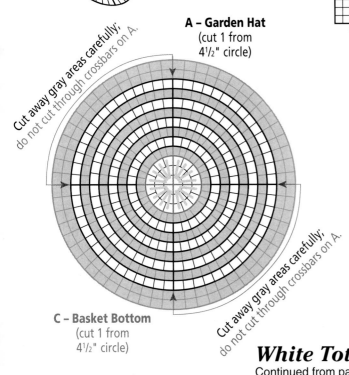

Cut away gray areas carefully;
do not cut through crossbars on A.

C – Basket Bottom
(cut 1 from
4½" circle)

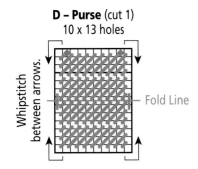

Straw Hat
Assembly Diagram

Overlap

STRAW HAT & PURSE COLOR KEY:
Raffia straw	Amount
■ Lt. Brown	7 yds.

STITCH KEY:
◆ Handle Attachment

D – Purse (cut 1)
10 x 13 holes

Whipstitch between arrows.

Fold Line

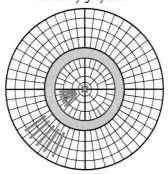

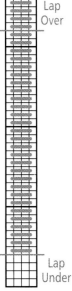

B – Basket Side
(cut 1)
4 x 28 holes

Lap Under

Lap Over

A – Straw Hat Brim (cut 1 from 3" circle)
B – Staw Hat Top (cut 1 from 3" circle)
Cut away gray area.

Continue Long Stitch pattern to
cover each entire piece.

C – Straw Hat Side
(cut 1)
4 x 36 holes

Lap Over

Lap Under

White Tote
Continued from page 77

around. At end of last rnd, join with sl st in first sc.

Rnd 25: Ch 3, skip next st, (hdc in next st, ch 1, skip next st) around, join with sl st in 2nd ch of ch-3 (20 hdc, 20 ch sps).

Rnd 26: Ch 1, sc in each st and in each ch sp around.

Rnd 27: Sc in each st around, join with sl st in first sc, fasten off.

NOTE: For **picot,** ch 3, sl st in top of last st made.

Rnd 28: Join lavender with sc in first st, sc in next st, picot, (sc in each of next 2 sts, picot) around, join, fasten off.

TIE (make 2)
Leaving an 8" length for sewing, ch 2, sc in 2nd ch from hook, ch 3, (sc in same ch, ch 3) 4 times, join with sl st in first sc, ch 50, fasten off.

Beginning and ending on one side of Tote, weave one tie through rnd 25; sew ends together just below flower. Repeat with other tie beginning and ending

on opposite side of Tote.

FLOWER
Leaving an 8" length for sewing, ch 2, sc in 2nd ch from hook, ch 3, (sc in same ch, ch 3) 4 times, join with sl st in first sc, fasten off.

Sew Flower to Tote as shown in photo.❦

Springtime in Paris

*Mon Chère–
Your Creativity
Blooms when
Wearing this
Chic Fashion
Statement*

*Artist's Costume (page 81);
Art Easel & Palette (page 82)*

ARTIST'S COSTUME

Designed by Joyce Bishop

TECHNIQUE: Crochet
SIZE: Fits 11-11½" fashion doll.
MATERIALS FOR ALL THREE:
Sport yarn — 1½ oz. variegated yellow, 1 oz. white, ¾ oz. yellow and ½ oz. green; White sewing thread; Three size 3/0 snaps; Miniature artist's palette; Black, yellow, green and blue felt pens; Two round toothpicks; Craft glue or hot glue gun; Sewing and Tapestry needles; E crochet hook or size needed to obtain gauge.
GAUGE: 5 sts = 1"; 11 sc rows = 2"; 11 dc rows = 4".

DRESS
Skirt
Row 1: Starting at waistline, with variegated, ch 18, sc in 2nd ch from hook, sc in each ch across, turn (17 sc).

Row 2: Ch 3, dc in same st, 2 dc in each st across, turn (34).

Row 3: Ch 3, 2 dc in next st, (dc in next st, 2 dc in next st) across, turn (51).

Rnd 4: Working in rnds, ch 3, dc in each st around, join with sl st in top of ch-3.

Rnd 5: Ch 3, dc in next st, 2 dc in next st, (dc in each of next 2 sts, 2 dc in next st) around, join (68).

Rnd 6: Ch 3, dc in each st around, join.

Rnd 7: Ch 3, dc in each of next 2 sts, 2 dc in next st, (dc in each of next 3 sts, 2 dc in next st) around, join (85).

Rnd 8: Repeat rnd 6.

Rnd 9: Ch 3, dc in each of next 3 sts, 2 dc in next st, (dc in next 4 sts, 2 dc in next st) around, join (102).

Rnd 10: Repeat rnd 6.

Rnd 11: Ch 3, dc in next 4 sts, 2 dc in next st, (dc in next 5 sts, 2 dc in next st) around, join (119).

Rnd 12: Repeat rnd 6.

Rnd 13: Ch 3, dc in next 5 sts, 2 dc in next st, (dc in next 6 sts, 2 dc in next st) around, join (136).

Rnd 14: Repeat rnd 6.

Rnd 15: Ch 3, dc in next 6 sts, 2 dc in next st, (dc in next 7 sts, 2 dc in next st) around, join (153).

Rnds 16-17: Repeat rnd 6. Fasten off at end of last rnd.

Rnd 18: For **ruffle,** join white with sl st in first st, ch 3, 2 dc in same st, (2 dc in next st, 3 dc in next st) around, join (383).

Rnd 19: Ch 3, dc in same st, dc in each st around, join, fasten off (384).

Rnd 20: Join variegated with sc in first st, ch 3, skip next st, (sc in next st, ch 3, skip next st) around, join, fasten off.

Bodice
Row 1: Working on opposite side of starting ch on Skirt, with right side of work facing you, join white with sc in firs ch, sc in each ch across, turn (17 sc).

Row 2: Ch 1, sc in first 4 sts, 2 sc in next st, (sc in each of next 3 sts, 2 sc in next st) 2 times, sc in last 4 sts, turn (20).

Row 3: Ch 1, sc in each st across, turn.

Row 4: Ch 1, sc in first 6 sts, 2 sc in each of next 2 sts, sc in next 4 sts, 2 sc in each of next 2 sts, sc in last 6 sts, turn (24).

Row 5: Repeat row 3.

Row 6: Ch 1, sc in first 8 sts, 2 sc in each of next 2 sts, sc in each of next 2 sts, 2 sc in each of next 3 sts, sc in last 8 sts, turn (30).

Rows 7-8: Repeat row 3.

Row 9: Ch 1, sc in first 8 sts, (sc next 2 sts tog) 7 times, sc in last 8 sts, turn (23).

Row 10: Ch 1, sc in first 4 sts; for **first armhole,** ch 6, skip next 3 sts, sc in next 9 sts; for **second armhole,** ch 6, skip next 3 sts, sc in last 4 sts, turn (17 sc, 2 ch-6 sps).

Row 11: Ch 1, sc in each st and in each ch across, turn (29).

Row 12: Ch 1, sc in first 4 sts, (sc next 2 sts tog) 3 times, sc in next 4 sts, sc next 2 sts tog, sc in each of next 3 sts, (sc next 2 sts tog) 3 times, sc in last 4 sts, turn (22).

Row 13: Repeat row 3.

Row 14: Ch 1, sc in first 4 sts, (sc next 2 sts tog) 3 times, sc in each of next 2 sts, (sc next 2 sts tog) 3 times, sc in last 4 sts, fasten off.

Sew snaps evenly spaced across back opening.

APRON
Skirt
Row 1: Starting at waistline, ch 10, sc in 2nd ch from hook, sc in each ch across, turn (9 sc).

Row 2: Ch 3, dc in same st, 2 dc in each st across, turn (18).

Rows 3-4: Ch 3, dc in each st across, turn.

Row 5: Ch 3, 2 dc in next st, (dc in next st, 2 dc in next st) across, turn (27).

Rows 6-7: Repeat row 3.

Row 8: Ch 3, dc in next st, 2 dc in next st, (dc in each of next 2 sts, 2 dc in next st) across, turn (36).

Rows 9-12: Repeat row 3. Fasten off at end of last row.

Bib
Row 1: With wrong side of row 1 of Skirt facing you, working on opposite side of starting ch, skip first ch, join with sl st in next ch, ch 3, dc in next 6 chs leaving last ch unworked, turn (7 sc).

Rows 2-5: Ch 3, dc in each st across, turn. Fasten off at end of last row.

Edging
Working in sts and in ends of rows around entire Apron, join green with sc in row 5 of Bib, sc in same row, 2 sc in each of next 4 rows, sc in skipped ch on row 1 of Apron; (for **tie,** ch 50, sl st in 2nd ch from hook, sl st in each ch across), sc in next row, 2 sc in each of next 11 rows, ch 1, sc in each st across, ch 1, 2 sc in each of next 11 rows, sc in next row; repeat between ( ), sc in skipped ch on row 1 of Apron, 2 sc in each of next 5 rows, ch 1, sc in each st across, ch 1, join with sl st in first sc, fasten off.

For **neck tie,** join green with sl st in first ch-1 sp on top corner of Bib, ch 15, sl st in next ch-1 sp on top corner of Bib, fasten off.

Pocket
Row 1: With yellow, ch 7, sc in 2nd ch from hook, sc in each ch across, turn (6).

Rows 2-3: Ch 1, sc in each st across, turn. Fasten off at end of last row.

Sew long sides and one short end of Pocket at a slight angle over rows 6-8 of Apron leaving one short end open (see photo).

BERET
Rnd 1: With green, ch 2, 6 sc in 2nd ch from hook, join with sl st in first sc (6 sc).

Rnd 2: Ch 1, 2 sc in each st around, join (12).

Continued on page 82

Artist's Costume
Continued from page 81

Rnd 3: Ch 1, (sc in next st, 2 sc in next st) around, join (18).

Rnd 4: Ch 1, (sc in each of next 2 sts, 2 sc in next st) around, join (24).

Rnd 5: Ch 1, (sc in each of next 3 sts, 2 sc in next st) around, join (30).

Rnd 6: Repeat rnd 4 (40).

Rnd 7: Ch 1, (sc in next 4 sts, 2 sc in next st) around, join (48).

Rnd 8: Working in **back lps** this rnd only, ch 1, sc in each st around, join.

Rnd 9: Ch 1, (sc in next st, sc next 2 sts tog) around, join (32).

Rnd 10: Ch 1, (sc in each of next 2 sts, sc next 2 sts tog) around, join, fasten off (24).

Rnd 11: Join yellow with sc in first st, sc in each of next 3 sts, sc next 2 sts tog, (sc in next 4 sts, sc next 2 sts tog) around, join, fasten off.

FINISHING

1: Place Dress on doll. Place Apron over Dress with neck tie over head. Cross ties on waist around back of doll and tie into bow at front. Place Beret on head.

2: Clip point from one end of each toothpick. With blue felt pen, color ¼" of clipped end on one toothpick. With yellow felt pen, color ⅛" of toothpick next to blue. With black felt pen, color remain-

der of toothpick. Repeat on other toothpick using green on one end instead of blue. Place pointed ends of toothpicks inside Pocket on Apron when completely dry.

3: Cut 4" piece of yellow. Glue center of piece to underside of palette and tie to doll's arm.❧

ART EASEL & PALETTE

Designed by Lynne L. Langer

PHOTO on page 80
TECHNIQUE: Plastic Canvas
SIZE: Easel is 8½" tall; Palette is 1⅜" x 1¾".
MATERIALS: ¼ sheet of 7-count plastic canvas; Three 12" bamboo skewers; One brown 12" chenille stem; Black permanent felt tip marker; Craft glue or glue gun; Worsted-weight or plastic canvas yarn (for amounts see Color Key).

CUTTING INSTRUCTIONS:

A: For tray sides and bottom, cut three 3 x 34 holes (no graph).

B: For tray ends, cut two 3 x 3 holes.

C: For Easel hinge sides, cut two according graph.

D: For Palette, cut one according to graph.

E: For Painting, cut one 20 x 26 holes.

ART EASEL & PALETTE COLOR KEY:

	Worsted-weight	Nylon Plus™	Need-loft™	Yarn Amount
	Maple	#35	#13	11 yds.
	Royal	#09	#32	5 yds.
	Dk. Green	#31	#27	3 yds.
	White	#01	#41	2 yds.
	Black	#02	#00	1½ yds.
	Purple	#21	#46	1 yd.
	Yellow	#26	#57	1 yd.
	Red	#19	#02	1 yd.
	Pumpkin	#50	#12	¼ yd.

STITCHING INSTRUCTIONS:

1: Using colors and stitches indicated, work B-E pieces according to graphs. Using black and Continental Stitch, work one A piece for tray bottom; using maple and Slanted Gobelin Stitch over narrow width, work remaining A pieces for tray sides.

2: With maple for Palette and with matching colors, Overcast unfinished edges of D and E pieces.

NOTES: Cut skewers into three 9" and two 1½" lengths. Cut chenille stem into two 4½" lengths.

3: For Easel, with maple, Whipstitch and assemble A-C pieces as indicated on graph and according

to Easel Assembly Diagram.

4: For each brush, flatten one end of one 1½" skewer and mark with permanent marker. Glue one brush to tray and one to Palette as shown in photo.❧

E – Painting
(cut 1) 20 x 26 holes

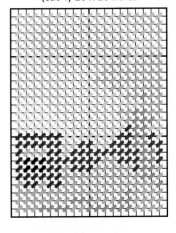

C – Easel Hinge Side
(cut 2) 4 x 8 holes

Whipstitch

B – Tray End
(cut 2)
3 x 3 holes

D – Palette
(cut 1) 8 x 11 holes

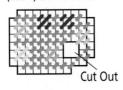

Cut Out

Easel Assembly Diagram

Step 1:
For hinge, Whipstitch C pieces together; Overcast unfinished edges.

Step 2:
For tray, Whipstitch A and B pieces together; Overcast unfinished edges.

Step 3:
For legs, glue 9" skewers to tray and hinge.

Step 4:
Bend ends of each stem tightly around legs.

Chenille Stems

Skewers

Fabulous Furnishings
Set the Mood for
a Romantic Evening

DINING ROOM SET

Designed by Sandra Miller-Maxfield

TECHNIQUE: Plastic Canvas
SIZE: Table is 7⅝" x 9⅞" x 5⅜" tall;
Captain's Chair is 3" x 4¾" x 7½"
tall; Chair is 3" x 3¼" x 7½" tall.
MATERIALS: Three sheets of 7-
count plastic canvas; Three 18"
lengths of 18-gauge floral wire;
Sewing needle and monofilament fishing line; Craft glue or
glue gun; Worsted-weight or
plastic canvas yarn (for amounts
see Color Key on page 84).

CUTTING INSTRUCTIONS:
NOTE: Graphs and diagrams on
pages 84 and 85.
A: For Table top, cut one 46 x
61 holes.
B: For Table center layer, cut
one 48 x 63 holes (no graph).
C: For Table bottom layer, cut
one 50 x 65 holes.
D: For Table side legs, cut two
according to graph.
E: For Table end legs, cut two
according to graph.
F: For Chair backs, cut four
according to graph.
G: For Chair fronts, cut four
according to graph.
H: For Chair front legs, cut four
according to graph.
I: For Chair side legs, cut eight

according to graph.
J: For Chair back brace, cut four
3 x 19 holes (no graph).
K: For Chair seat, cut four 18 x
21 holes.
L: For Captain's Chair right arm,
cut one according to graph.
M: For Captain's Chair left arm,
cut one according to graph.
N: For Captain's Chair arm
braces, cut two 1 x 9 holes (no
graph).

STITCHING INSTRUCTIONS:
NOTES: B and C pieces are
unworked.
Cut eight 5" lengths of wire.
1: Using colors and stitches indicated, work A, D and E (hold one

Continued on page 84

Dining Room Set

Continued from page 83

wire along wrong side of each Table leg and stitch over wire as you work), F-I and K-M pieces according to graphs; with maple, Overcast unfinished edges of L-N pieces.

2: Using maple and Slanted Gobelin Stitch over narrow width, work J pieces.

3: With maple, Whipstitch A-E pieces together as indicated on graphs and according to Dining Table Assembly Diagram. With fishing line, sew through all thicknesses of Table top along table extender board seams and around center motif to stabilize.

4: Whipstitch and assemble F-N pieces according to Dining Chair Assembly Diagram.

E – Table End (cut 2) 34 x 46 holes

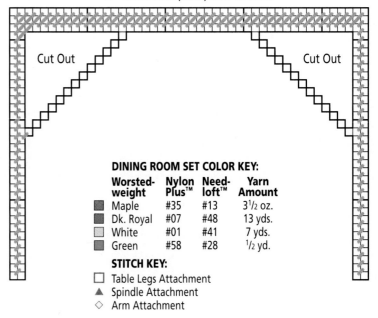

DINING ROOM SET COLOR KEY:

	Worsted-weight	Nylon Plus™	Need-loft™	Yarn Amount
	Maple	#35	#13	3 1/2 oz.
	Dk. Royal	#07	#48	13 yds.
	White	#01	#41	7 yds.
	Green	#58	#28	1/2 yd.

STITCH KEY:
- □ Table Legs Attachment
- ▲ Spindle Attachment
- ◇ Arm Attachment

I – Chair Side Legs
(cut 8) 18 x 18 holes

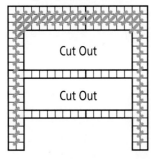

Cut Out

Cut Out

K – Chair Seat (cut 4) 18 x 21 holes

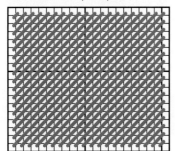

A – Table Top (cut 1) 46 x 61 holes

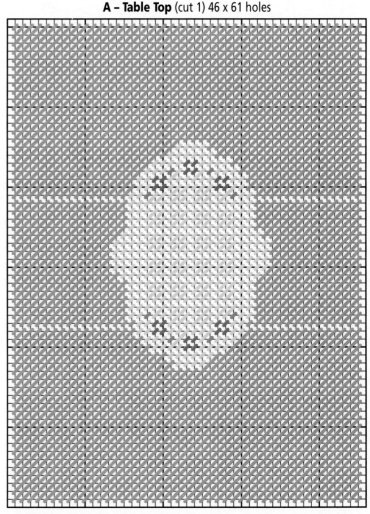

Dining Table Assembly Diagram

Step 1: Whipstitch A and B pieces together.

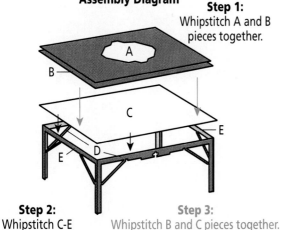

Step 2: Whipstitch C-E pieces together.

Step 3: Whipstitch B and C pieces together. Overcast unfinished edges.

C – Table Bottom Layer (cut 1) 50 x 65 holes

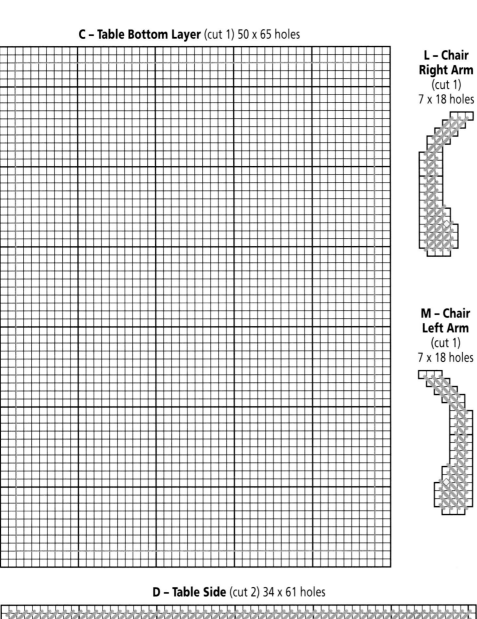

L – Chair Right Arm (cut 1) 7 x 18 holes

M – Chair Left Arm (cut 1) 7 x 18 holes

F – Chair Back (cut 4) 21 x 49 holes

Cut Out

Cut Out

G – Chair Front (cut 4) 21 x 31 holes

Cut Out

H – Chair Front Legs (cut 4) 18 x 21 holes

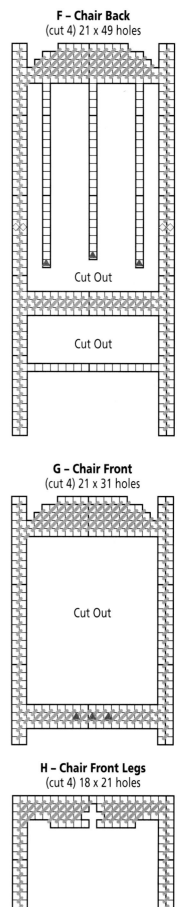

D – Table Side (cut 2) 34 x 61 holes

Cut Out

Cut Out

Dining Chair Assembly Diagram

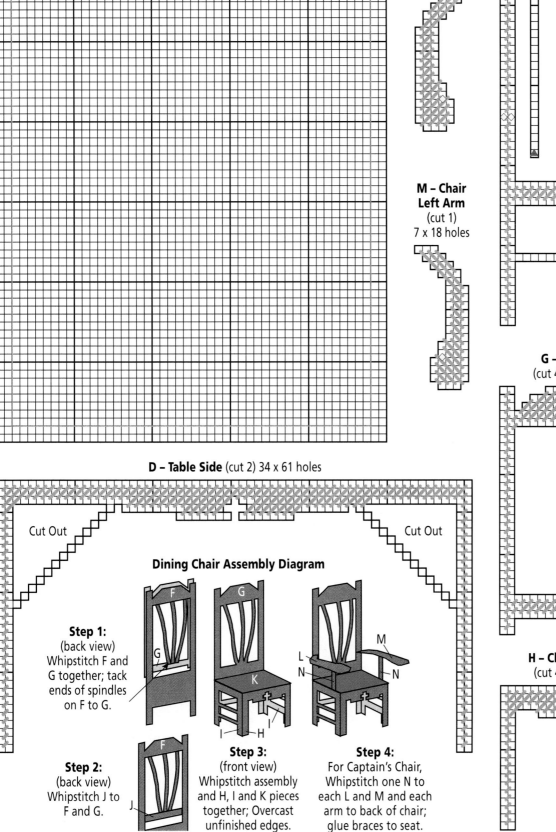

Step 1:
(back view) Whipstitch F and G together; tack ends of spindles on F to G.

Step 2:
(back view) Whipstitch J to F and G.

Step 3:
(front view) Whipstitch assembly and H, I and K pieces together; Overcast unfinished edges.

Step 4:
For Captain's Chair, Whipstitch one N to each L and M and each arm to back of chair; glue braces to seat.

Welcome Home

LIVING ROOM

LIVING ROOM

Designed by Lilo Fruehwirth

TECHNIQUE: Plastic Canvas
SIZE: Love Seat is 4½" x 10" x
6½" tall; Arm Chair is 4½" x
6½" x 6½" tall; Chair is 3" x
3⅜" x 6½" tall; Coffee Table is
3¾" x 5½" x 3" tall; End Table
is 2¾" x 3½" x 3" tall; Rug is
13¼" x 15"; Vase is 2⅜" across
x 3".
MATERIALS: Four sheets of 5-
count plastic canvas; 3½" x 7"
piece of clear acetate or vinyl
plastic; Polyester fiberfill;
Sewing needle and matching
color quilting thread; Long
quilting pins; Silk greenery;
Craft glue or glue gun; 44"-
wide cotton fabric (for amounts
see Color Key on page 88).

FABRIC PREPARATION INSTRUCTIONS:

1: For fabric strips, measuring
along one selvage edge of fabric,
mark every ¾" and snip with
sharp scissors to begin tear. If selvage will not tear easily, trim off
with scissors before snipping.

2: Holding fabric firmly with
both hands, starting at cut, tear
into strips. Discard first and last
strips if not correct width.
Remove any long threads from
strips.

NOTE: To thread needle, fold
one short end of strip in half and
slide through eye of needle.
Handle strips carefully to prevent
excessive fraying.

Continued on page 88

*Relax with your Friends
in a Room Furnished with
the Latest Comfy Decor*

Living Room

Continued from page 86

LOVE SEAT
CUTTING INSTRUCTIONS:
A: For outer back, cut one according to graph.

B: For inner back, cut one according to graph.

C: For cushion, cut two according to graph.

D: For outer sides, cut two according to graph.

E: For inner sides, cut two according to graph.

STITCHING INSTRUCTIONS:
1: Using colors and stitches indicated, work A-E (one of each

LIVING ROOM COLOR KEY:

44"-wide cotton fabric	Amount
Dk. Blue Print	1³/₄ yds.
Dk. Blue Solid	1³/₄ yds.
Eggshell	1³/₄ yds.
Rose	1 yd.

A – Love Seat Outer Back (cut 1) 31 x 45 holes

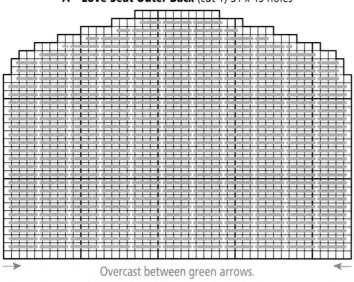

Overcast between green arrows.

B – Love Seat Inner Back (cut 1) 31 x 45 holes

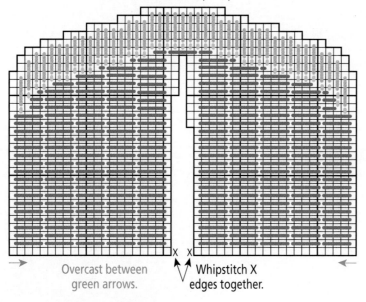

Overcast between green arrows.

Whipstitch X edges together.

D – Love Seat Outer Side
(cut 2) 17 x 22 holes

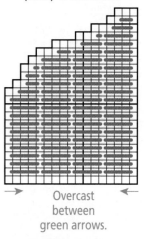

Overcast between green arrows.

E – Love Seat Inner Side
(cut 2) 17 x 24 holes

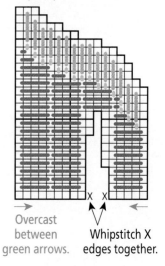

Overcast between green arrows.

Whipstitch X edges together.

Love Seat/Arm Chair Assembly Diagram

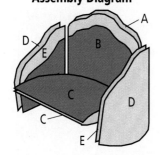

C – Love Seat Cushion (cut 2) 18 x 47 holes

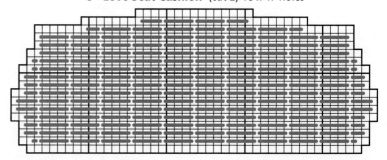

D and E on opposite side of canvas) pieces according to graphs.

2: With thread, Whipstitch X edges of B and E pieces together as indicated on graphs. Using dk. blue solid and Long Stitch, work established pattern over each seam; Overcast unfinished bottom edges of inner pieces as indicated.

3: For back, holding A and B pieces wrong sides together and curving A to fit, with dk. blue print, Whipstitch side and top edges together; Overcast unfinished bottom edge of A.

4: For cushion, holding C pieces wrong sides together, with dk. blue print, Whipstitch together, stuffing with fiberfill before closing.

5: For each side, using D and E pieces, repeat as for back in Step 3.

6: With thread, Whipstitch sides and back together according to Love Seat/Arm Chair Assembly Diagram. Glue cushion to sides and back (see diagram) and secure with pins while glue is drying.

ARM CHAIR
CUTTING INSTRUCTIONS:
A: For outer back, cut one according to graph.

B: For inner back, cut one according to graph.

C: For cushion, cut two according to graph.

D: For outer sides, cut two according to Love Seat D graph.

E: For inner sides, cut two according to Love Seat E graph.

STITCHING INSTRUCTIONS:
1: Using Arm Chair pieces in place of Love Seat pieces, follow Stitching Instructions for Love Seat.

CHAIR
CUTTING INSTRUCTIONS:
NOTE: Graphs and diagrams on page 91.

A: For outer back, cut one according to graph.

B: For inner back, cut one according to graph.

C: For cushion, cut two according to graph.

D: For front legs, cut one according graph.

E: For side legs, cut two according to graph.

STITCHING INSTRUCTIONS:
1: Using colors and stitches indicated, work A-E (one E on opposite side of canvas) pieces according to graphs. Using A-C pieces, follow Steps 2-4 of Love Seat.

2: With dk. blue print, Overcast unfinished edges of D and E pieces. With thread, Whipstitch and assemble pieces according to Chair Assembly Diagram.

TABLES
CUTTING INSTRUCTIONS:
NOTE: Graphs and diagrams on page 90.

A: For Coffee Table top, cut one according to graph.

B: For Coffee Table side legs, cut two according to graph.

C: For Coffee Table end legs, cut two according to graph.

D: For End Table top, cut one according to graph.

E: For End Table side legs, cut two according to graph.

F: For End Table end legs, cut two according to graph.

G: For top coverings, using A and D pieces as patterns, cut one each from acetate or vinyl plastic.

STITCHING INSTRUCTIONS:
1: Using colors and stitches indicated, work A-F pieces according to graphs; with rose, Overcast unfinished edges.

2: With thread, Whipstitch and assemble corresponding pieces according to Table Assembly Diagram; glue G pieces to corresponding table tops.

RUG & VASE
CUTTING INSTRUCTIONS:
NOTE: Graphs and diagrams on pages 91 and 92.

A: For Rug, cut one 65 x 74 holes.

B: For Vase sides, cut six according to graph.

C: For Vase bottom, cut one according to graph.

STITCHING INSTRUCTIONS:
1: Using colors and stitches indicated, work A-C pieces according to graphs; with eggshell for Rug and rose for Vase pieces, Overcast unfinished edges.

2: For Vase, with thread, Whipstitch B pieces together as indicated on graph and to C.❧

C – Arm Chair Cushion
(cut 2) 16 x 26 holes

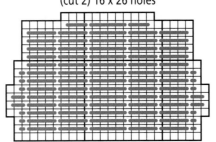

A – Arm Chair Outer Back
(cut 1) 25 x 30 holes

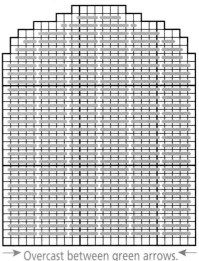

→ Overcast between green arrows. ←

B – Arm Chair Inner Back
(cut 1) 25 x 30 holes

→ Overcast between green arrows.

Whipstitch X edges together.

Living Room
Instructions on page 89

A – Coffee Table Top (cut 1) 16 x 25 holes

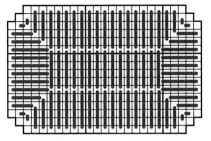

C – Vase Bottom
(cut 1) 10 x 10 holes

B – Vase Side
(cut 6)
5 x 15 holes

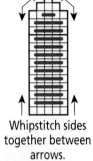

Whipstitch sides
together between
arrows.

B – Coffee Table Side Legs
(cut 2) 14 x 24 holes

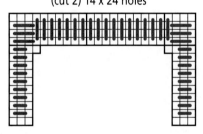

C – Coffee Table End Legs
(cut 2) 14 x 15 holes

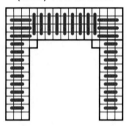

E – End Table Side Legs
(cut 2) 14 x 14 holes

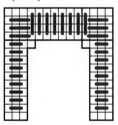

D – End Table Top
(cut 1) 11 x 15 holes

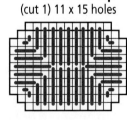

F – End Table End Legs
(cut 2) 10 x 14 holes

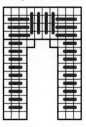

Table Assembly Diagram

Step 1:
Whipstitch side and
end legs together.

Step 2:
Bending each leg
to join, Whipstitch
bottom ½" of each
leg together at
inside corners.

Step 3:
Glue top to legs
slightly below
top edge.

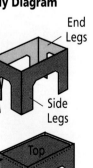

End Legs

Side Legs

Top

- 90 -

Chair Assembly Diagram

Step 1:
Whipstitch cushion, D and E pieces together; Whipstitch back and side legs together.

Step 2:
Glue back edge of cushion to back of chair.

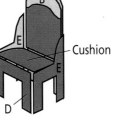

A

B

Cushion

Step 3:
Bending each leg to join, Whipstitch bottom 1/2" of each leg together at inside corners.

E

E

D

A – Chair Outer Back
(cut 1) 14 x 31 holes

C – Chair Cushion
(cut 2) 14 x 15 holes

LIVING ROOM COLOR KEY:

44"-wide cotton fabric	Amount
Dk. Blue Print	1 3/4 yds.
Dk. Blue Solid	1 3/4 yds.
Eggshell	1 3/4 yds.
Rose	1 yd.

B – Chair Inner Back
(cut 1) 14 x 18 holes

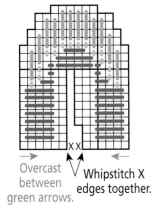

→ Overcast between green arrows.

X X

↓ Whipstitch X edges together.

←

D – Chair Front Legs
(cut 1) 12 x 14 holes

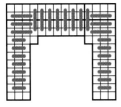

E – Chair Side Legs
(cut 2)
12 x 21 holes

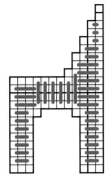

A – Rug (cut 1) 65 x 74 holes

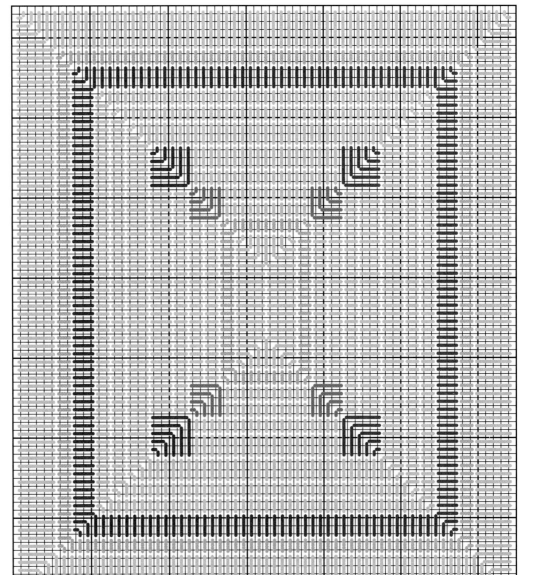

Jam Session

*Let your Hair Down
and Have a Rockin' Good
Time with your Friends*

*Electric Guitar & Amp (page 93); Tennis
Time (page 94); Bean Bag Chair (page 95)*

ELECTRIC GUITAR & AMP

Designed by Brenda R. Wendling

TECHNIQUE: Plastic Canvas
SIZE: Guitar is 2¼" x 5½"; Amp is 1¼" x 2⅝" x 3⅜" tall, including handle; Tambourine is ¼" x 1½" across.
MATERIALS: ½ sheet of black 7-count plastic canvas; ¼ sheet of neon pink 7-count plastic canvas; 6" plastic canvas circle; Twenty assorted-color 5-mm. round sequins; Four gold 3-mm. beads; Sewing needle and matching color thread; Fine metallic braid (for amount see Color Key); Metallic cord (for amounts see Color Key); Worsted-weight or plastic canvas yarn (for amount see Color Key).

CUTTING INSTRUCTIONS:

NOTES: Use pink for J and two A pieces and black canvas for remaining pieces. Graphs and diagrams continued on page 95.

A: For Guitar, cut three according to graph.

B: For Guitar shoulder pad, cut one 1 x 4 holes.

C: For Amp front and back, cut one 16 x 16 holes and one 16 x 18 holes.

D: For Amp sides, cut two according to graph.

E: For Amp top and bottom, cut one 6 x 16 holes and one 8 x 16 holes (no bottom graph).

F: For Amp control panel, cut one 3 x 16 holes.

G: For Amp speaker, cut one from 6" circle according to graph.

H: For Amp speaker support, cut one 5 x 27 holes (no graph).

I: For Amp handle, cut one according to graph.

J: For Tambourine, cut one according to graph.

STITCHING INSTRUCTIONS:

NOTE: Clear and one pink A, bottom E and H pieces are unworked.

1: Using colors and stitches indicated, work one pink A (work metallic braid stitches under bridge nearest neck), C, D (one on opposite side of canvas), top E, F

and G pieces according to graphs. Using colors indicated and French Knot, embroider buttons on worked A and F pieces as indicated on graphs.

NOTE: Cut one 14" and one 8" length of black metallic cord.

2: For shoulder strap, attach and knot one end of 8" strand of cord at ◆ holes as indicated on body end of unworked pink A. Leaving about 3½" of cord between, work B according to graph for shoulder pad. Leaving about 1½" of cord between, attach and knot opposite end of cord at ◆ holes on neck end of piece.

3: For Amp cord, attach and knot one end of 14" strand of cord at ▲ holes as indicated on

unworked pink A; thread opposite end from front to back on F as indicated; knot to secure.

4: For Guitar, holding pink A pieces together with clear piece between, with bright pink, Whipstitch together. With thread, sew beads to neck as shown in photo.

5: For Amp, with black, Overcast unfinished edges of I; Whipstitch and assemble C-I pieces as indicated and according to Amp Assembly Diagram.

6: For Tambourine, glue centers of two sequins to each cut bar on J. Overlapping three holes, with silver, Whipstitch ends of J together; wrap overlap area to cover as shown, and glue ends to secure.

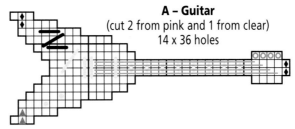

A – Guitar
(cut 2 from pink and 1 from clear)
14 x 36 holes

B – Guitar Shoulder Pad
(cut 1)
1 x 4 holes

C – Amp Back
(cut 1) 16 x 18 holes

C – Amp Front
(cut 1) 16 x 16 holes

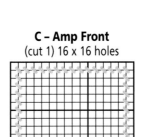

D – Amp Side
(cut 2)
8 x 18 holes

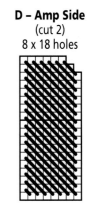

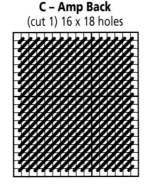

E – Amp Top
(cut 1) 6 x 16 holes

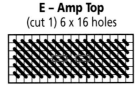

I – Amp Handle
(cut 1)
3 x 4 holes

Tack to E.

F – Amp Control Panel
(cut 1) 3 x 16 holes

J – Tambourine (cut 1 from pink) 1 x 29 holes
Cut through orange-crossed bars carefully.

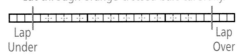

Lap Under   Lap Over

ELECTRIC GUITAR & AMP COLOR KEY:

Fine metallic braid		Amount
▩ Gold		1 yd.

Metallic cord		Amount
■ Black		10 yds.
▨ Silver		4 yds.
☐ Gold		2 yds.

Worsted-weight	Need-loft™	Yarn Amount
■ Bt. pink	#62	3 yds.

STITCH KEY:
— Backstitch/Straight Stitch
● French Knot
◆ Shoulder Strap Attachment
▲ Amp Cord Attachment
○ Bead Attachment
☐ Handle Attachment

TENNIS TIME

Designed by Barbara Tipton

TECHNIQUE: Plastic Canvas
SIZE: Tote is ½" x 1¾" x 3" tall, including handles; Tennis Racket is 1½" x 3⅝".
MATERIALS: ½ sheet of 7-count plastic canvas; Two white ¼" pom-poms (optional); Metallic cord (for amounts see Color Key); Worsted-weight or plastic canvas yarn (for amounts see Color Key).

CUTTING INSTRUCTIONS:

A: For Tote front and back, cut one each 11 x 16 holes.

B: For Tote ends, cut two 3 x 16 holes (no graph).

C: For Tote bottom, cut one 3 x 11 holes (no graph).

D: For Tennis Racket cutout and solid sides, cut one each according to graphs.

STITCHING INSTRUCTIONS:

NOTE: D pieces are unworked.

1: Using white/silver cord and Continental Stitch, work front A according to graph. Fill in uncoded areas and work B and C pieces using hot pink/silver cord and Continental Stitch.

NOTE: Cut two 4" lengths of white/silver cord.

2: For Tote, with indicated colors, Whipstitch A-C pieces together as indicated on graph and accord-ing to Tote Assembly Diagram.

3: For Tennis Racket, with silver, Whipstitch D pieces together as indicated. Using cinnamon and Running Stitch (see Stitch Illustration), work one or two stitches across length and Overcast bottom edge of handle to secure yarn (see Handle Wrap Diagram). Wrap handle with cinnamon as indicated; secure ends under wraps. Wrap remainder of handle with silver until completely covered; secure ends under wraps.

4: If desired, use pom-poms as tennis balls. ❧

Tote Assembly Diagram

Step 1:
For each handle, knot one end of one 4" strand of cord, thread from back to front through one ◆ hole, then from front to back through neighboring ◆ hole; knot opposite end of cord at back to secure.

Handles

Step 2:
With white/silver for bottom edges and with hot pink/silver, Whipstitch A-C pieces together; with white/silver, Overcast unfinished top edges.

D – Tennis Racket Cutout Side
(cut 1) 9 x 23 holes

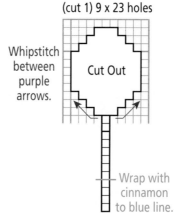

Whipstitch between purple arrows.

Cut Out

— Wrap with cinnamon to blue line.

D – Tennis Racket Solid Side
(cut 1) 9 x 23 holes

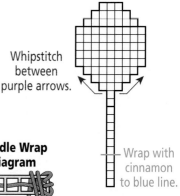

Whipstitch between purple arrows.

— Wrap with cinnamon to blue line.

Handle Wrap Diagram

Running Stitch Illustration

6 5 4 3 2 1

A – Tote Front & Back
(cut 1 each) 11 x 16 holes

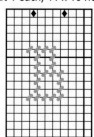

BEAN BAG CHAIR

Designed by Trudy Bath Smith

PHOTO on page 92
TECHNIQUE: Sewing
SIZE: 2½" x 6".
MATERIALS: ¼ yd. denim knit fabric; Heavy cardboard; Plastic stuffing pellets or navy beans; Craft glue or glue gun; Sewing needle and thread to match fabric.

CUTTING INSTRUCTIONS:

1: From denim knit fabric, cut six Side pieces following Side pattern, and Top and Bottom pieces following Top and Bottom pattern.

2: From cardboard, cut two Lining pieces following Lining pattern.

STITCHING INSTRUCTIONS:

1: With right sides together and with ¼" seams, stitch side pieces together along curved edges, leaving an opening where indicated on pattern. Press. Trim seams and turn right side out.

2: Place lining pieces centered on wrong side of top and bottom pieces; fold fabric over lining and glue to secure.

3: Glue top piece to unopen end of assembled sides, covering points. Fill assembled sides with plastic stuffing pellets or navy beans. Slip stitch side pieces together along curved edges on open end and glue bottom piece over slip stitches, covering points. ❧

Bean Bag Chair
Lining Pattern
(cut 2)

Bean Bag Chair
Top/Bottom
Pattern
(cut 1 of each)

Bean Bag Chair
Side Pattern
(cut 6)

Leave open

Electric Guitar & Amp

Instructions on page 93

G – Amp Speaker
(cut 1 from center of 6" circle)
Cut away gray area.

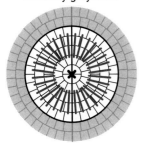

ELECTRIC GUITAR & AMP COLOR KEY:

Fine metallic braid		Amount
▩ Gold		1 yd.
Metallic cord		**Amount**
■ Black		10 yds.
▨ Silver		4 yds.
☐ Gold		2 yds.
Worsted-weight	**Need-loft™**	**Yarn Amount**
■ Bt. pink	#62	3 yds.

STITCH KEY:
— Backstitch/Straight Stitch
● French Knot
◆ Shoulder Strap Attachment
▲ Amp Cord Attachment
○ Bead Attachment
☐ Handle Attachment

Amp Assembly Diagram

Step 1:
Overlapping 3 holes, Whipstitch ends of H together.

Step 2:
Glue wrong side of G to H and H to wrong side center of back C.

Step 3:
For back assembly, Whipstitch back C and D pieces together.

Step 4:
For front assembly, Whipstitch front C, E, F and I pieces together.

Step 5:
Whipstitch front and back assemblies together.

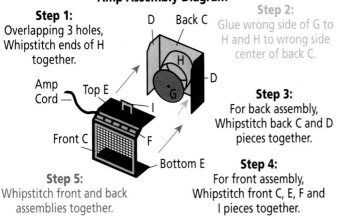

Summer Gardens

GIBSON GIRL

Designed by Joyce Bishop

TECHNIQUE: Crochet & Plastic Canvas

SIZE: Dress fits 11"-11½" fashion doll; Swing is 16" x 22".

MATERIALS FOR DRESS: 3-ply sport yarn — 2 oz. black and 1 oz. white; 2 yds. black 1" satin ribbon; 12" white 7" lace; 6½" white ⅜" gathered lace; 12" black ⅛" ribbon; ⅜"-long oval cameo shank button; Three size 3/0 snaps; White and black sewing thread; Sewing and tapestry needles; E crochet hook or size needed to obtain gauge.

GAUGE: 5 sc sts = 1", 5 sc rows = 1"; 5 dc sts = 1", 5 dc rows = 2".

MATERIALS FOR SWING: ¼ sheet of 7-count plastic canvas; 24" flat hanging vine arch; Silk leaves or vines; Dried baby's breath; 2¼ yds. of 1⅜" wide ribbon; 12 twist ties; 1 yd. white ¼" cord; Craft glue or glue gun; Worsted-weight yarn (for amount see Color Key).

Wile Away the Afternoon Swinging in the Shade of an Old Magnolia

DRESS

SKIRT

Row 1: Beginning at back waist, with black, ch 18, sc in 2nd ch from hook, sc in each ch across, turn (17 sc).

Row 2: Ch 3, 2 dc in each of next 15 sts, dc in last st, turn (32).

Row 3: Ch 3, (2 dc in next st, dc in next st, 2 dc in next st) 10 times, dc in last st, turn (52).

Rnd 4: Working in rnds, ch 3, dc in each st around, join with sl st in top of ch-3.

Rnd 5: Ch 3, (dc in each of next 2 sts, 2 dc in next st, dc in each of next 2 sts) 10 times, dc in last st, join (62).

Rnd 6: Ch 3, dc in each st around, join.

Rnd 7: Ch 3, (dc in each of next 2 sts, 2 dc in next st, dc in each of next 3 sts) 10 times, dc in last st, join (72).

Rnd 8: Ch 3, (dc in each of next 3 sts, 2 dc in next st, dc in each of next 3 sts) 10 times, join (82).

Rnd 9: Ch 3, dc in each of next 3 sts, (2 dc in next st, dc in each of next 2 sts) around, join (108).

Rnd 10: Ch 3, dc in each of next 3 sts, 2 dc in next st, dc in next 4 sts, (dc in next 4 sts, 2 dc in next st, dc in next 4 sts) around, join (120).

Rnd 11: Ch 3, dc in each of next 3 sts, 2 dc in next st, dc in next 5 sts, (dc in next 4 sts, 2 dc in next st, dc in next 5 sts) around, join (132).

Rnd 12: Ch 3, (dc in next 6 sts, 2 dc in next st, dc in next 6 sts) 10 times, dc in last st, join (142).

Rnd 13: Ch 3, (dc in next 6 sts, 2 dc in next st, dc in next 7 sts) 10 times, dc in last st, join (152).

Rnd 14: Ch 3, (dc in next 7 sts, 2 dc in next st, dc in next 7 sts) 10 times, dc in last st, join (162).

Rnd 15: Ch 3, dc in each st around, join.

Rnd 16: Ch 3, (dc in next 4 sts, 2 dc in next st, dc in each of next 3 sts) 20 times, dc in last st, join (182).

Rnd 17: Ch 3, (dc in next 4 sts, 2 dc in next st, dc in next 5 sts) 18 times, dc in last st, join (200).

Rnd 18: Ch 3, dc in each st around, join, fasten off.

BODICE

Row 1: Working in opposite side of starting ch on Skirt, join white with sc in first ch, sc in each ch across, turn (17 sc).

Row 2: Ch 1, sc in first 4 sts, (2 sc in next st, sc in each of next 3 sts) 2 times, 2 sc in next st, sc in last 4 sts, turn (20).

Row 3: Ch 1, sc in each st across, turn.

Row 4: Ch 1, sc in first 6 sts, 2 sc in each of next 2 sts, sc in next 4 sts, 2 sc in each of next 2 sts, sc in last 6 sts, turn (24).

Row 5: Ch 1, sc in each st across, turn.

Row 6: Ch 1, sc in first 8 sts, 2 sc in each of next 3 sts, sc in each of next 2 sts, 2 sc in each of next 3 sts, sc in last 8 sts, turn (30).

Rows 7-8: Ch 1, sc in each st across, turn.

Row 9: Ch 1, sc in first 8 sts, (sc next 2 sts tog) 7 times, sc in last 8 sts, turn (23).

Row 10: Ch 1, sc in first 5 sts; for **first armhole,** ch 6, skip next 2 sts; sc in next 9 sts; for **second armhole,** ch 6, skip next 2 sts; sc in last 5 sts, turn (19 sc, 2 ch-6 lps).

Row 11: Ch 1, sc in first 4 sts, (sc next st and next ch tog, sc in next 4 chs, sc next ch and next st tog), sc in next 7 sts; repeat between ( ), sc in last 4 sts, turn (27 sc).

Row 12: Ch 1, sc in first 4 sts, (sc next 2 sts tog, sc in each of next 2 sts, sc next 2 sts tog), sc in next 7 sts; repeat between ( ), sc in last 4 sts, turn (23).

Row 13: Ch 1, sc in first 4 sts, (sc next 2 sts tog) 2 times, sc in next 7 sts, (sc next 2 sts tog) 2 times, sc in last 4 sts, turn (19).

Row 14: Ch 1, sc in first 6 sts, sc next 2 sts tog, sc in each of next 3 sts, sc next 2 sts tog, sc in last 6 sts, turn (17).

Row 15: Ch 1, sc in first 4 sts, sc next 2 sts tog, sc in next 5 sts, sc next 2 sts tog, sc in last 4 sts, turn.

Row 16: Ch 2, hdc in each st across to last st, ch 2, sl st in last st; for **placket,** ch 1, sc in end of rows 15-1, fasten off.

Row 17: Working in ends of rows on opposite side, join white with sc in end of row 1, sc in end of rows across to row 15, sl st in bottom of ch-2 on row 16, fasten off.

RIGHT SLEEVE

Rnd 1: With back opening facing you, join white with sc in second skipped st of row 10, sc in same st, 2 sc in end of next row; working on opposite side of ch-6, 2 sc in each of next 6 chs; 3 hdc in end of next row, 2 sc in last skipped st on row 10, join with sl st in first sc (21 sts).

Rnd 2: Ch 3, dc in next st, (2 dc in next st, dc in each of next 2 sts) 2 times, 2 dc in next st, dc in each of next 3 sts, (2 dc in next st, dc in each of next 2 sts) 3 times, join (27).

Rnd 3: Ch 3, dc in each st around, join.

Rnd 4: Ch 1, sc in each of first 3 sts, hdc in each of next 3 sts, dc in next 15 sts, hdc in each of next 3 sts, sc in each of last 3 sts, join.

Rnd 5: Ch 1, sc in first st, sc next 2 sts tog, hdc in next st, hdc next 2 sts tog, (dc in next st, dc next 2 sts tog) 5 times, hdc next 2 sts tog, hdc in next st, sc next 2 sts tog, sc in last st, join (18 sts).

Rnd 6: Ch 1, sc first 2 sts tog, hdc next 2 sts tog, (dc next 2 sts tog) 5 times, hdc next 2 sts tog, sc last 2 sts tog, join (9 sts).

Rnd 7: Ch 1, sc in each of first 3 sts, (sc next 2 sts tog) 2 times, sc in each of last 2 sts, join (7).

Rnds 8-14: Ch 1, sc in each st around, join. Fasten off at end of last rnd.

LEFT SLEEVE

Rnd 1: With front facing you, join white with sc in second skipped st of row 10, sc in same st, 3 hdc in end of next row; working on opposite side of ch-6, 2 sc in each of next 6 chs; 2 sc in end of next row, 2 sc in last skipped st on row 10, join with sl st in first sc (21 sts).

Rnds 2-14: Repeat same rnds of Right Sleeve.

FINISHING

1: Sew snaps evenly spaced to placket on Bodice.

2: Sew 3½" piece of lace trim around top edge of neckline. Fold remaining 3" of lace in half to form a "U" and sew to center front of Bodice with cut ends at neckline. Sew cameo button at top of neck, centered over lace.

3: Sew 45" of 1" ribbon over rnds 17 and 18 around bottom of Skirt.

4: Cut 7" of 1" ribbon, fold into thirds; wrap center of ⅛" ribbon tightly around middle of folded ribbon and tie securely, leaving ends free to tie into doll's hair.

5: Fold center 3" of remaining 20" of 1" ribbon in half lengthwise; tie folded area around doll's waist, making bow from unfolded ends.

6: For **slip,** with right sides together, sew cut edges of 7" lace together, forming tube. Turn. Weave a strand of white yarn through top edge of lace and pull to gather. Tie around doll's waist, gathering to fit.

SWING

CUTTING INSTRUCTIONS:

A: For swing, cut two from plastic canvas according to graph.

Continued on page 100

GIBSON GIRL SWING COLOR KEY:

	Worsted-weight	Nylon Plus™	Need-loft™	Yarn Amount
■ Camel		#34	#43	10 yds.

A – Swing (cut 2) 10 x 25 holes
Cut out gray areas.

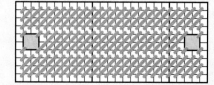

– 97 –

EGYPTIAN COSTUME

Designed by Greg Smith

TECHNIQUE: Plastic Canvas & Crochet

SIZE: Fits 11½" fashion doll.

MATERIALS: ¼ sheet of 7-count plastic canvas; Five 4½" plastic canvas radial circles; One 13-mm. round, one 12-mm. square and one 12- x 18-mm. oval topaz foil-backed acrylic stones; 7" wooden ⅜" dowel or stick; Two hook and eye sets; Sewing needle and matching color thread; Two straight pins; Craft glue or glue gun; Raffia straw (for amounts see Color Key); Metallic flat braid or ribbon (for amount see Color Key); Metallic braid or cord (for amount see Color Key); G crochet hook or size needed to obtain gauge.

GAUGE: 4 sts = 1"; 4 rows = 1".

COLLAR, SKIRT & HEADDRESS CUTTING INSTRUCTIONS:

A: For collar, cut one from circle according to graph.

B: For skirt pieces, cut two from circles according to graph.

C: For headdress, cut one from circle according to graph.

D: For front and back panels, cut two (one for front and one for back) according to graph.

E: For fan, cut one from circle according to graph.

F: For fan frond holder, cut one from circle according to graph.

STITCHING INSTRUCTIONS:

1: Using colors and stitches indicated, work A-E pieces according to graphs; with rainbow/black for collar and with matching colors, Overcast unfinished edges of A, C (omit side edges of top as indicated on graph) and D pieces.

2: With thread, sew one end of each D to A as indicated; overlapping gold border areas as shown in photo, sew B pieces together as indicated.

NOTE: Cut remaining raffia into 12" lengths.

3: Using colors indicated and Lark's Head Knot, attach fronds on F as indicated. Folding fan in half with frond holder between, sew sides of E and F together at center top of F. Glue one end of dowel inside cutout at bottom of fan.

4: Glue stones to headdress, skirt and collar and dowel to F as shown.

TUBE TOP

INSTRUCTIONS:

Row 1: With G hook and metallic flat braid or ribbon, ch 18, sc in 2nd ch from hook, sc in each ch across, turn (17 sc).

Row 2: Ch 1, sc in next 7 sts, 2 sc in each of next 3 sts, sc in next 7 sts, turn (20).

Row 3: Ch 1, sc in next 7 sts, (sc next 2 sts tog) 3 times, sc in next 7 sts, turn (17).

Row 4: Ch 1, sc in each st across, fasten off.

FINISHING:

1: Sew hook and eye sets to back of tube top.

2: To dress doll, place tube top on doll. Slip collar over doll's head with neck area in front as indicated; slip small opening of skirt up over panels to rest on hips. Pin headdress to head.

EGYPTIAN COSTUME COLOR KEY:

Raffia straw	Amount
Aqua	24 yds.
Black	22 yds.
Gold	10 yds.
Metallic flat braid or ribbon	**Amount**
Gold	35 yds.
Metallic braid or cord	**Amount**
Rainbow/Black	27 yds.

STITCH KEY:
- ···· Collar/Panel Attachment
- O Frond Attachment

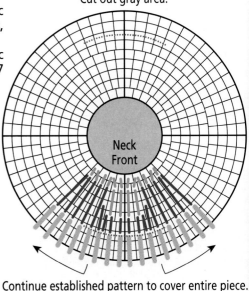

A – Collar (cut 1 from 4½" circle)
Cut out gray area.

Neck Front

Continue established pattern to cover entire piece.

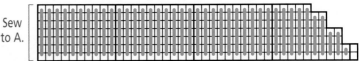

D – Front & Back Panel (cut 1 each) 7 x 41 holes

Sew to A.

B – Skirt Piece (cut 2 from 4½" circles)
Cut out gray center.

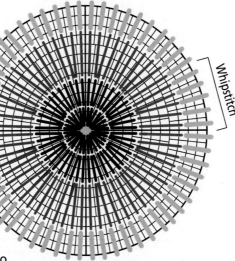

Whipstitch

Whipstitch

E – Fan (cut 1 from 4½" circle)

C – Headdress (cut 1 from 4½" circle)
Cut away gray areas.

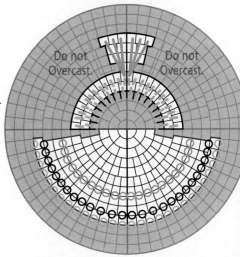

Do not Overcast.

Do not Overcast.

F – Fan Frond Holder (cut 1 from 4½" circle)

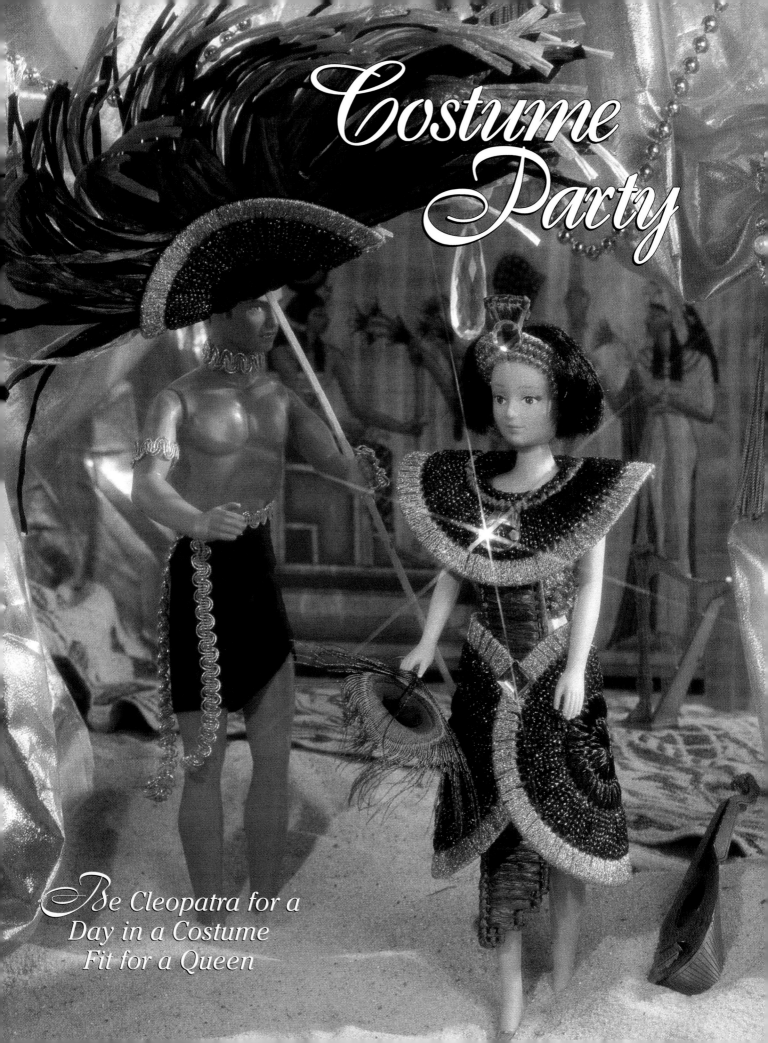

Costume Party

Be Cleopatra for a
Day in a Costume
Fit for a Queen

CAT COSTUME

Designed by Pamela J. McKee

TECHNIQUE: Crochet
SIZE: Fits 11"-11½" fashion doll.
MATERIALS: Size 10 bedspread cotton — 250 yds. black; 3" piece black chenille stem; Black sewing thread; Sewing and tapestry needles; No. 4 steel crochet hook or size needed to obtain gauge.
GAUGE: 8 dc sts = 1"; 7 dc rows = 2".

BODY & LEGS

Row 1: Starting at neckline, ch 26, sc in 2nd ch from hook, sc in each ch across, turn (25 sc).

Row 2: Ch 3, dc in same st, 2 dc in each st across, turn (50).

Row 3: Ch 3, dc in each st across, turn.

Row 4: Ch 3, dc in next 7 sts; for **first armhole,** ch 4, skip next 8 sts; dc in next 4 sts, 2 dc in each of next 4 sts, dc in each of next 2 sts, 2 dc in each of next 4 sts, dc in next 4 sts; for **second armhole,** ch 4, skip next 8 sts; dc in last 8 sts, turn (42 dc, 2 ch-4 sps).

Row 5: Ch 3, dc in each st and in each ch across, turn (50).

Row 6: Ch 3, dc in next 13 sts, (dc in next 2 sts tog) 2 times, *dc in next 5 sts, (dc next 2 sts tog) 2

Gibson Girl
Continued from page 97

STITCHING INSTRUCTIONS:

1: Using camel and stitches indicated, work A pieces according to graph. Holding pieces wrong sides together, Whipstitch together around outer edge, leaving cutout edges unfinished.

2: Arrange greenery over front of vine arch and secure with twist ties. Glue baby's breath at random among leaves.

3: With ribbon, make a 12-loop bow and secure to center top of arch.

4: Thread ends of cord through bottom of Swing. Tie cord ends to bottom of arch centered so Swing hangs evenly; glue ends to secure. Hang arch as desired; seat girl in Swing. ❧

times; repeat from *, dc in last 14 sts, turn (44).

Row 7: Ch 3, dc in next 7 sts, (dc next 2 sts tog, dc in next 4 sts) 2 times, (dc next 2 sts tog) 2 times, (dc in next 4 sts, dc next 2 sts tog) 2 times, dc in last 8 sts, turn (38).

Row 8: Ch 3, dc in each of next 2 sts, dc next 2 sts tog, (dc in next 4 sts, dc next 2 sts tog) 5 times, dc in each of last 3 sts, turn (32).

Row 9: Ch 3, (dc in each of next 2 sts, dc next 2 sts tog) 7 times, dc in each of last 3 sts, turn (25).

Rows 10-12: For **waist,** ch 1, sc in each st across, turn.

Row 13: Ch 3, (dc in next st, 2 dc in next st) across with dc in each of last 2 sts, turn (36).

Rnd 14: Working in rnds, ch 3, dc in next st, 2 dc in next st, (dc in next 5 sts, 2 dc in next st) 5 times, dc in each of last 3 sts, join with sl st in top of ch-3 (42).

Rnds 15-16: Ch 3, dc in each st around, join.

Rnd 17: Ch 3, skip first 21 sts; for **first leg,** sl st in next st, ch 3, dc in next 20 sts, dc in each of last 3 chs, join with sl st in top of ch-3 (24).

Rnd 18: Ch 3, dc in each st around, join.

Rnd 19: Ch 3, dc in each st around to last 2 sts, dc last 2 sts tog, join (23).

Rnds 20-33: Repeat rnds 18 and 19 alternately, ending with 16 sts in last rnd.

Rnds 34-35: Repeat rnd 19 (15, 14).

Rnd 36: Ch 1, sc in each st around, join with sl st in first sc, fasten off.

Rnd 17: For **second leg,** join with sl st in first skipped st on rnd 16, ch 3, dc in next 20 sts, dc in each of last 3 chs, join (24).

Rnds 18-36: Repeat same rnds of first leg.

ARMS

Rnd 1: Working in one armhole, join with sl st in first skipped st, (ch 3, dc) in same st, 2 dc in next st, (dc in next st, 2 dc in

each of next 2 sts) 2 times, sl st in end of next row, sc in last 4 chs, sl st in end of next row, join with sl st in top of ch-3 (14 dc, 4 sc).

Rnd 2: Ch 3, dc in next 13 dc, sc in last 4 sc, join (18 sts).

Rnd 3: Ch 3, dc in next 13 sts, (dc next 2 sts tog) 2 times, join (16 dc).

Rnds 4-8: Ch 3, dc in each st across to last 2 sts, dc last 2 sts tog, join, ending with 11 sts in last rnd.

Rnds 9-10: Ch 1, dc in each st around, join.

Rnd 11: Ch 1, sc in each st around, join with sl st in first sc, fasten off.

Repeat in other armhole.

TAIL

Row 1: Join with sl st in bottom
Continued on page 105

SOUTH SEAS COSTUME

Designed by Minette Collins Smith

TECHNIQUE: Plastic Canvas and Crochet

SIZE: Fits 11½" fashion doll.

MATERIALS FOR PLASTIC CANVAS: Scraps of 7-count plastic canvas; One hook and eye set; Raffia straw (for amounts see Color Key).

MATERIALS FOR CROCHET: Raffia straw — 4 yds. gold and 1 yd. each lt. green, purple and white; G and I crochet hooks or sizes needed to obtain gauges.

GAUGES: With G hook, 4 sc sts = 1"; 4 sc rows = 1". With I hook, 3 sc sts = 1".

SKIRT BAND & HEADBAND CUTTING INSTRUCTIONS:

A: For skirt band, cut one 2 x 25 holes.

B: For headband, cut one 1 x 33 holes.

STITCHING INSTRUCTIONS:

NOTE: Cut twenty five 14" lengths each of gold and green raffia.

1: Using colors indicated and Lark's Head Knot, attach 14" strands of gold to A as indicated on graph; turn piece over and attach green strands as indicated.

2: With green, Overcast unfinished top edge of A securing hook and eye set as indicated and edges of B piece.

3: Using white and French Knot, embroider flowers on B as indicated; tack ends of B together, forming ring.

HALTER TOP INSTRUCTIONS:

Row 1: With G hook and gold, leaving a 7" length on each end for ties, ch 14, **do not** turn, fasten off (14 ch).

Row 2: For **first side**, join gold with sc in eighth ch, sc in next 4 ch, leaving last 2 chs unworked, turn (5 sc).

Row 3: Ch 1, sc in each st across, turn.

Row 4: Ch 1, skip first st, sc in each of last 2 sts, turn (2).

Row 5: Ch 1, skip first st, sc in last st, ch 1, turn; leaving 7" length for tie, fasten off.

Row 2: For **second side**, join gold with sc in next unworked ch on row 1, sc in next 4 chs, leaving last 2 chs unworked, turn (5 sc).

Rows 3-5: Repeat rows 3-5 of first side.

SOUTH SEAS COSTUME STITCH KEY:

- ○ Gold Strand Attachment
- ○ Green Strand Attachment
- ● French Knot

LEI INSTRUCTIONS:

NOTE: Make one each green, purple and white.

With I hook and color, ch 20, sl st in first ch to form ring, fasten off.

A – Skirt Band (cut 1) 2 x 25 holes

B – Headband (cut 1) 1 x 33 holes

CLOWN COSTUME

Designed by Minette Collins Smith

TECHNIQUE: Plastic Canvas and Sewing

SIZE: Fits 11½" or 10" fashion doll.

MATERIALS: One 4¼" plastic canvas radial circle; Two 3" plastic canvas radial circles; Two 14" x 14" scraps of coordinating color fabric; Seam binding; ½ yd. small yellow rickrack; Fourteen ¼" and two ½" yellow pom-poms; Raffia straw (for amounts see Color Key).

COLLARS & HAT BAND
CUTTING INSTRUCTIONS:

A: For top collar, cut one from 3" circle according to graph.

B: For bottom collar, cut one from 4½" circle according to graph.

C: For hat band, cut one from 3" circle according to graph.

STITCHING INSTRUCTIONS:

NOTES: Use a doubled strand of raffia throughout. Use raffia lengths no longer than 24"; longer lengths may split. Use shorter lengths for Overcast. Untwist and flatten raffia strands before stitching.

1: Using colors and stitches indicated, work A and B pieces according to graphs; With matching colors, Overcast unfinished edges.

2: Glue small pom-poms evenly spaced around outer edge.

3: With red, Overcast unfinished edges of C.

SUIT & HAT
CUTTING INSTRUCTIONS:

1: From one fabric piece, following patterns, cut one Front, one Back, one Sleeve and one Hat Side on right side of fabric.

2: From remaining fabric piece, repeat Step 1 on wrong side of fabric to reverse shaping of pieces.

CLOWN COSTUME COLOR KEY:

Raffia straw		Amount
■	Red	10 yds.
▨	Aqua	7 yds.

STITCHING INSTRUCTIONS:

NOTE: All seams are ¼" unless otherwise noted.

1: With right sides together, stitch front and back together at inside leg seams. Turn pant legs under ¼" and hem. Stitch bias tape slightly above hem, for elastic casing. Cut rickrack to fit around bottom edge of each pant leg; stitch in place as shown in photo. Measure elastic slightly larger than fashion doll's ankle; pull elastic through casing and secure ends.

2: With right sides together, stitch center front and back seam, stopping at dot where indicated on pattern. Stitch side seams. Hem

Continued on page 105

B – Bottom Collar (cut 1 from 4½" circle)
Cut away gray areas.

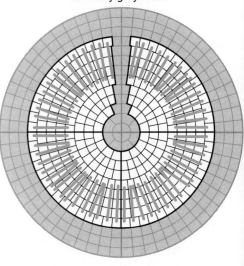

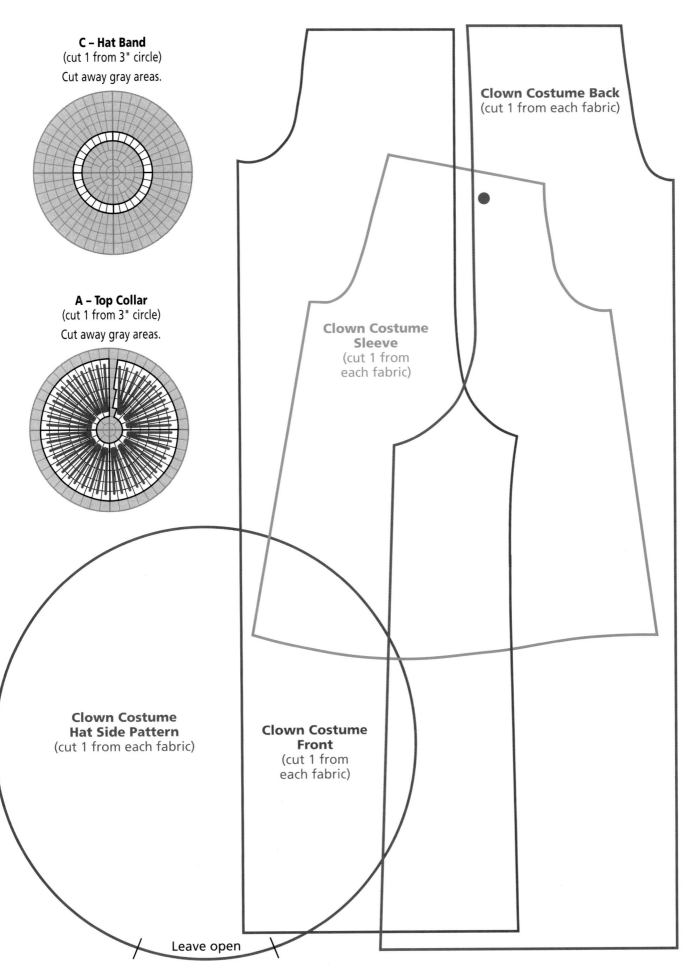

C – Hat Band
(cut 1 from 3" circle)
Cut away gray areas.

A – Top Collar
(cut 1 from 3" circle)
Cut away gray areas.

Clown Costume Back
(cut 1 from each fabric)

Clown Costume Sleeve
(cut 1 from each fabric)

Clown Costume Hat Side Pattern
(cut 1 from each fabric)

Clown Costume Front
(cut 1 from each fabric)

Leave open

METALLIC MASKS

Designed by Trudy Bath Smith

TECHNIQUE: Plastic Canvas
SIZE: Each Mask is 1" x 1⅜".
MATERIALS FOR ONE OF EACH: ¼ sheet of 10-count plastic canvas; Toothpicks (optional); Craft glue or glue gun (optional); Fine metallic braid or metallic thread (for amount see Color Key); Heavy metallic braid or metallic cord (for amounts see Color Key).

CUTTING INSTRUCTIONS:
A: For Masks, cut one each according to graphs.

B: For backs, cut five 2 x 7 holes (no graph).

STITCHING INSTRUCTIONS:
NOTE: B pieces are unworked.
1: Using colors indicated and Continental Stitch, work one A according to each graph. With gold for Comedy, Tragedy and Heart, white for Teardrop and with matching colors, Overcast unfinished cutout edges.
2: Curving each mask slightly to fit, with matching colors, Whipstitch ends of one B to wrong side of each A as indicated on graphs; Overcast remaining unfinished edges.
3: Using colors indicated, Straight

A – Tragedy
(cut 1) 14 x 14 holes
Cut out gray areas carefully.

Whipstitch to one B.

Whipstitch to one B.

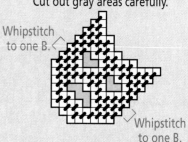

A – Comedy
(cut 1) 14 x 14 holes
Cut out gray areas carefully.

Whipstitch to one B.

Whipstitch to one B.

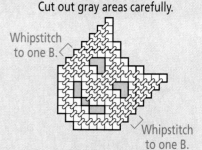

A – Split Heart
(cut 1) 12 x 12 holes
Cut out gray areas carefully.

Whipstitch to one B.

Whipstitch to one B.

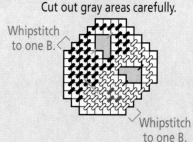

A – Teardrop
(cut 1) 12 x 12 holes
Cut out gray areas carefully.

Whipstitch to one B.

Whipstitch to one B.

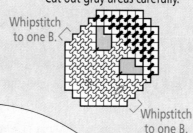

Stitch and Lazy Daisy Stitch, embroider detail as indicated.

4: If desired, glue toothpicks to backs.❧

A – Heart
(cut 1) 12 x 12 holes
Cut out gray areas carefully.

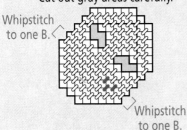

Whipstitch to one B.◁

▷Whipstitch to one B.

METALLIC MASKS COLOR KEY:

	Fine metallic braid or metallic thread	Amount
▦	Gold	¼ yd.
	Heavy metallic braid or metallic cord	**Amount**
▨	White	6 yds.
■	Black	3 yds.
▥	Gold	2 yds.
▦	Dk. Pink	½ yd.
▦	Red	¼ yd.

STITCH KEY:
— Backstitch/Straight Stitch
◦ Lazy Daisy Stitch

Cat Costume
Continued from page 100

of back opening, ch 25, sc in 2nd ch from hook, sc in each ch across, sl st in same sp as first sl st, turn (24 sc).

Row 2: Working in **front lps** and in **remaining lps** of starting ch at same time, sc in each st across with sl st in last st, fasten off leaving long end. Weave end through sts on last row, pull to make Tail curl as desired, secure ends.

NOTE: For **picot,** ch 4, sl st in 4th ch from hook.

For **edging,** working in sts and in ends of rows around back opening, join with sl st in base of Tail, *2 sc in each dc row and sc in each sc row across*; working on opposite side of starting ch, sc in first ch, (picot, skip next ch, sc in next ch) across; repeat between **, join with sl st in first sl st, fasten off.

Sew snaps evenly spaced to edging on back opening.

EARS
Row 1: For **first ear,** working over chenille stem, starting 1"

from one end, join with sc over stem, 4 sc over stem, turn (5 sc).

Rows 2-5: Ch 1, skip first st, sc in each st across, turn, ending with 1 st in last row, fasten off.

Row 1: For **second ear,** working over chenille stem, starting ¼" from first ear, join with sc over stem, 4 sc over stem, turn (5 sc).

Rows 2-5: Repeat same rows of first ear.

Bend chenille stem into headband and place on head.❧

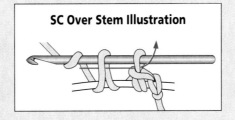

SC Over Stem Illustration

Clown Costume
Continued from page 102

sleeves and finish same as legs. With right sides together, stitch sleeves to armholes of front and back; stitch sleeve seams.

3: Turn neck edge under ⅜" and hem. Stitch along edge, forming elastic casing. Cut a 3" length of ⅛" elastic; pull through casing, secure ends. Finish back opening and stitch snap in place at neck edge. Glue ½" pom-poms to front seam as shown in photo.

4: For hat, with right sides together, stitch pieces together, leaving an opening where indicated on pattern. Turn right side out; press. Slip stitch opening closed. Secure hat on doll's head with plastic canvas hat band.❧

Baby Shower

Swing (page 107); Cradle & Playpen (page 107); Toy Chest &
Rocking Horse (page 108); Stroller (page 110); Walker (page 110)

~106~

Welcome the New Baby in your Life with a Complete Nursery

Designed by Nanette M. Seale

TECHNIQUE: Plastic Canvas
SIZE: Swing is 6½" x 8⅜" at base x 8¼" tall; Cradle is 3¼" x 5½" x 3¾" tall; Playpen is 4⅝" square x 3" tall; Toy Chest is 2" x 4¾" x 2½" tall; Rocking Horse is 2⅝" x 4⅜" x 4" tall; Stroller is 2" x 2⅜" x 6¼" tall; Walker is 4⅜" across x 3⅛" tall.
MATERIALS: Five sheets of 7-count plastic canvas; Four 6" Darice® or four 4" Uniek® Crafts plastic canvas circles; Eight white ½" two-hole buttons; One 6-mm. pearl bead or shank button; Four blue 10-mm. faceted beads; Six pink 6-mm. rondell beads; Alphabet beads to spell "BABY"; 6" of 18-gauge floral wire; 2" of white ⅛" elastic; Sewing needle and white thread; Monofilament fishing line; Worsted-weight or plastic canvas yarn (for amounts see individual Color Keys on pages 107-112).
NOTE: For entire set, use the following yarn amounts: White – 7 oz., Camel – 20 yds., Lt. Pink – 13 yds., Lt. Blue – 9 yds., Black – ½ yd.

SWING
CUTTING INSTRUCTIONS:

NOTE: Graphs and diagrams on page 112.

A: For chair back, cut one according to graph.

B: For chair seat, cut one 12 x 13 holes (no graph).

C: For chair sides, cut two 5 x 12 holes (no graph).

D: For chair hangers, cut two 1 x 17 holes and two 1 x 28 holes (no graphs).

E: For base, cut one 43 x 55 holes (no graph).

F: For leg pieces, cut twelve 2 x 53 holes (no graph).

G: For leg brace pieces, cut four 2 x 12 holes (no graph).

H: For hanger bar pieces, cut four 1 x 32 holes (no graph).

I: For top cover sides, cut two 7 x 33 holes.

J: For top cover ends, cut two according to graph.

STITCHING INSTRUCTIONS:

1: Using colors indicated and Continental Stitch, work A and I pieces according to graphs; fill in uncoded areas and work B, C, F, G (hold two pieces together and work through both thicknesses as one) and J pieces using white and Continental Stitch. Using white and stitches indicated, work E according to Swing Base Stitch Pattern Guide. Overcast unfinished edges of base and D pieces.

NOTE: Cut ⅛" elastic in half.

2: With white, Whipstitch and assemble A-D pieces and elastic according to Swing Chair Assembly Diagram. Whipstitch I and J pieces together as indicated on graph and according to Swing Top Cover Assembly Diagram; Overcast unfinished edges.

3: For each leg, with white, Whipstitch long edges of three F pieces together according to Leg Assembly Diagram; Overcast unfinished edges.

4: For hanger bar, Whipstitch H pieces together according to Swing Hanger Bar Assembly Diagram. Slide hanger bar through elastic chair hangers; with thread, tack each elastic piece together according to diagram.

5: Assemble pieces according to Swing Assembly Diagram.

CRADLE & PLAYPEN
CUTTING INSTRUCTIONS:

NOTE: Cradle graphs and diagram on page 108.

A: For Cradle front and back, cut one each according to graphs.

Continued on page 110

PLAYPEN COLOR KEY:

	Worsted-weight	Nylon Plus™	Need-loft™	Yarn Amount
☐	White	#01	#41	25 yds.
☐	Lt. Blue	#05	#36	1 yd.
☐	Lt. Pink	#10	#08	1 yd.

G – Playpen Side (cut 4) 19 x 30 holes

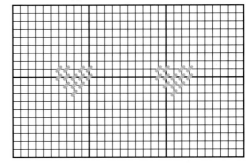

Nursery Set
Continued from page 107

B: For Cradle sides, cut two 7 x 35 holes.

C: For Cradle rocker supports, cut two according to graph.

D: For Cradle rocker bottoms, cut two 1 x 24 holes (no graph).

E: For Cradle bottom, cut one 20 x 35 holes.

F: For Cradle hood, cut one 7 x 34 holes (no graph).

G: For Playpen sides, cut four 19 x 30 holes (graph on page 107).

H: For Playpen bottom, cut one 30 x 30 holes (no graph).

STITCHING INSTRUCTIONS:

1: Using colors indicated and Continental Stitch, work A, B (reverse color of hearts on second piece), E and G pieces according to graphs. Fill in uncoded areas of A and B pieces (uncoded areas of G pieces are unworked) and work C, F and H pieces using white and Continental Stitch.

2: For Cradle, with white, Whipstitch A-F pieces together as indicated on graphs and according to Cradle Assembly Diagram.

3: For Playpen, with right side of H facing up, Whipstitch G and H pieces together as shown in photo; Overcast unfinished edges.

TOY CHEST & ROCKING HORSE CUTTING INSTRUCTIONS:

A: For Toy Chest front and back, cut one 8 x 30 holes and one 16 x 30 holes.

B: For Toy Chest ends, cut two 8 x 13 holes.

C: For Toy Chest lid, cut one 13 x 30 holes.

D: For Toy Chest bottom, cut one 13 x 30 holes (no graph).

E: For Rocking Horse sides, cut two from circles according to graph.

F: For Rocking Horse rocker, cut one 17 x 45 holes (no graph).

G: For Rocking Horse seat, cut one 17 x 25 holes (no graph).

STITCHING INSTRUCTIONS:

1: For Toy Chest, using colors indicated and Continental Stitch, work A-C pieces according to graphs; leaving indicated area unworked, fill in uncoded areas and work D using white and Continental Stitch. Overcast unfinished edges of C as indicated on graph.

CRADLE COLOR KEY:

Worsted-weight	Nylon Plus™	Need-loft™	Yarn Amount
White	#01	#41	47 yds.
Lt. Blue	#05	#36	3 yds.
Lt. Pink	#10	#08	3 yds.

STITCH KEY:
☐ Rocker Support Attachment
☐ Cradle Bottom Attachment

A – Cradle Front (cut 1) 18 x 20 holes

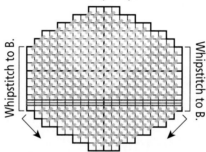

Whipstitch to B.
Whipstitch to B.
Whipstitch to D between arrows.

A – Cradle Back (cut 1) 20 x 24 holes

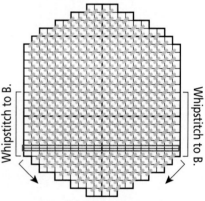

Whipstitch to B.
Whipstitch to B.
Whipstitch to D between arrows.

B – Cradle Side
(cut 2) 7 x 35 holes
Whipstitch to F.

C – Cradle Rocker Support
(cut 2) 6 x 20 holes
Whipstitch to E.

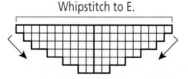

Whipstitch to D between arrows.

E – Cradle Bottom
(cut 1) 20 x 35 holes
Whipstitch to A.
Whipstitch to A.

Cradle Assembly Diagram

Step 2: With right side of cradle back and wrong side of cradle front pieces facing in, Whipstitch A pieces to ends of E.

Step 6: Whipstitch F to back A and B pieces; Overcast unfinished edges.

Step 1: With right sides facing in, Whipstitch C pieces to wrong side of E.

Step 4: Whipstitch one D to bottom edges of front and support.

Step 3: Whipstitch A, B and E pieces together.

Step 5: Whipstitch remaining D to bottom edges of back and support.

2: With white, Whipstitch A-D pieces together and attach loop and bead as indicated on graphs and according to Toy Chest Assembly Diagram on page 110.

3: For Rocking Horse, using colors and stitches indicated, work E pieces on opposite sides of canvas. Using white and Continental Stitch, work F and G pieces.

4: With indicated colors, Whipstitch E-G pieces together according to Rocking Horse Assembly Diagram.

NOTE: Cut twenty-four 3" lengths of lt. pink.

5: For mane and tail, knot 3" strands to sides as indicated. Trim ends and fray to fluff.

Continued on page 110

ROCKING HORSE COLOR KEY:

	Worsted-weight	Nylon Plus™	Need-loft™	Yarn Amount
☐	White	#01	#41	40 yds.
▨	Camel	#34	#43	20 yds.
☐	Lt. Pink	#10	#08	2 yds.
■	Black	#02	#00	½ yd.

STITCH KEY:
— Seat Attachment
◆ Mane & Tail Attachment

Rocking Horse Assembly Diagram

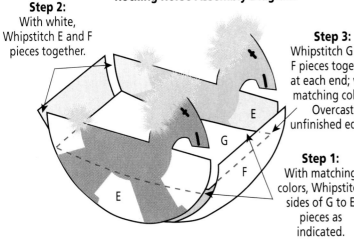

Step 2:
With white, Whipstitch E and F pieces together.

Step 3:
Whipstitch G and F pieces together at each end; with matching colors, Overcast unfinished edges.

Step 1:
With matching colors, Whipstitch sides of G to E pieces as indicated.

E – Rocking Horse Side
(cut 2 from circles - if using 6" circles, cut away outer 5 rows of holes)
Cut away gray areas.

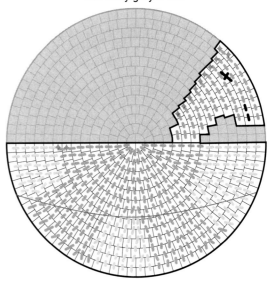

A – Toy Chest Back (cut 1) 16 x 30 holes

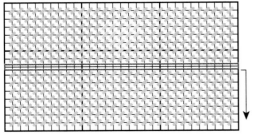

Work stitches below this line on opposite side of canvas.

TOY CHEST COLOR KEY:

	Worsted-weight	Nylon Plus™	Need-loft™	Yarn Amount
☐	White	#01	#41	30 yds.
▨	Lt. Pink	#10	#08	4 yds.
☐	Lt. Blue	#05	#36	3 yds.

STITCH KEY:
☐ Unworked Area/Lid Attachment
◆ Bead Attachment

C – Toy Chest Lid
(cut 1) 13 x 30 holes

Do not Overcast; Whipstitch to back A.

B – Toy Chest End
(cut 2) 8 x 13 holes

A – Toy Chest Front (cut 1) 8 x 30 holes

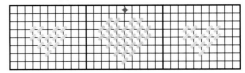

Nursery Set

Continued from page 109

STROLLER

CUTTING INSTRUCTIONS:

A: For seat back, cut one 13 x 17 holes.

B: For seat bottom, cut one 12 x 13 holes (no graph).

C: For seat sides, cut two according to graph.

D: For leg pieces, cut eight 1 x 16 holes (no graph).

E: For leg brace pieces, cut two 1 x 12 holes (no graph).

F: For handle pieces, cut two 1 x 10 holes and two 1 x 4 holes (no graphs).

STITCHING INSTRUCTIONS:

1: Using colors indicated and Continental Stitch, work A and C (one on opposite side of canvas) pieces according to graphs; fill in uncoded areas and work B using white and Continental Stitch.

2: For leg brace, with white, Whipstitch E pieces together along each long edge, leaving ends unfinished; for each leg, leaving one hole at one end unfinished to attach wheels, repeat with two D pieces.

NOTE: Cut floral wire in half.

3: For each handle, holding 3" wire along one end and tacking one 1 x 4-hole piece to one 1 x 10-hole piece as you work (see Stroller Assembly Diagram), with white, Overcast F pieces. Bend short handle piece down at angle.

4: For each wheel, attach two buttons to each leg according to

Wheel Assembly Diagram. For Stroller, with white, Whipstitch and assemble pieces according to Stroller Assembly Diagram.

WALKER

CUTTING INSTRUCTIONS:

A: For top, cut one from circle according to graph.

B: For top rim, cut one 1 x 88 holes (no graph).

C: For bottom pieces, cut two from circles according to graph.

D: For seat, cut one from remaining circle center according to graph.

E: For seat back, cut one 6 x 25 holes (no graph).

STROLLER COLOR KEY:

	Worsted-weight	Nylon Plus™	Need-loft™	Yarn Amount
▨	White	#01	#41	25 yds.
▨	Lt. Pink	#10	#08	1½ yds.
▨	Lt. Blue	#05	#36	1 yd.

Wheel Assembly Diagram

Thread yarn through buttons and unfinished end of leg as shown; tie ends in knot. Trim ends and glue to secure.

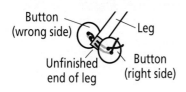

Button (wrong side) — Leg
Unfinished end of leg — Button (right side)

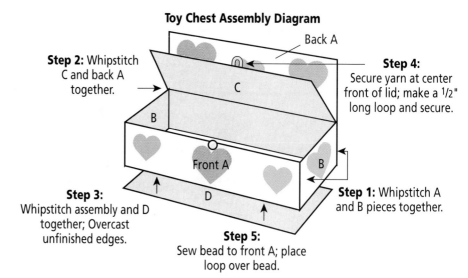

Toy Chest Assembly Diagram

Back A

Step 2: Whipstitch C and back A together.

Step 4: Secure yarn at center front of lid; make a ½" long loop and secure.

C

B

Front A

B

Step 3: Whipstitch assembly and D together; Overcast unfinished edges.

D

Step 1: Whipstitch A and B pieces together.

Step 5: Sew bead to front A; place loop over bead.

A – Stroller Seat Back
(cut 1) 13 x 17 holes

C – Stroller Seat Side
(cut 2) 12 x 12 holes

Whipstitch to A.

Whipstitch to B.

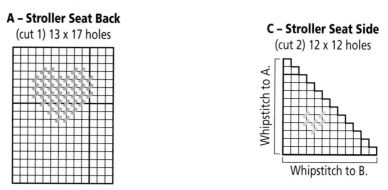

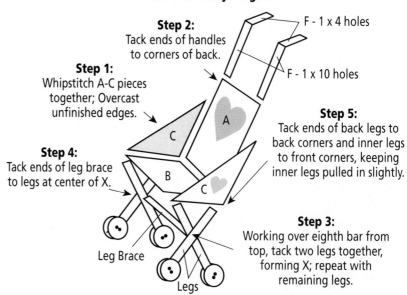

Stroller Assembly Diagram

Step 2: Tack ends of handles to corners of back.

F - 1 x 4 holes

F - 1 x 10 holes

Step 1: Whipstitch A-C pieces together; Overcast unfinished edges.

A

C

Step 5: Tack ends of back legs to back corners and inner legs to front corners, keeping inner legs pulled in slightly.

Step 4: Tack ends of leg brace to legs at center of X.

B

C

Step 3: Working over eighth bar from top, tack two legs together, forming X; repeat with remaining legs.

Leg Brace

Legs

F: For seat back hangers, cut three 1 x 4 holes (no graph).

G: For seat front strap, cut one 1 x 10 holes (no graph).

H: For leg pieces, cut eight 1 x 22 holes (no graph).

STITCHING INSTRUCTIONS:

1: Using white and Continental Stitch, work A, C (hold pieces together and work through both thicknesses as one), D and E pieces. Overcast unfinished cutout edges of A and unfinished edges of bottom, F, and G pieces. For each leg, Whipstitch two H pieces together.

2: For seat, with white, Whipstitch and tack pieces together according to Seat Assembly Diagram. For Walker, Whipstitch and assemble pieces as indicated and according to Walker Assembly Diagram. Glue pink and letter beads to spell "BABY" to front center of top as shown in Walker Bead Diagram.❧

WALKER COLOR KEY:

	Worsted-weight	Nylon Plus™	Need-loft™	Yarn Amount
☐	White	#01	#41	15 yds.

STITCH KEY:
✦ Strap Attachment

Walker Assembly Diagram

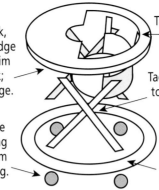

Step 1:
Starting at center back, Whipstitch B to outer edge of A, tacking ends of rim together as you work; Overcast unfinished edge.

Step 2:
Tack ends of seat straps to top as indicated.

Step 3:
Tack center of two legs together; repeat with remaining legs.

Step 4:
With ends centered 2" apart, tack legs to each side of top and bottom.

Step 5:
Glue one blue bead to wrong side of bottom under each leg.

Walker Seat Assembly Diagram

Step 1:
Whipstitch one long edge of E to outer edge of D; Overcast unfinished edges.

Step 2:
Tack ends of F and G pieces to seat and back.

Walker Bead Diagram

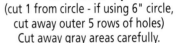

A – Walker Top
(cut 1 from circle - if using 6" circle, cut away outer 5 rows of holes)
Cut away gray areas carefully.

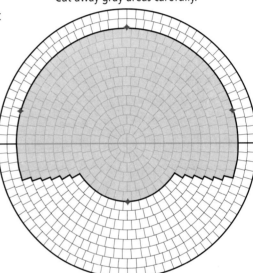

C – Walker Bottom Piece
(cut 2 from circles - if using 6" circles, cut away outer 5 rows of holes)
Cut away gray areas.

D – Walker Seat
(cut 1 from center of 6" circle)

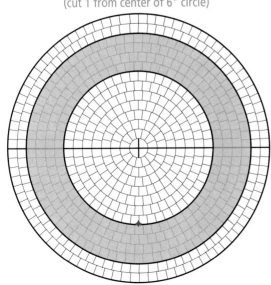

Nursery Set
Swing instructions on page 107

Swing instructions on page 107

Swing Top Cover Assembly Diagram

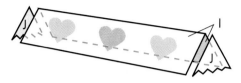

J   I   J

SWING COLOR KEY:

Worsted-weight	Nylon Plus™	Need-loft™	Yarn Amount
White	#01	#41	3 oz.
Lt. Pink	#10	#08	1½ yds.
Lt. Blue	#05	#36	1 yd.

Swing Hanger Bar Assembly Diagram

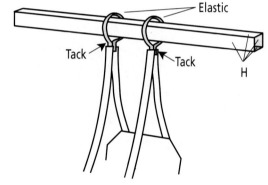

Elastic

Tack   Tack   H

Swing Base Stitch Pattern Guide

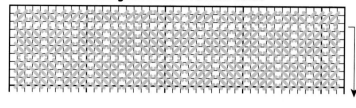

Continue established pattern across entire piece.

Swing Assembly Diagram

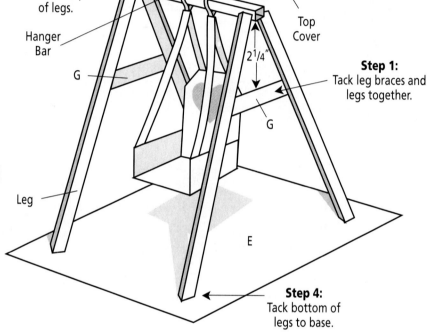

Step 2:
Tack ends of hanger bar between tops of legs.

Hanger Bar

Step 3:
Place top cover over legs and bar and tack ends together to secure.

Top Cover

Step 1:
Tack leg braces and legs together.

2¼"

G

G

Leg

E

Step 4:
Tack bottom of legs to base.

Swing Chair Assembly Diagram

Step 4:
With thread, sew ends of elastic pieces to hangers.

1" Elastic

D – 1 x 17 holes

D – 1 x 28 holes

Step 3:
Tack one end of each D piece to back and sides of chair.

C   A

B   C

Step 1:
Whipstitch one 13-hole edge of B and bottom edge of A together.

Step 2:
Whipstitch A–C pieces together; Overcast unfinished edges.

I – Swing Top Cover Side (cut 2) 7 x 33 holes

A – Swing Chair Back
(cut 1) 13 x 17 holes

Leg Assembly Diagram

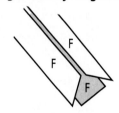

F

F

F

J – Swing Top Cover End
(cut 2) 7 x 7 holes

Whipstitch to I.

Whipstitch to I.

Winter Wonderland

Let it Snow! You're Ready for Every Occasion with this Winter Wardrobe

BLACK & TURQUOISE HAT & SCARF

Designed by Lucia Karge

TECHNIQUE: Crochet
SIZE: Fits 11"-11½" fashion doll.
MATERIALS FOR BOTH: Fuzzy sport yarn — small amount each black and turquoise; Tapestry needle; G crochet hook or size needed to obtain gauge.
GAUGE: 4 sts = 1"; 2 dc rows = 1".

HAT

Rnd 1: With black, ch 5, sl st in first ch to form ring, ch 3, 13 dc in ring, join with sl st in top of ch-3 (14 dc).

Rnd 2: Ch 3, dc in same st changing to turquoise, (2 dc in next st changing to black in last st made, 2 dc in next st changing to turquoise in last st made) around to last st, 2 dc in last st, join, fasten off black.

Rnds 3-5: Ch 2, hdc in each st around, join with sl st in top of ch-2. Fasten off at end of last rnd.

SCARF

Row 1: With black, ch 40, dc in 4th ch from hook, dc in each ch across, turn (38 dc).

Row 2: Ch 3, dc in next st changing to turquoise, dc in each of next 2 sts changing to black in last st made, (dc in each of next 2 sts changing to turquoise in last st made, dc in each of next 2 sts changing to black in last st made) across to last 2 sts, dc in each of last 2 sts, fasten off black and turquoise.

For **each fringe,** cut 6" strand of black. Fold strand in half, insert hook in st, draw fold through, draw both loose ends through fold, tighten. Trim ends.

Fringe 5 times on each short end of Scarf.

SWEATER, HAT & SCARF SET

Designed by Irene Stock

TECHNIQUE: Crochet
SIZE: Fits 11"-11½" fashion doll.
MATERIALS FOR ALL THREE:
Baby yarn — 3 oz.; 1" x 1½"
piece of Velcro®; ¾" safety pin;
Three white 3-mm. pearl beads;
Beading wire; Tapestry needle; E
crochet hook or size needed to
obtain gauge.
GAUGES: 5 sc sts = 1"; 6 sc rows
= 1".

SWEATER
Bottom Ribbing
Row 1: Ch 6, sc in 2nd ch from
hook, sc in each ch across, turn (5 sc).
Rows 2-34: Working the following rows in **back lps**, ch 1, sc in
each st across, turn. **Do not** fasten
off at end of last row.

Lower Body
Row 1: Working in end of rows,
ch 1, sc in each row across, turn (34
sc).
Rows 2-11: Ch 1, sc in each st
across, turn. Fasten off at end of
last row.

Sleeve (make 2)
Rows 1-8: For **ribbing**, repeat
same rows of Bottom Ribbing (5 sc).
Row 9: For **arm,** working in end
of rows, ch 1, sc in each row across,
turn (8).
Row 10: Ch 1, 2 sc in each st
across, turn (16).
Rows 11-15: Ch 1, sc in each st
across, turn. Fasten off at end of
last row.
Sew Sleeve seams.

Upper Body
Row 1: For **right front,** with
wrong side of row 11 facing you,
join with sc in first st on Lower
Body, sc in next 6 sts; to **join row
15 on Sleeve to Lower Body,**
working through both thicknesses
with Upper Body facing you, starting with 2nd st before seam on
Sleeve, sl st in next 3 sts; for **back,**
sc in next 14 sts on Lower Body;
join Sleeve to Lower Body as
before; for **left front,** sc in last 7
sts on Lower Body, turn (28 sc).
Row 2: Ch 1, sc in first 7 sts, sc in

next 13 unworked sts on Sleeve, sc
in next 14 sts, sc in next 13
unworked sts on Sleeve, sc in last 7
sts, turn (54).
Rows 3-4: Ch 1, sc in each st
across, turn.
Row 5: Ch 1, sc in first 4 sts, (sc
next 2 sts tog, sc in each of next 3
sts) across, turn (44).
Row 6: Repeat row 3.
Row 7: Repeat row 5 (36).
Row 8: Repeat row 3.
Row 9: Ch 1, sc in first 5 sts, sc
next 2 sts tog, (sc in each of next 3
sts, sc next 2 sts tog) across to last 4
sts, sc in last 4 sts, turn (30).
Rows 10-11: Ch 1, sc in first 4 sts,
sc next 2 sts tog, (sc in each of next
3 sts, sc next 2 sts tog) across to last
4 sts, sc in last 4 sts, turn, ending
with 21 sts in last row, fasten off.

Edging
Row 1: Working across front
opening, with wrong side of work

facing you, join with sc in first st on
Bottom Ribbing, sc in each st and in
ends of each row across with 3 sc in
each corner to last st on opposite
side of Bottom Ribbing, turn.
Row 2: Ch 1, sc in each st across
with 3 sc in each center corner st,
fasten off.
Cut Velcro® lengthwise into
four equal pieces. Attach one side
of Velcro® evenly spaced inside
Right Front on Edging and other
side to outside of Left Front on
Edging.

HAT
Crown
NOTE: Do not join rnds unless
otherwise stated. Mark first st on
each rnd.
Rnd 1: Ch 4, sl st in first ch to
form ring, ch 1, 6 sc in ring (6 sc).
Rnd 2: 2 sc in each st around (12).
Rnd 3: (Sc in next st, 2 sc in next
Continued on page 115

SLED

Designed by Michele Wilcox

PHOTO on page 113
TECHNIQUE: Plastic Canvas
SIZE: 5" x 7⅜" (not including cord) x 1¾" tall.
MATERIALS: ½ sheet of stiff 7-count plastic canvas; ½ yd. jute cord; Craft glue or glue gun; Worsted-weight or plastic canvas yarn (for amounts see Color Key).

CUTTING INSTRUCTIONS:
A: For sled top, cut one according to graph.
B: For runners, cut four according to graph.
C: For support pieces, cut two 4 x 16 holes (no graph).

STITCHING INSTRUCTIONS:
1: Using colors and stitches indicated, work A and B (two on opposite side of canvas) pieces according to graphs; with beige, Overcast unfinished edges of A. Using red and Slanted Gobelin Stitch over narrow width, work C pieces.
2: For each runner, holding two B pieces wrong sides together, with red, Whipstitch together; for support, holding C pieces wrong sides together, Whipstitch together.

SLED COLOR KEY:

	Worsted-weight	Nylon Plus™	Need-loft™	Yarn Amount
☐	Beige	#43	#40	20 yds.
■	Red	#19	#02	15 yds.

3: Thread one end of jute cord through from front to back through each cutout on A; knot on wrong side to secure. Glue pieces together according to Sled Assembly Diagram. ❦

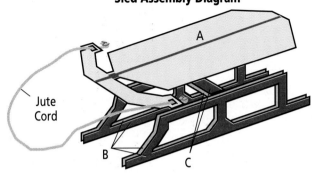

Sled Assembly Diagram

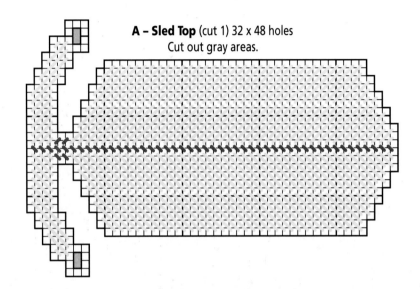

A – Sled Top (cut 1) 32 x 48 holes
Cut out gray areas.

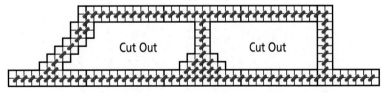

B – Runner (cut 4) 10 x 48 holes

Sweater, Hat & Scarf Set

Continued from page 114
st) around (18).
Rnd 4: (Sc in each of next 2 sts, 2 sc in next st) around (24).
Rnds 5-9: Sc in each st around.
Rnd 10: For **brim,** working the following rnds in **back lps,** 2 sc in each st around (48).
Rnds 11-13: Sc in each st around. At end of last rnd, join with sl st in first sc, fasten off.

Ear Flap (make 2)
Row 1: Ch 5, sc in 2nd ch from hook, sc in each ch across, turn (4).
Rows 2-3: Ch 1, sc in each st across, turn.
Row 4: Ch 1, (insert hook in next st, yo, draw lp through) 4 times, yo, draw through all 5 lps on hook; for **tie,** ch 40, fasten off.
Sew each Ear Flap to underside of Brim on each side of rnd 9.
For **bow,** ch 75, fasten off. Weave through every other st on rnd 9 of Crown, pulling ends even. Tie ends into a bow.

SCARF
Row 1: Ch 6, sc in 2nd ch from hook, sc in each ch across, turn (5 sc).

Rows 2-32: Ch 1, sc in each st across, turn. Fasten off at end of last row.

Fringe
For **each fringe,** cut two strands each 2" long. With both strands held together, fold in half, insert hook in st, draw fold through, draw all loose ends through fold, tighten, trim.
Fringe in each st on short ends of Scarf.
For **pin,** place beads onto beading wire. Twist ends of wire between each bead and around one side of safety pin. ❦

CREAM MITTENS & TAM

Designed by Priscilla Cole

TECHNIQUE: Crochet
SIZE: Fits 11"-11½" fashion doll.
MATERIALS FOR BOTH:
Acrylic punch embroidery yarn or size 20 crochet cotton — 75 yds. cream; No. 4 steel crochet hook or size needed to obtain gauge.
GAUGE: 10 sc sts = 1"; 10 sc rnds = 1".

TAM

NOTE: Do not join rnds unless otherwise stated. Mark first st of each rnd.

Rnd 1: For **button on top,** ch 8; 8 sc in 8th ch from hook (8 sc).

Rnd 2: Skipping button, (2 sc in each of next 2 sts, sc in next st) 2 times, 2 sc in next st, sc in last st (13).

Rnd 3: (2 sc in next st, sc in each of next 2 sts) 4 times, 2 sc in last st (18).

Rnd 4: (Sc in each of next 2 sts, 2 sc in next st) around (24).

Rnd 5: (Sc in each of next 3 sts, 2 sc in next st) around (30).

Rnd 6: (Sc in next 4 sts, 2 sc in next st) around (36).

Rnd 7: (Sc in next 5 sts, 2 sc in next st) around (42).

Rnd 8: (Sc in next 6 sts, 2 sc in next st) around (48).

Rnd 9: (Sc in next 7 sts, 2 sc in next st) around (54).

Rnd 10: (Sc in next 8 sts, 2 sc in next st) around (60).

Rnd 11: (Sc in next 9 sts, 2 sc in next st) around (66).

Rnd 12: (Sc in next 10 sts, 2 sc in next st) around (72).

Rnd 13: (Sc in next 10 sts, sc next 2 sts tog) around (66).

Rnd 14: (Sc in next 9 sts, sc next 2 sts tog) around (60).

Rnd 15: (Sc in next 8 sts, sc next 2 sts tog) around (54).

Rnd 16: (Sc in next 7 sts, sc next 2 sts tog) around (48).

Rnd 17: (Sc in next 6 sts, sc next 2 sts tog) around (42).

Rnd 18: (Sc in next 5 sts, sc next 2 sts tog) around (36).

Rnd 19: (Sc in next 4 sts, sc next 2 sts tog) around (30).

Rnd 20: (Sc in each of next 3 sts, sc next 2 sts tog) around (24).

Rnd 21: Sc in each st around, join with sl st in first sc.

Rnd 22: Ch 1, reverse sc in each st around, join with sl st in first sc, fasten off.

MITTEN (make 2)

Rnd 1: For **hand,** ch 2, 5 sc in 2nd ch from hook (5 sc).

Rnd 2: Sc in first st, 2 sc in each of last 4 sts (9).

Rnds 3-5: Sc in each st around. Fasten off at end of last rnd. Set aside.

Rnd 6: For **thumb,** ch 2, 5 sc in 2nd ch from hook (5 sc).

Rnds 7-8: Sc in each st around.

Rnd 9: Sc in first st of rnd 5 on hand, sc in next 7 sts, sc last st of hand and first st of thumb tog, sc in each of next 3 sts on thumb, sc last st of thumb and first st of this rnd tog (13 sc).

Rnd 10: Sc in next 7 sts, sc next 2 sts tog, sc in each of last 3 sts (11).

Rnds 11-12: Sc in each st around.

Rnd 13: Sl st in next st, ch 1, reverse sc in each st around, join with sl st in first sc, fasten off.

– 116 –

HOODED CAPE

Designed by Michele Wilcox

TECHNIQUE: Crochet
SIZE: Fits 11"-11½" fashion doll.
MATERIALS: Worsted-weight yarn — 2 oz. burgundy; Tapestry needle; F crochet hook or size needed to obtain gauge.
GAUGE: 9 sc sts = 2"; 5 sc rows = 1".

CAPE

Row 1: Beginning at neckline, ch 13, sc in 2nd ch from hook, sc in each ch across, turn (12 sc).

Row 2: Ch 1, 2 sc in each st across, turn (24).

Row 3: Ch 1, sc in first 5 sts, 2 sc in each of next 2 sts, sc in next 10 sts, 2 sc in each of next 2 sts, sc in last 5 sts, turn (28).

Row 4: Ch 1, sc in first 6 sts, 2 sc in each of next 2 sts, sc in next 12 sts, 2 sc in each of next 2 sts, sc in last 6 sts, turn (32).

Row 5: Ch 1, sc in first 7 sts, 2 sc in each of next 2 sts, sc in next 14 sts, 2 sc in each of next 2 sts, sc in last 7 sts, turn (36).

Row 6: Ch 1, sc in first 8 sts, 2 sc in each of next 2 sts, sc in next 16 sts, 2 sc in each of next 2 sts, sc in last 8 sts, turn (40).

Row 7: Ch 1, sc in first 9 sts, 2 sc in each of next 2 sts, sc in next 18 sts, 2 sc in each of next 2 sts, sc in last 9 sts, turn (44).

Rows 8-9: Ch 1, sc in each st across, turn.

Row 10: Ch 1, sc in first 20 sts, 2 sc in each of next 4 sts, sc in last 20 sts, turn (48).

Row 11: Ch 1, sc in first 20 sts, 2 sc in each of next 8 sts, sc in last 20 sts, turn (56).

Rows 12-32: Ch 1, sc in each st across, turn. Fasten off at end of last row.

HOOD

Row 1: Ch 13, sc in 2nd ch from hook, sc in each ch across, turn (12 sc).

Rows 2-30: Ch 1, sc in each st across, turn. Fasten off at end of last row.

Fold hood in half crosswise and sew ends of rows together along one edge. Easing to fit, sew Hood to row 1 of Cape.

FINISHING

With right side facing you, join with sc in end of row 32 on Cape, 2 sc in same row, sc in end of each row across Cape to neck edge, sc in first row on Hood; *for **tie**, ch 30, sl st in 5th ch from hook, (ch 4, sl st in same ch as last sl st) 2 times, sl st in each ch across*; sc in end of each row across Hood to neck edge; repeat between **, sc in end of each row across Cape to bottom edge with 3 sc in end of row 32; working across bottom edge, (ch 3, skip next st, sl st in next st) across, ch 3, join with sl st in first sc, fasten off.

Career Mates

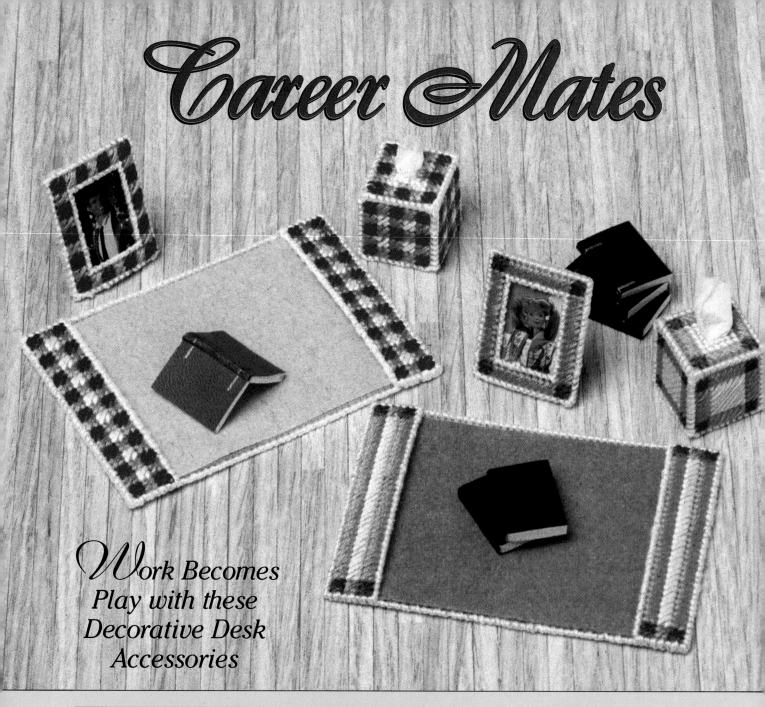

Work Becomes Play with these Decorative Desk Accessories

HIS & HER DESK SETS

Designed by Nancy Marshall

TECHNIQUE: Plastic Canvas
SIZE: Tissue Box is ⅞" square x ⅞" tall; Picture Frame is 1⅛" x 1⅜" tall; Blotter is 2½" x 3⅝".
MATERIALS FOR ONE SET: ½ sheet of 14-count plastic canvas; 2⅜" x 3½" piece of coordinating color construction paper; 1" x 1¼" picture; Tissue; Six-strand embroidery floss (for amounts see individual Color Keys).

CUTTING INSTRUCTIONS:

A: For Tissue Box top, cut one according to graph.

B: For Tissue Box sides, cut four 11 x 11 holes.

C: For Picture Frame front, cut one according to graph.

D: For Picture Frame back, cut one 15 x 19 holes.

E: For Picture Frame support, cut one 5 x 13 holes (no graph).

F: For Desk Pad flaps, cut two 7 x 35 holes.

G: For Desk Pad back, cut one 35 x 50 holes (no graph).

STITCHING INSTRUCTIONS:

NOTES: D, E and G pieces are unworked. Separate floss into 3-ply strands.

1: Using colors and stitches indicated, work A, B, C and F pieces according to graphs of choice.

NOTE: For Whipstitching and Overcasting, use tan for His Set or white for Her Set.

2: For Tissue Box, Overcast unfinished cutout edges of A. Whipstitch A and B pieces together, forming box; Overcast unfinished bottom edges. Tear one end off tissue and fold up; stuff into box and pull corner through top cutout.

3: For Picture Frame, Overcast unfinished cutout edges of C and bottom edge as indicated on graph. Whipstitch one short end of E to D as indicated. Holding C and D wrong sides together, Whipstitch unfinished edges together. Insert picture in frame.

4: For Desk Pad, Overcast one long edge of each F piece. Matching unfinished edges, Whipstitch one F to each end of G as shown in photo. Overcast unfinished edges. Insert construction paper in Desk Pad.🍎

A – Her Tissue Box Top
(cut 1) 11 x 11 holes

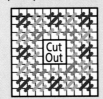

B – Her Tissue Box Side
(cut 4) 11 x 11 holes

HER DESK SET COLOR KEY:

Embroidery floss	Amount
White	4 1/2 yds.
Pink	2 1/2 yds.
Rose	2 1/2 yds.

STITCH KEY:
☐ Stand Attachment

C – Her Frame Front
(cut 1) 15 x 19 holes

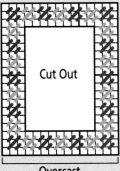

Cut Out

Overcast

F – Her Desk Pad Flap
(cut 2) 7 x 35 holes

D – His or Her Frame Back
(cut 1) 15 x 19 holes

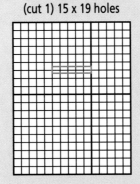

HIS DESK SET COLOR KEY:

Embroidery floss	Amount
Beige	4 1/2 yds.
Tan	2 1/2 yds.
Brown	1 1/2 yds.

STITCH KEY:
☐ Stand Attachment

Picture Frame Assembly Diagram

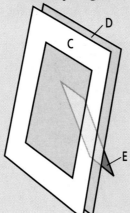

C – His Frame Front
(cut 1) 15 x 19 holes

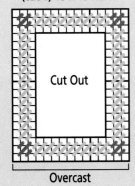

Cut Out

Overcast

A – His Tissue Box Top
(cut 1) 11 x 11 holes

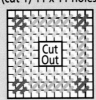

Cut Out

B – His Tissue Box Side
(cut 4) 11 x 11 holes

F – His Desk Pad Flap
(cut 2) 7 x 35 holes

Ready, Set, Stitch!

Basic Instructions to Get You Started

Most needlecrafters love getting their projects organized before they even step out the door in search of supplies. A few moments of careful planning can make the creation of your project even more fun.

First of all, prepare your work area. You will need a flat surface for cutting and assembly, and you will need a place to store your materials. Good lighting is essential, and a comfortable chair will make your stitching time even more enjoyable.

Do you plan to make one project, or will you be making several of the same item? A materials list appears at the beginning of each pattern. If you plan to make several of the same item, multiply your materials accordingly.

Supplies

Yarn, canvas, needles, cutters and most other supplies needed to complete the projects in this book are available through craft and needlework stores and mail order catalogs. Other supplies are available at fabric, hardware and discount stores. For mail order information, see page 127.

Marking & Cutting Canvas

To avoid wasting canvas, careful cutting of each piece is important. For some pieces with square corners, you might be comfortable cutting the canvas without marking it beforehand. But for pieces with lots of angles and cutouts, you may want to mark your canvas before cutting.

To count holes on the graphs, look for the bolder lines showing each ten holes. These ten-count lines begin in the lower left-hand corner of each graph and are on the graph to make counting easier. To count holes on the canvas, you may use your tapestry needle, a toothpick or a plastic hair roller pick. Insert the needle or pick slightly in each hole as you count.

Most stitchers have tried a variety of marking tools and have settled on a favorite, which may be crayon, permanent marker or grease pencil. One of the best marking tools is a fine-point overhead projection marker, available at office supply stores. The ink is dark and easy to see and washes off completely with water. After cutting and before stitching, it's important to remove all marks so they won't stain yarn as you stitch or show through stitches later. Cloth and paper toweling remove grease pencil and crayon marks, as do used fabric softener sheets.

Canvas

Most projects can be made using standard-size sheets of canvas. Standard-size sheets of 7-count (7 holes per inch) are 70 x 90 holes and are about 10½"x 13½". For larger projects, 7-count canvas also comes in 12" x 18" (80 x 120 holes) and 13½" x 22½" (90 x 150 holes) sheets. Other shapes are available in 7-count, including circles, diamonds, ovals and purse forms.

10-count canvas (10 holes per inch) comes only in standard-size sheets, which vary slightly depending on brand. They are 10½" x 13½" (106 x 136 holes) or 11" x 14" (108 x 138 holes).

Newer canvas like 5-count (5 holes per inch) and 14-count (14 holes per inch) are also becoming popular with plastic canvas designers.

Some canvas is soft and pliable, while other canvas is stiffer and more rigid. To prevent canvas from cracking during or after stitching, you'll want to choose pliable canvas for projects that require shaping, like round baskets with curved handles. If your project is a box or an item that will stand alone, stiffer canvas is more suitable.

Both 7- and 10-count canvas are available in a rainbow of colors. Most designs can be stitched on colored as well as clear canvas. When a pattern does not specify color in the materials list, you can assume clear canvas was used in the photographed model. If you'd like to stitch only a portion of the design, leaving a portion unstitched, use colored canvas to coordinate with yarn colors.

Buy the same brand of canvas for each entire project. Different brands of canvas may differ slightly in the distance between each bar.

Cutting Canvas

Follow all Cutting Instructions, Notes and labels above graphs to cut canvas. Each piece is labeled with a letter of the alphabet. Square-sided pieces are cut according to hole count, and some may not have graphs.

Unlike sewing patterns, graphs are not designed to be used as actual patterns but rather as counting, cutting and stitching guides. Therefore, graphs may not be actual size. Count the holes on the graph (see Marking & Cutting Canvas on page 120), mark your canvas to match, then cut. Trim off the nubs close to the bar, and trim all corners diagonally.

If you accidentally cut or tear a bar or two on your canvas, don't worry! Boo-boos can usually be repaired in one of several ways: heat the tip of a metal skewer and melt the canvas back together; glue torn bars with a tiny drop of craft glue, Super Glue® or hot glue; or reinforce the torn section with a separate piece of canvas placed at the back of your work. When reinforcing with extra canvas, stitch through both thicknesses.

Needles & Other Stitching Tools

Blunt-end tapestry needles are used for stitching plastic canvas. Choose a No. 16 needle for stitching 7-count and a No. 18 for stitching 10-count. Keep a small pair of embroidery scissors handy for snipping yarn. Try using needle-nose jewelry pliers for pulling the needle through several thicknesses of canvas and out of tight spots too small for your hand.

Yarn & Other Stitching Materials

You may choose two-ply nylon plastic canvas yarn (the color numbers of two popular brands are found in Color Keys) or four-ply worsted-weight yarn for stitching on 7-count canvas. There are about 42 yards per ounce of plastic canvas yarn and 50 yards per ounce of worsted-weight yarn.

Worsted-weight yarn is widely available and comes in wool, acrylic, cotton and blends. If you decide to use worsted-weight yarn, choose 100% acrylic for best coverage. Select worsted-weight yarn by color instead of the color names or numbers found in the Color Keys. Projects stitched with worsted-weight yarn often "fuzz" after use. "Fuzz" can be removed by shaving with a fabric shaver to make your project look new again.

Plastic canvas yarn comes in over 60 colors and is a favorite of many plastic canvas designers. These yarns "wear" well both while stitching and in the finished product. When buying plastic canvas yarn, shop using the color names or numbers found in the Color Keys, or select colors of your choice.

Stitching the Canvas

Stitching Instructions for each section are found after the Cutting Instructions. First, refer to the illustrations of basic stitches to familiarize yourself with the stitches used. Illustrations will be found near the graphs for pieces worked using special stitches. Follow the numbers on the tiny graph beside the illustration to make each stitch — bring your needle up from the back of the work on odd numbers and down through the front of the work on the even numbers.

Before beginning, read the Stitching Instructions to get an overview of what you'll be doing. You'll find that some pieces are stitched using colors and stitches indicated on graphs, and for other pieces, you will be told which color and stitch to use to cover the entire piece.

Cut yarn lengths no longer than 18" to prevent fraying. Thread needle; do not tie a knot in the end. Bring your needle up through the canvas from the back, leaving a short length of yarn on the wrong side of the canvas. As you begin to stitch, work over this short length of yarn. If you are beginning with Continental Stitches, leave a 1" length, but if you are working longer stitches, leave a longer length.

In order for graph colors to contrast well, graph colors may not match yarn colors. For instance, a light yellow may have been selected to represent the metallic cord color gold, or a light blue may represent white yarn.

When following a graph showing several colors, you may want to work all the stitches of one color at the same time. Some stitchers prefer to work with several colors at once by threading each on a separate needle and letting the yarn not being used hang on the wrong side of the work. Either way, remember that strands of yarn run across the wrong side of the work may show through the stitches from the front.

As you stitch, try to maintain an even tension on the yarn. Loose stitches will look uneven, and tight stitches will let the canvas show through. If your yarn twists as you work, you may want to let your needle and yarn hang and untwist occasionally.

When you end a section of stitching or finish a thread, weave the yarn through the back side of your last few stitches, then trim it off.

Ready, Set, Stitch!

Finishing Tips

To combat glue strings when using a hot glue gun, practice a swirling motion as you work. After placing the drop of glue on your work, lift the gun slightly and swirl to break the stream of glue, as if you were making an ice cream cone. Have a cup of water handy when gluing. For those times when you'll need to touch the glue, first dip your finger into the water just enough to dampen it. This will minimize the glue sticking to your finger, and it will cool and set the glue more quickly.

To attach beads, use a bit more glue to form a cup around the bead. If too much shows after drying, use a craft knife to trim off excess glue.

Scotchguard® or other fabric protectors may be used on your finished projects. However, avoid using a permanent marker if you plan to use a fabric protector, and be sure to remove all other markings before stitching. Fabric protectors can cause markings to bleed, staining yarn.

Construction & Assembly

After all pieces of an item needing assembly are stitched, you will find the order of assembly is listed in the Stitching Instructions and sometimes illustrated in diagrams found with the graphs. For best results, join pieces in the order written. Refer to the Stitch Key and to the directives near the graphs for precise attachments.

For More Information

Sometimes even the most experienced needlecrafters can find themselves having trouble following instructions. If you have difficulty completing your project, write to: **Fashion Doll Fantasy Editors**, *The Needlecraft Shop*, 23 Old Pecan Road, Big Sandy, Texas 75755.

Cutting Tools

You may find it helpful to have several tools on hand for cutting canvas. When cutting long, straight sections, scissors, craft cutters or kitchen shears are the fastest and easiest to use. For cutting out detailed areas and trimming nubs, you may like using manicure scissors, nail clippers or the Ultimate Plastic Canvas Cutters, available from The Needlecraft Shop catalog (see address on page 127). If you prefer laying your canvas flat when cutting, try a craft knife and cutting surface — self-healing mats designed for sewing, as well as kitchen cutting boards, work well.

Continental Stitch can be used to stitch designs or fill in background areas.

Long Stitch can be used to stitch designs or fill in background areas. Can be stitched over two or more bars.

Slanted Gobelin Stitch can be used to stitch designs or fill in background areas. Can be stitched over two or more bars in vertical or horizontal rows.

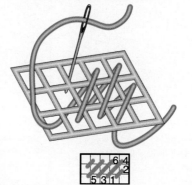

Overcast Stitch is used to finish edges. Stitch two or three times in corners for complete coverage.

Whipstitch is used to join two or more pieces together.

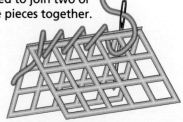

French Knot is usually used as an embroidery stitch to add detail. Can be made in one hole or over a bar. If dot on graph is in hole as shown, come up and go down with needle in same hole. If dot is across a bar, come up in one hole and go down one hole over.

Straight Stitch is usually used as an embroidery stitch to add detail. Stitches can be any length and can go in any direction. Looks like Backstitch, except stitches may not touch.

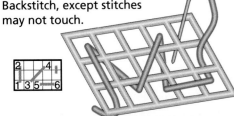

Cross Stitch can be used as a needlepoint stitch on plastic canvas alone, or as an embroidery stitch, stitched over background stitches with contrasting yarn or floss.

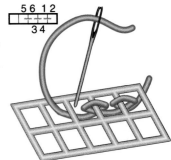

Lark's Head Knot

Step 1   Step 2

Lazy Daisy Stitch

Backstitch is usually used as an embroidery stitch to outline or add detail. Stitches can be any length and can go in any direction.

Running Stitch

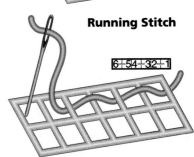

CROSS STITCH

CROSS STITCH AND EMBROIDERY

For best results, choose a #24 or #26 blunt-end tapestry needle for cross stitching on evenweave fabric and Aida cloth. Choose a sharp-pointed needle for embroidery. Secure fabric in a hoop to keep fabric taut.

For cross stitch, work all cross stitches and fractional cross stitches first, then Backstitches, then other embroidery stitches.

WORKING FROM CROSS STITCH GRAPHS

Graphs or charts are made up of colors and symbols to tell you the exact color, type and placement of each stitch. Each square represents the area for one complete Cross Stitch. Next to each graph, there is a key with information about stitches and floss colors represented by the graph's colors and symbols.

Three-quarter Cross Stitch (¾x):
A Half Cross Stitch plus a Quarter Cross Stitch. Stitch may slant in any direction, as shown on graph.

CROSS STITCH STITCHES

Cross Stitch (x): There are two ways of making a basic Cross Stitch. The first method is used when working rows of stitches in the same color. The first step makes the bottom half of the stitches across the row, and the second step makes the top half.

The second method is used when making single stitches. The bottom and top halves of each stitch are worked before starting the next stitch.

EMBROIDERY STITCHES

Lazy Daisy Stitch can be any length and can go in any direction. Insert needle through fabric as shown and gently pull needle through until loop is snug. Insert needle back through at same point.

French Knot   **Satin Stitch**

Outline or Stem Stitch

Backstitch is usually used as an embroidery stitch to outline or add detail. Stitches can be any length and can go in any direction.

Ready, Set, Stitch!

Chain (ch)
Yo, draw hook through lp.

Slip Stitch (sl st)
Insert hook in st, yo, draw through st and lp on hook.

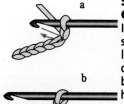

Single Crochet (sc)
Insert hook in st (a), yo, draw lp through, yo, draw through both lps on hook (b).

Front Loop (a) **/ Back Loop** (b)
(front lp/back lp)

Abbreviations

Chain(s) ....ch(s)
Decrease ....dec
Double Crochet ....dc
Half Double Crochet...........hdc
Increase................................inc
Loop(s) ....lp(s)
Round(s)..............................rnd(s)
Single Crochet.......................sc
Slip Stitch ....sl st
Space(s) ....sp(s)
Stitch(s) ....st(s)
Together................................tog
Treble Crochet........................tr
Yarn Over ....yo

Gauge

Always check your gauge before beginning a project. The purpose of checking gauge is to determine which hook size to use. The tightness or looseness of your stitches determines gauge, and is affected by hook size. Gauge is measured by counting the number of rows or stitches per inch.

Make a swatch at least 2" square in the stitch indicated in the gauge section of the pattern. Lay the swatch flat and measure the stitches and rows. If you determine you have more stitches or rows per inch than specified in the pattern, your gauge is too tight and you need to choose a larger hook. If you have fewer stitches or rows per inch than needed, a smaller hook is required.

For some patterns, especially small patterns like flowers or motifs, gauge is given as a size measurement for the entire motif. In this case, make one motif and measure.

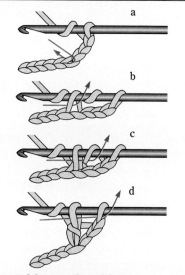

Double Crochet (dc)
Yo, insert hook in st (a), yo, draw lp through (b), (yo, draw through 2 lps on hook) 2 times (c and d).

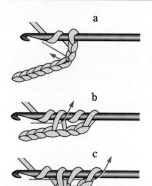

Half Double Crochet (hdc)
Yo, insert hook in st (a), yo, draw lp through (b), yo, draw through all 3 lps on hook (c).

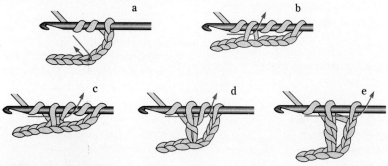

Treble Crochet (tr)
Yo 2 times, insert hook in st (a), yo, draw lp through (b), (yo, draw through 2 lps on hook) 3 times (c, d and e).

Parentheses, Asterisks & More

For clarity, written instructions may include symbols such as parentheses, asterisks, brackets and diamonds. These symbols are used as signposts to set off a portion of instructions which will be worked more than once.

( ) Parentheses enclose instructions which are to be worked the number of times indicated after the parentheses. For example, "(2 dc in next st, skip next st) 5 times" means to follow the instructions within parentheses a total of five times. Parentheses may also be used to enclose a group of stitches which should be worked in one space or stitch. For example, "(2 dc, ch 2, 2 dc) in next st" means to work all the stitches within parentheses in the next stitch.

*Asterisks may be used alone or in pairs, many times in combination with parentheses. If used in pairs, a set of instructions enclosed within asterisks will be followed by instructions for repeating. These repeat instructions may appear later in the pattern or immediately after the last asterisk. For example, "*Dc in next 4 sts, (2 dc, ch 2, 2 dc) in corner sp*, dc in next 4 sts; repeat between ** 2 times" means to work through the instructions for repeating, then repeat only the instructions that are enclosed within the asterisks twice.

If used alone, an asterisk marks the beginning of instructions which are to be repeated. For example, "Ch 3, dc in same st, *ch 2, skip next 2 sts, dc in next st, ch 1, skip next st, 2 dc in next st; repeat from * across" means to work from the beginning, then repeat only the instructions after the *, working all the way across the row. Instructions for repeating may also specify a number of times to repeat, and this may be followed by further instructions. For example, instructions might say, "...repeat from * 5 more times; dc in last st." To follow these instructions, work through from the beginning once, then repeat from * five more times for a total of six times. Then, follow remaining instructions, which in this example are "dc in last st."

[ ] Brackets and ◊ diamonds are used to clarify and set off sections of instructions.

In some patterns, all types of symbols are used together. As you can see, there is no need to be intimidated by symbols! These signposts will get you where you're going — to the end of a beautiful finished project.

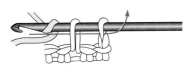

Single Crochet Color Change (sc color change)
Drop first color; yo with 2nd color, draw through last 2 lps of st.

Double Crochet Color Change (dc color change)
Drop first color; yo with 2nd color, draw through last 2 lps of st.

Half Double Crochet next 2 stitches together (hdc next 2 sts tog)
(Yo, insert hook in next st, yo, draw lp through) 2 times, yo, draw through all 5 lps on hook.

Single Crochet next 2 stitches together (sc next 2 sts tog)
Draw up lp in each of next 2 sts, yo, draw through all 3 lps on hook.

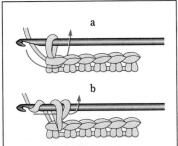

Reverse Single Crochet (reverse sc)
Working from left to right, insert hook in next st to the right (a), yo, draw through st, complete as sc (b).

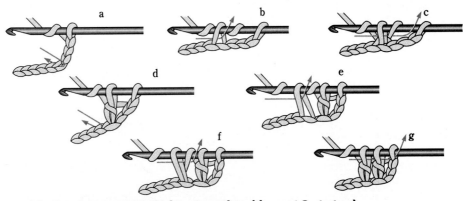

Double Crochet next 2 stitches together (dc next 2 sts tog)
*Yo, insert hook in next st (a), yo, draw lp through (b), yo, draw through 2 lps on hook (c); repeat from * one time (d, e and f), yo, draw through all 3 lps on hook (g).

Acknowledgments

We would like to express our appreciation to the many people who helped create this book. Our special thanks go to each of the talented designers who contributed original designs.

Thanks, also, to all the talented and skilled editors, art directors, photographers and production staff whose technical expertise made the book come together.

In addition, we would like to thank the companies and individuals who provided doll clothes and accessories, props or other contributions.

Finally we wish to express our gratitude to the following manufacturers for their generous contribution of materials and supplies:

ALEENE'S™
- Fabric stiffener — Crown & Scepter
- Thick Designer Tacky Glue — Living Room

BEL-TREE CORP.
- Animal eyes — Bearskin Rug

COATS & CLARK
- Size 10 bedspread cotton — Bath Set, Kitchen Set, Elegant Dinnerware, Turquoise Beach Set,
- Size 30 crochet cotton — Bath Set

DARICE®
- Nylon Plus™ yarn — Recliner, Concession Stand, Sled
- Metallic Cord — Equestrian Beauties, Concession Stand, Electric Guitar & Amp, Egyptian Costume
- 5-count canvas — Living Room
- 10-count canvas — Tray, Acoustic Guitar, Swim Fins & Masks, Concession Stand
- 14-count canvas — His & Her Desk Sets, Concession Stand
- Ultra Stiff™ canvas — Sled
- Plastic canvas radial circles — Watermelon Summer Outfit, Egyptian Costume, Clown Costume
- Raffia straw — Concession Stand, Clown Costume
- Gemstones — Crown & Scepter
- Doll joints — Recliner

DELTA
- Wood stain — Fish Plaque

DMC®
- Pearl cotton — Rug & Floor Pillow, Tray
- Embroidery floss — Place Mat & Bread Cover, His & Her Desk Sets

J. & P. COATS®
- Embroidery floss — Acoustic Guitar, Concession Stand

KREINIK
- Metallic ribbon — Beaded Accessories
- Metallic braid — Elegant Dinnerware, Crown & Scepter, Electric Guitar & Amp, Metallic Masks

MILL HILL
- Seed beads — Beaded Accessories

ONE & ONLY CREATIONS®
- Wavy doll hair — Equestrian Beauties

RAFF-IT
- Raffia straw — Watermelon Summer Outfit, Egyptian Costume, Hawaiian Costume

RAINBOW GALLERY
- Metallic flat braid — Egyptian Costume

SHAFAII COMPANY
- Metal nailheads — Fish Plaque

SLOMON'S
- Sobo glue — Eyelet Suit

TULIP™
- Glitter paint — Crown & Scepter

UNIEK® CRAFTS
- Needloft® yarn — Rug & Floor Pillow, Nursery Set, Equestrian Beauties, Travel Cases, Dining Room Set
- Colored canvas — Electric Guitar & Amp, Travel Cases

WICHELT IMPORTS
- 16-count Aida — Place Mat & Bread Cover

WRIGHT'S®
- Eyelet — Eyelet Suit
- Ribbon — Eyelet Suit

Index

For supplies, first shop your local craft and needlework stores. If you are unable to find the supplies you need, write to the address below for a free catalog. The Needlecraft Shop *carries plastic canvas in a variety of shapes, sizes and colors, 60 colors of plastic canvas yarn and a large selection of pattern books.*

23 Old Pecan Road
Big Sandy, Texas 75755   (903) 636-4000